Write for Business

A Compact Guide to Writing
& Communicating in the Workplace

Verne Meyer

Pat Sebranek

John Van Rys

UPWRITE PRESS™

Burlington, Wisconsin

Acknowledgements

The authors wish to thank the many business people in for-profit and not-for-profit organizations across the United States and Canada who contributed samples of business writing for this project. In addition, we want to thank the following people for sharing their valuable time, energy, and ideas by reviewing *Write for Business* at various stages of its development: Julia Blackmore, Bernard De Wit, Jim Evers, Tip Haagsma, Erik Hoekstra, Richard Kobes, Heidi Mosher, Gloria Pickering, Marcy Stravers, Pam Ten Napel, Jon Van Gorp, Keith Van Rys, Loren Veldhuizen, and Daniel Walker.

Editorial Director: Patrick Sebranek
Director of Marketing: Thomas Spicuzza
Cover Design: Colleen Belmont
Illustrations: Chris Krenzke
Creative Director: Julie Spicuzza
CD: Chris Erickson, Kathy Kahnle, Ben Meyer, Jason Reynolds, Janae Sebranek, Lester Smith, Claire Ziffer
Editorial: Laura Bachman, Ron Bachman, Mariellen Hanrahan, Kathy Henning, Stuart Hoffman,
    Dave Kemper, Pat Kornelis, Lois Krenzke, Barb Lund, Randy VanderMey
Designers: Colleen Belmont, Sherry Gordon
Production: Colleen Belmont, Sherry Gordon, Ellen Leitheusser, Jean Varley, Sandy Wagner

Printed in the U.S.A.

Library of Congress Control Number: 2003104597

ISBN (hardcover): 1-932436-00-6
ISBN (spiral): 1-932436-01-4

1 2 3 4 5 6 7 8 9 −RRDC− 07 06 05 04 03

Right for Business

THE BOTTOM LINE

Good communication is good business. Every day, business people write, read, speak, and listen to do their work—sending e-mail messages, reporting on projects, making presentations, and developing proposals. The success of their work—and yours—often depends upon the quality and speed of the communication.

Write for Business can help you achieve that success. First, this handbook contains proven strategies that will help you produce top-quality documents. Second, the book contains guidelines, models, checklists, and templates that will save you time drafting, revising, and proofreading. Third, the book will enable you to develop and deliver a full range of oral presentations—from impromptu sales talks to full-length reports.

So whatever your communication task, *Write for Business,* along with its interactive CD, is your tool for success! The companion CD offers a complete e-book, writing templates, and interactive lessons—all aimed at helping you turn good communication into good business.

Write for Business:
A Compact Guide

The Companion CD:
An e-book with
interactive lessons
and writing templates

Using *Write for Business*

By helping you successfully connect with your readers, *Write for Business* will save you time and money. Often, you'll simply check the book for a quick answer to a specific writing question. Other times, you'll use guidelines, models, and checklists to help you compose a complete document. The handbook also offers instruction for improving specific writing skills, such as voice and clarity. Illustrated below are the kinds of materials included in the handbook.

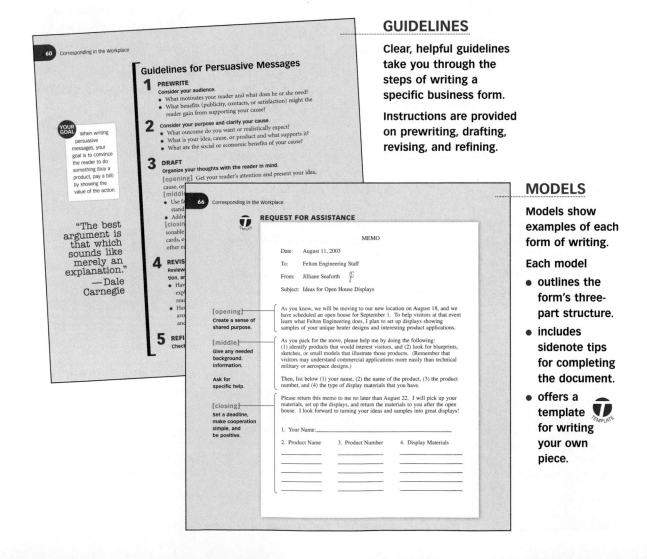

GUIDELINES

Clear, helpful guidelines take you through the steps of writing a specific business form.

Instructions are provided on prewriting, drafting, revising, and refining.

MODELS

Models show examples of each form of writing.

Each model

- **outlines the form's three-part structure.**
- **includes sidenote tips for completing the document.**
- **offers a template for writing your own piece.**

CHECKLISTS

A checklist at the end of each chapter will help you complete that type of document successfully. You can double-check your writing for

- ideas
- organization
- voice
- word choice
- sentence smoothness
- correctness
- design

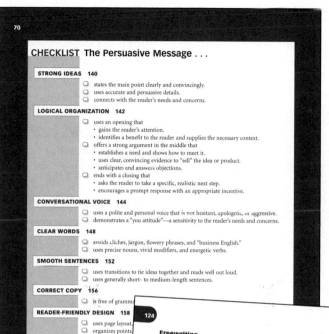

70

CHECKLIST The Persuasive Message . . .

STRONG IDEAS 140

- states the main point clearly and convincingly.
- uses accurate and persuasive details.
- connects with the reader's needs and concerns.

LOGICAL ORGANIZATION 142

- uses an opening that
  - gains the reader's attention.
  - identifies a benefit to the reader and supplies the necessary context.
- offers a strong argument in the middle that
  - establishes a need and shows how to meet it.
  - uses clear, convincing evidence to "sell" the idea or product.
  - anticipates and answers objections.
- ends with a closing that
  - asks the reader to take a specific, realistic next step.
  - encourages a prompt response with an appropriate incentive.

CONVERSATIONAL VOICE 144

- uses a polite and personal voice that is not hesitant, apologetic, or aggressive.
- demonstrates a "you attitude"—a sensitivity to the reader's needs and concerns.

CLEAR WORDS 148

- avoids cliches, jargon, flowery phrases, and "business English."
- uses precise nouns, vivid modifiers, and energetic verbs.

SMOOTH SENTENCES 152

- uses transitions to tie ideas together and reads well out loud.
- uses generally short- to medium-length sentences.

CORRECT COPY 156

- is free of gramma

READER-FRIENDLY DESIGN 158

- uses page layout
- organizes points

EXPLANATIONS

Additional pages provide helpful explanations, instructions, graphics, and more—each designed to supply practical information.

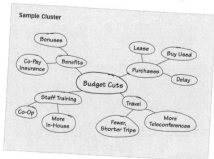

124

Freewriting

Writing whatever comes to mind on a particular topic is called *freewriting*. Freewriting is really brainstorming on paper (or on the computer). It helps you record, develop, and understand your thinking.

1 Write nonstop about your subject or project, *following* rather than *directing* your thoughts.

2 Resist the temptation to stop and judge or edit what you write.

3 If you get stuck, switch directions and follow a different line of thinking.

4 When you finish, reread your material and highlight passages you think might be useful.

Clustering

Clustering creates a web of connections between a general topic and specific subtopics. A cluster allows you to see the structure of your topic and plan your writing.

1 Write a key word or phrase in the middle of your page.

2 Record or "cluster" related words and phrases around this key word.

3 Circle each idea and link it to related ideas in your cluster.

4 Continue recording related ideas until you have covered the topic.

Sample Cluster

Bonuses · Co-Pay Insurance · Benefits · Lease · Buy Used · Purchases · Delay · Budget Cuts · Staff Training · Travel · Co-Op · More In-House · Fewer, Shorter Trips · More Teleconferences

Using the *Write for Business* CD

The *Write for Business* companion CD contains an e-book version of the print book. In addition, the CD provides interactive lessons related to key chapters of the book, as well as ready-to-use templates for nearly all the writing models in the book.

E-BOOK

The e-book version of *Write for Business* contains the entire text of the print book in popular Adobe® PDF format. (A free copy of Adobe® Acrobat® Reader® software is included on the CD. Simply run the "Setup" program to install it automatically.)

Hyperlinks: Every page-number reference in the e-book has been hyperlinked to the page it identifies. That includes every entry in the table of contents, the index, and all the cross references within the text itself. Just click a page-number link to go directly to the designated page.

Bookmarks: The bookmarks panel in the e-book lists every chapter title and major heading. Click the arrow next to a heading to reveal any subheadings it contains. Click on a heading or subheading to be taken directly to its first page in the book.

Find Function: Clicking the "Find" button on the e-book's toolbar brings up a panel where you can enter a word or phrase and search for it in the book.

INTERACTIVE LESSONS

Video lessons are included on the CD for the key chapters in the book. Each lesson is followed by an interactive exercise to test and reinforce your understanding of the material.

WRITING TEMPLATES

Most writing models in the book are included on the CD, pre-designed in Microsoft® Word format. Just open the model that matches your current writing task, replace its text with your own, and print it out—it's that simple.

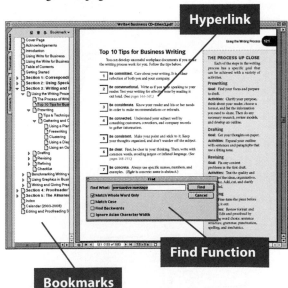

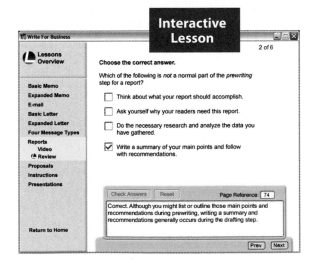

Table of Contents

Getting Started

Good business writing is informative, clear, and convincing. It helps facilitate business transactions and strengthen business relationships. To produce better business writing—and communicating as a whole—follow the bottom-line principles listed below.

BOTTOM-LINE WRITING PRINCIPLES

1 **Set positive goals.** To complete each document successfully,
- establish a reasonable deadline,
- decide what you want to accomplish, and
- align your writing goals with the company's mission and values.

2 **Write directly to readers.** Think about each reader's knowledge, motivation, and position. How will he or she react to your message? How can you build common ground? Consider the diversity of your audience and then write respectfully to that audience. (See page 122.)

3 **Master the writing process.** Be prepared to do the necessary work—prewriting, drafting, revising, and refining. Develop efficient writing habits. (See pages 120-138.)

4 **Follow good models.** To save time and money, avoid starting each document from scratch. Keep a file for samples of good writing, check the models in this book, and use the templates on the companion CD. Then copy, paste, and modify models to fit any given situation.

5 **Benchmark your writing with the seven traits.** Practice quality control by measuring your writing in each document against these traits: strong ideas, logical organization, conversational voice, clear words, smooth sentences, correct copy, and reader-friendly design. (See pages 139-160.)

6 **Produce a professional look.** The appearance of your writing is almost as important as the content. So always use appropriate stationery, inks, fonts, logos, envelopes, and so on.

7 **Be a team writer.** Work together for the benefit of the project, the company, and the reader. Test important documents before sending or distributing them. Ask for and give honest feedback in order to improve each piece of writing.

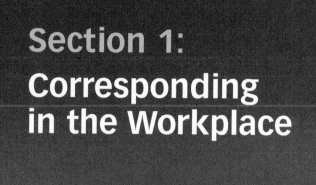

Section 1:
Corresponding in the Workplace

In this section

LESSON

Writing Memos, E-Mail, Letters, and Faxes

Good communication is good business. This has been true throughout history. Well-written memos, e-mails, and letters help your business serve its clients well—to everyone's benefit.

When sending correspondence, your goal is for your reader to understand and respond to your message as planned. You also want to initiate or maintain a good working relationship. In other words, you want results. If you write messages that are clear, complete, and focused on your reader, you will get results.

Guidelines for Memos

1 PREWRITE
Consider your purpose and your audience.
- Ask yourself why you are writing. What outcome do you want?
- Consider your readers. Who needs this memo? Why? How should the memo be sent?

2
Prepare to draft. Gather necessary facts, figures, and attachments. Brainstorm for more details and make a list of your main points.

3 DRAFT
Organize your memo clearly.

[opening] Type "memo" or "memorandum" at the top of the page and complete the memo heading (name only one subject on the subject line).

[middle] Provide details that answer readers' questions: What is this memo about? What does it mean to me? Why is it important?

[closing] Clarify any action needed, especially who is responsible for what.

Note: For good or neutral news, put your key point in the subject line and introduction. For bad-news or persuasive memos, use a neutral subject line and then build to your main point.

4 REVISE
Review your draft for ideas, organization, and voice.
- Have you given clear, accurate information?
- Have you arranged your points logically?
- Have you used a team attitude, focusing on company goals?
- Have you used a polite, professional voice?

5 REFINE
Check your writing line by line for the following:
- ☐ precise word choice, smooth sentences, and effective transitions.
- ☐ a reader-friendly format and design that uses lists, headings, tables, boxes, and white space effectively.
- ☐ correct grammar, punctuation, and spelling.

YOUR GOAL When writing a memo, your goal is to make your point quickly, clearly, and effectively. If possible, keep your memo to a single page.

"Good writing sounds like talking on paper."

BASIC MEMO

Center "Memo" or company name.

Complete and align all four items in the heading. Add your initials.

Type "Subject" or "Re" and add your subject.

[opening]

Expand on the subject line.

[middle]

Use lists where appropriate.

Double-space between paragraphs and items in a list.

[closing]

Focus on action.

Memo

Date: August 8, 2003

To: Josie James

From: Ike Harris   Single- or double-space the heading.

Subject: Promotion of Mona Veal to Full-Time Graphic Artist

Triple Space

For the past 18 months, Mona Veal has done outstanding work as a part-time graphic artist in our Marketing Department. I recommend that she be promoted to full-time status and be given the necessary $5.50 per hour wage increase and full benefits.

Double Space

The promotion is warranted for two reasons:

1. Throughout the past 18 months, Mona has demonstrated those traits that Slenk Manufacturing most values in its graphic artists: creativity, dependability, and the ability to work well with others.

2. Presently we have four full-time and two part-time graphic artists. While this group was able to complete its projects on time last year, Allison Christian in Accounting tells me that the full-time employees averaged 3.5 hours of overtime per week throughout the year. Given that fact, our new contract with LEE-MAR Industries will soon put a strain on both the group and our budget.

Please let me know by August 15 whether you approve this promotion. I'd like Mona to begin full-time work on September 1.

Use 1" to 1.5" margins and a block style.

Expanded Memo

While each memo includes the basic elements shown on page 5, sometimes you may need to add more elements. The guidelines below, which are numbered and modeled on the next page, show your options.

HEADING

1 You can type the word "Memo" or the company name at the top, but do not include the company's address or phone number.

2 For sensitive messages, label your memo **CONFIDENTIAL** and seal it in an envelope that is also marked **CONFIDENTIAL**.

3 Complete your heading with job titles, phone numbers, e-mail addresses, or a checklist showing the memo's purpose. Initial the memo after your name in the heading or after your job title, if one is used. If you have more than one reader, use one of these options:
- List the names after *To:* and highlight a different one on each copy of the memo.
- Put *See distribution* after *To:* and list all the readers at the end of the memo.
- Type a department's name after *To:*

CLOSING

4 Use quick-response options such as checklists, fill-in-the-blanks, or boxes.

5 Add an identification line showing the initials of who wrote the memo (in caps) and who typed it (in lowercase) separated by a slash.

6 If you're sending documents with the memo, type *Attachment(s)* or *Enclosure(s),* followed by either (a) the number of documents or (b) a colon and the document titles listed vertically.

7 If you want to send copies to secondary readers, type *c* or *cc* and a colon; then list the names and job titles stacked vertically (when job titles are included). To send a copy to someone without the main reader knowing it, add *bc* (blind copy) ONLY on the copy sent to the person listed after this notation.

Ike Harris   Page 2   8 August 2003

Page 2
Ike Harris
8 August 2003

FYI If your memo is longer than one page, carry over at least two lines of the message onto a plain sheet of stationery. Use one of the heading formats shown on the left.

EXPANDED MEMO

1 Slenk Manufacturing

2 C O N F I D E N T I A L

Date: August 8, 2003

3 **To:**   Josie James, Director of Personnel
Rebecca Tash, LAHW Representative

From: Ike Harris, Graphic Arts Director   *IH*

Subject: Promotion of Mona Veal to Full-Time Graphic Artist

For the past 18 months, Mona Veal has done outstanding work as a part-time graphic artist in our Marketing Department. I recommend that she be promoted to full-time status. The promotion is warranted for two reasons:

1. Throughout the past 18 months, Mona has demonstrated those traits that Slenk Manufacturing most values in its graphic artists: creativity, dependability, and the ability to work well with others.

2. Presently we have four full-time and two part-time graphic artists. While this group was able to complete its projects on time last year, Allison Christian in Accounting tells me that the full-time employees averaged 3.5 hours of overtime per week throughout the year. Given that fact, our new contract with LEE-MAR Industries will soon put a strain on both the group and our budget.

If you approve the promotion, please initial below and return this memo.

4 Yes, proceed with Mona Veal's promotion to full-time graphic artist. _____

5 IH/gm
6 Attachment: Evaluation report of Mona Veal
7 cc: Elizabeth Zoe
      Mark Moon

Guidelines for E-Mail Messages

1 **PREWRITE**
Consider your purpose and your audience.
- Clarify what you want your e-mail message to accomplish.
- Think about your reader's position and possible reaction.
- Gather necessary information and arrange your points.

2 **DRAFT**
Write with the computer screen in mind.
- Complete the routing information required by your program.
- Give an informative subject line. Don't leave it blank.
- Limit the length of your message to one screen if possible.
- Send longer messages as attachments, pointing to them in the e-mail.

3 **Organize the message into three parts.**
[opening] If appropriate, use a greeting to personalize the message. Then state your reason for writing the message.
[middle] Provide details that answer readers' questions: What is this message about? What does it mean to me? Why is it important? (Try to restrict each e-mail message to a single topic.)
[closing] Indicate any follow-up needed. Who will be responsible for what? Then close politely.

4 **REVISE**
Review your e-mail for ideas, organization, and voice.
- Have you included all the necessary information?
- Is the information accurate and well organized?
- Have you used a friendly but professional voice or tone?

5 **REFINE**
Check your e-mail for the following:
- ☐ precise word choice, smooth sentences, and correct grammar.
- ☐ use of short paragraphs, white space, lists, and headings.
- ☐ correctness—always reread your e-mail before hitting "Send."
- ☐ attachments—have you attached the right files?

YOUR GOAL
In writing an e-mail message, your goal is to provide clear, concise information in a fast, efficient manner. Follow the steps on this page before clicking "Send."

"I try to leave out the parts that people skip."
—Elmore Leonard

BASIC E-MAIL

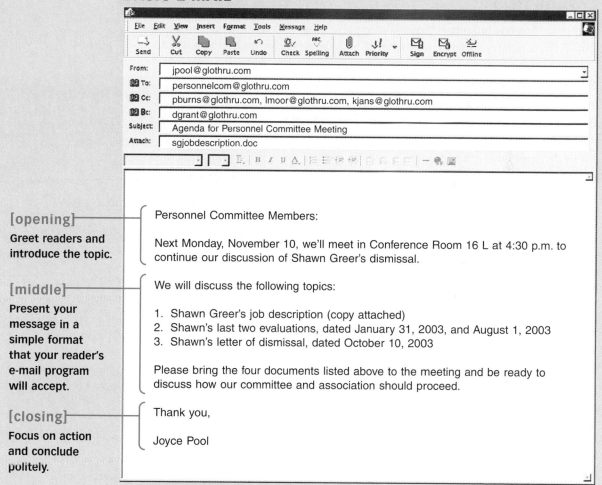

[opening]

Greet readers and introduce the topic.

Personnel Committee Members:

Next Monday, November 10, we'll meet in Conference Room 16 L at 4:30 p.m. to continue our discussion of Shawn Greer's dismissal.

[middle]

Present your message in a simple format that your reader's e-mail program will accept.

We will discuss the following topics:

1. Shawn Greer's job description (copy attached)
2. Shawn's last two evaluations, dated January 31, 2003, and August 1, 2003
3. Shawn's letter of dismissal, dated October 10, 2003

Please bring the four documents listed above to the meeting and be ready to discuss how our committee and association should proceed.

[closing]

Focus on action and conclude politely.

Thank you,

Joyce Pool

From: jpool@glothru.com
To: personnelcom@glothru.com
Cc: pburns@glothru.com, lmoor@glothru.com, kjans@glothru.com
Bc: dgrant@glothru.com
Subject: Agenda for Personnel Committee Meeting
Attach: sgjobdescription.doc

FORMAT TIPS
- Use short paragraphs and double-space between them.
- Create lists with numbers, bullets, or asterisks.
- Begin with an appropriate greeting and conclude with a fitting closing.
- In the subject line, clarify the nature of your message and use labels when appropriate (FOR ACTION, FYI, URGENT).
- Keep line lengths between 65-80 characters and use the word-wrap feature rather than hitting *return*.

E-Mail Tips

E-mail has revolutionized business communication. But when should you choose e-mail over a phone call, letter, or memo? Check the tips below to help you decide.

STRONG POINTS

Simplicity and Speed ■ An e-mail message is composed on-screen through simple key strokes and travels instantly to the reader.

Flexibility and Power ■ With e-mail, you can send, receive, and store messages easily, communicating with both on-site coworkers and far-off customers. In addition, you can embed Web address hyperlinks for reader convenience.

Clarity ■ E-mail replies can include the original correspondence, establishing a clear electronic trail.

Economy ■ Once an e-mail system is set up, maintenance costs are minimal—no postage, no paper.

WEAK POINTS

Quality and Reliability ■ Because e-mail is easy to use, writers may overload readers with poorly written messages. Also, e-mail systems occasionally malfunction.

Accessibility and Respect ■ Reading e-mail on a computer screen is harder than reading print. Some readers may look at e-mail as lightweight correspondence—easy to delete or ignore.

Confidentiality ■ E-mail can sometimes end up in the wrong place, so confidentiality cannot be guaranteed. In addition, your message may be forwarded, so think twice before sending sensitive information by e-mail.

Global Issues ■ Because e-mail can travel around the globe to diverse readers, be sensitive to cultural differences. Avoid slang and colloquialisms.

SPECIAL FEATURES

- *Address book* allows easy access to your e-mail addresses.
- *Mailing lists* allows you to distribute e-mail to groups of users.
- *Copy* allows you to send your message to more than your primary readers. *Blind copy* allows you to send your message to someone without the original reader's knowledge.
- *Reply* allows you to respond to an e-mail on screen—with the option of including the original message. Use cut, copy, and paste with the original message: Don't automatically include the whole message or reply to "all" instead of the writer.
- *Forward* allows you to distribute to others a message you have received.
- *Signature file* allows you to automatically attach contact info to your messages. Include your name, organization, department, and so on, stacked vertically.
- *Search* allows you to do a search of saved e-mail messages.
- *Folders* allows you to save, order, and group messages.
- *Attach documents* allows you to send digital files with your message.

E-Mail Etiquette and Shorthand

How should you behave in the digital world of e-mail? It's simple: Follow the rules of etiquette and use initialisms and emoticons carefully.

Note: Emoticons and initialisms are e-mail shorthand symbols that are informal and can easily be misunderstood. Don't use either in business correspondence.

ETIQUETTE

Appropriate Use ■ Use e-mail for group projects, bulletins, routine messages, and immediate follow-up. Generally, avoid e-mail for sensitive issues, serious topics, or bad news. As always, follow your company's policies about e-mail use.

Formality Level ■ Use language appropriate for your reader, whether a coworker or a client. Distinguish between in-house e-mail and messages to people outside your organization.

Message Checking ■ Check your e-mail several times a day. If you can't respond immediately, send a short message to indicate that you received the message and that you will reply by a specific time.

Distribution ■ Instead of distributing e-mail messages too widely, send them only to those who need them. Otherwise readers may routinely delete your messages.

Flaming ■ Use of anger or sarcasm, called *flaming* (it is often signaled with uppercase), is never appropriate. Cool off and avoid sending an angry message.

Spamming ■ Avoid sending unsolicited ads by e-mail, a practice called *spamming*.

Forwarding ■ Think carefully before forwarding messages. When in doubt, get permission from the original sender.

Ethics ■ Because companies are legally responsible for their computer network activity, e-mail is company property. In addition, networks typically store messages for years. So only write messages you would not mind seeing in the company newsletter.

EMOTICONS

You make emoticons, often called *smileys*, with simple keyboard strokes. To get the picture, turn your head to the left.

:) or :-)	a smile
:D	a big smile
:-(	a frown, unhappy
:-O	shocked or amazed
:-	undecided
:-/	skeptical or puzzled
:-*	oops!
II*(	handshake offered
II*)	handshake accepted

INITIALISMS

Initialisms are abbreviations written in all capital letters with no periods.

OTOH	On The Other Hand
F2F	Face To Face
BTW	By The Way
FYI	For Your Information
IMHO	In My Humble Opinion
TIA	Thanks In Advance
WRT	With Respect To
IOW	In Other Words
FWIW	For What It's Worth

Guidelines for Letters

1 **PREWRITE**
Consider your purpose and your audience.
- Ask yourself what you want the letter to accomplish.
- Consider the reader's concerns about, knowledge of, and history with your organization.

2 **Gather information.**
- Gather files and other necessary resources.
- Jot down your main points in a logical order.
- Use the letter format (full-block, semiblock, or simplified) that your company prefers.

3 **DRAFT**
Organize the body of your letter into three parts.
[opening] State the situation (reason for writing, background).
[middle] Give the full explanation, supporting points, and details. If your message is good or neutral news, make your key point early. For a bad-news or persuasive message, build up to the main point.
[closing] End with a call for action (who should do what, when), and, if appropriate, mention future contact.

4 **REVISE**
Review your draft for ideas, organization, and voice.
- Are all names, dates, and details accurate?
- Is information presented in a logical order?
- Do you use a conversational but professional tone?
- Do you emphasize the reader's perspective?

5 **REFINE**
Check your writing line by line for the following:
- ☐ precise wording and positive use of personal pronouns, especially "you."
- ☐ smooth sentences that pass the "read aloud" test.
- ☐ correct spelling (especially double-check names).
- ☐ correct grammar, punctuation, and mechanics.
- ☐ appropriate format and design.

YOUR GOAL   When writing a business letter, your goal is to communicate your message and give a positive impression of yourself and your organization.

"Be yourself when you write. You will stand out as a real person among robots."
—William Zinsser

Professional Appearance of Letters

Before your readers catch a word of your message, they've already read your letter's overall appearance. What does it say to them? Use the guidelines on this page to ensure a good impression.

FIRST IMPRESSIONS

Choose your look. ■ Do you want your letter to look traditional and conservative or friendly and contemporary? (See "Letter Formats," page 18.)

Frame your letter in white space. ■ Make your margins 1 to 1.5 inches left and right, top and bottom. Create a balanced, open look by centering the message vertically and adjusting the space between the parts of the letter.

Make reading easy. ■ Use sensible type sizes and styles.

- Keep type size at 10-12 points.
- Choose a user-friendly font. Serif type has fine lines finishing off the main strokes of the letter. (This is serif type.) Sans serif type has a block-letter look. (This is sans serif type.) Serif typefaces are easier to read and understand; sans serif typefaces work well for headings.
- Avoid flashy and frequent type changes, as well as overuse of italics or boldface.

Print for quality. ■ Use a quality printer and avoid any handwritten editing changes. Always print a clean final copy.

LETTER PERFECT

Use 20- to 24-pound bond paper. ■ The 20- to 24-pound bond paper folds cleanly, takes ink crisply, and works well in most office machines.

Use 8.5- by 11-inch paper. ■ It's standard and files easily. Other sizes may be used for personal correspondence, executive letters, or mass mailings.

Use white or off-white paper. ■ Be careful with other colors. Light, subtle colors mean business. Bold colors scream, "I'm an ad!"

Match, don't mix. ■ Letterhead pages, continuation sheets, and envelopes should match in paper weight, size, color, and design.

LETTERHEAD DESIGN

If you are asked to design or redesign your company's letterhead stationery—or if you want to design a letterhead specific to your position—be sure to include the following:

- the company's complete legal name;
- the company logo or slogan;
- complete contact information—full address, phone number (including area code), a fax number, a Web-site address; and
- names of key people (perhaps in the left-margin sidebar).

Note: Make sure your design reflects your company's mission and character.

Basic Letter

All letters should include a clear message and information about the writer and the reader. Details for both are listed below and on page 16.

Basic Letter Guidelines

- Do not indent paragraphs.
- Single-space within paragraphs.
- Double-space between paragraphs.
- Leave the right margin ragged (uneven).
- Set margins from 1 to 1.5 inches.

1 The **heading** provides the reader a return address. Type the address (minus the writer's name) at the top of the letter. Spell out words like *Road, Street, West*. Omit the address if you are using a letterhead.

2 The **date** shows when the letter was drafted or dictated. Write the date as *month, day, year* for U.S. correspondence (August 5, 2003); write *day, month, year* for international or military correspondence (5 August 2003).

3 The **inside address** gives the reader's name and complete mailing address. Type it flush left and include as many details as necessary, in this order:
  - reader's courtesy title, name, and job title (if the job title is one word)
  - reader's job title (if two or more words)
  - office or department
  - organization name
  - street address/p.o. box/suite/room (comma precedes *NE, SE,* etc.)
  - city, state, zip code (or city, country, postal code)

4 The **salutation** personalizes the message. Capitalize all first letters and place a colon after the name. (See "Forms of Address," pages 24-27.)

5 The **body** contains the message, usually organized into three parts:
  - an opening that states why you are writing,
  - a middle that gives readers the details they need, and
  - a closing that focuses on what should happen next.

6 The **complimentary closing** provides a polite word or phrase to end the message. Capitalize the first word only and add a comma after the closing.

7 The **signature block** makes the letter official. Align the writer's name with the complimentary closing. Place a one-word job title on the same line as the typed name or below the name; place a longer title below the typed name.

8 Use an **enclosure note** whenever you enclose something. Type *Enclosure(s)* or *Enc(s). a*nd the number of enclosures. To list enclosures by name, type *Enclosure(s)* or *Enc(s).*, a colon, and the names stacked vertically. (See an alternate format of a vertical list on page 93.)

9 A **postscript** contains a personal or final note. Type *P.S.* (with periods but no colon) followed by the message. (Shown on page 50.)

BASIC LETTER

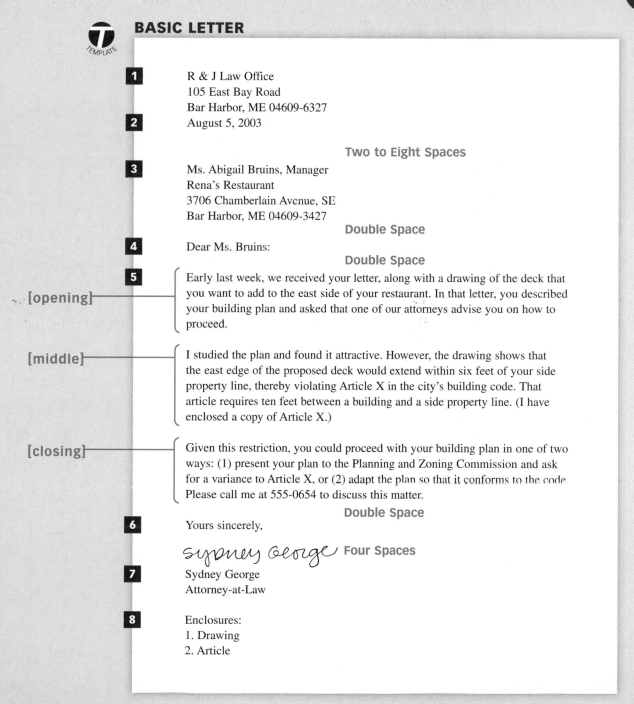

1
R & J Law Office
105 East Bay Road
Bar Harbor, ME 04609-6327

2
August 5, 2003

Two to Eight Spaces

3
Ms. Abigail Bruins, Manager
Rena's Restaurant
3706 Chamberlain Avenue, SE
Bar Harbor, ME 04609-3427

Double Space

4
Dear Ms. Bruins:

Double Space

5
[opening]
Early last week, we received your letter, along with a drawing of the deck that you want to add to the east side of your restaurant. In that letter, you described your building plan and asked that one of our attorneys advise you on how to proceed.

[middle]
I studied the plan and found it attractive. However, the drawing shows that the east edge of the proposed deck would extend within six feet of your side property line, thereby violating Article X in the city's building code. That article requires ten feet between a building and a side property line. (I have enclosed a copy of Article X.)

[closing]
Given this restriction, you could proceed with your building plan in one of two ways: (1) present your plan to the Planning and Zoning Commission and ask for a variance to Article X, or (2) adapt the plan so that it conforms to the code. Please call me at 555-0654 to discuss this matter.

Double Space

6
Yours sincerely,

Sydney George   Four Spaces

7
Sydney George
Attorney-at-Law

8
Enclosures:
1. Drawing
2. Article

Expanded Letter

Adding Information

When you, your reader, a typist, a filing clerk, or future readers need additional information, include one or more of the items from this list.

1 A **method of transmission note** indicates how a letter should be or has been sent: via facsimile, via registered mail, via overnight courier.

2 A **reference line** begins with a guide word and a colon (*Reference:*, *In reply to:*) followed by a file, an account, an invoice, or a database number.

3 When appropriate, use a **confidential notation** on both the letter and the envelope. CAPITALIZE or underline the word *confidential* for emphasis.

4 In the **inside address**, stack names by alphabet or position for two or more readers. For two readers at separate addresses, stack the addresses (including names) with a line between.

5 The **attention line** designates a reader or department but encourages others to read the letter. Place it two lines below the inside address, flush left or centered. CAPITALIZE or underline for emphasis. (See page 47 for a model.)

6 The **subject line** announces the topic and is placed flush left two lines below the salutation. CAPITALIZE or underline for emphasis.

7 The **signature block** may include the writer's courtesy title typed in front of the name to clarify his or her gender or a preferred form of address. If two people must sign the letter, place the second name beside the first starting at the center of the page—or place it four spaces below the first name.

8 In the **identification line**, type the writer's initials in capitals and the typist's in lowercase, separated by a slash (but no spaces).

9 Use the **copies notation** by typing *c* or *cc*, followed by a colon and a vertical list of people (with job titles in parentheses). To send a copy to someone else without the reader knowing it, type *bc* or *bcc* (blind copy), but only on the copy sent to the person listed.

10 **Continuation pages** follow a letter's first page. On blank stationery, carry over at least two lines and use a heading in one of the formats below:

Page 2
Abigail Bruins
Paul Meyer
August 5, 2003

Abigail Bruins   Page 2   August 5, 2003
Paul Meyer

EXPANDED LETTER

R&J Law Office
105 East Bay Road, Bar Harbor, ME 04609-6327 ● 207-555-0645 ● rjlawoffice.com

August 5, 2003

Two to Eight Spaces

1 Via facsimile

Double Space

2 Reference: Article X

Double Space

3 CONFIDENTIAL

Double Space

4 Ms. Abigail Bruins
Mr. Paul Meyer
Rena's Restaurant
3706 Chamberlain Avenue, SE
Bar Harbor, ME 04609-3427

Double Space

Dear Ms. Bruins and Mr. Mcyer:

Double Space

6 BUILDING PERMIT

Double Space

Early last week we received your letter, along with a drawing of the deck that you want to add to the east side of your restaurant. I studied the plan and found it attractive. However, the drawing shows that the proposed deck would extend within six feet of your property line, thereby violating Article X in the city's building code. That article requires ten feet between a building and a side property line.

Given this restriction, you could proceed with your building plan in one of two ways: (1) present your plan to the Planning and Zoning Commission and ask for a variance to Article X, or (2) adapt the plan so that it conforms to the code. Please call me at 555-0654 to discuss this matter.

Double Space

Yours sincerely,

Four Spaces

7 *Sydney George*

Ms. Sydney George
Attorney-at-Law

Double Space

8 SG/mbb
Enclosures 2
9 cc: Leah Theodore (Senior Partner)

Special Note: Item 5 from page 16 is not shown in this model. See 47 to see an *attention line.*

Letter Formats

You can arrange a letter in a full-block, semi-block, or simplified format. Choose the letter format that best fits the situation and your organization's guidelines.

FULL-BLOCK FORMAT

Rules:	All parts flush left
Character:	Professional, clean, contemporary
Plus:	Easy to set up and follow
Minus:	May appear unbalanced to the left of the page
Best Uses:	Routine letters, not social and executive letters
Note:	More traditional and international readers may not prefer this format.

SEMIBLOCK FORMAT

Rules:	Date line, method of transmission line, reference line, complimentary close, and signature block align with a vertical line at the center of the page; all other parts of the letter are flush left.
Character:	Professional, traditional
Plus:	Balanced appearance on the page
Minus:	More difficult setup than full block or simplified
Best Uses:	International and traditional letters, as well as executive and social letters
Note:	You may indent the subject line and all paragraphs to further soften the form. In addition, you may drop the space between paragraphs.

SIMPLIFIED FORMAT

Rules:	All parts flush left No salutation or complimentary close Subject line and writer's name in caps; dash between the writer's name and title
Character:	Bare-bones, functional
Plus:	Easy setup
Minus:	Impersonal format due to lack of courtesy elements
Best Uses:	Routine letters—regular reminders, notices, bulletins, orders, mass mailings Not appropriate for high-level or persuasive letters
Note:	You may drop courtesy titles from the inside address.

FULL BLOCK

R & J Law Office
105 East Bay Road, Bar Harbor, ME 04609-6327
207-555-0654   rjlawoffice.com

August 5, 2003

Ref. A. Bruins #2

CONFIDENTIAL

Ms. Abigail Bruins
Mr. Paul Meyer
Rena's Restaurant
Box 248
Bar Harbor, ME 04609-3427

Dear Ms. Bruins and Mr. Meyer:

BUILDING PERMIT

Early last week, we received your letter, along with drawings of the deck that you want to add to the east side of your restaurant. In that letter, you described your building plan and asked that one of our attorneys advise you on how to proceed.

I studied the plan and found it attractive. However, the drawings show that the east edge of the proposed deck would extend within six feet of your side property line, thereby violating Article X in the city's building code. That article requires ten feet between a building and a side property line.

Given this restriction, you could proceed with your building plan in one of two ways: (1) present your plan to the Planning and Zoning Commission and ask for a variance to Article X, or (2) adapt the plan so that it conforms to the code.

Please call me at 555-0654 to discuss this matter.

Yours sincerely,

Sydney George

Ms. Sydney George
Attorney-at-Law

SG/mbb
Enc.: Article X
cc: Leah Theodore

SEMIBLOCK

R & J Law Office
105 East Bay Road, Bar Harbor, ME 04609-6327
207-555-0654   rjlawoffice.com

August 5, 2003

Ref. A. Bruins #2

CONFIDENTIAL

Ms. Abigail Bruins
Mr. Paul Meyer
Rena's Restaurant
Box 248
Bar Harbor, ME 04609-3427

Dear Ms. Bruins and Mr. Meyer:

BUILDING PERMIT

Early last week, we received your letter, along with drawings of the deck that you want to add to the east side of your restaurant. In that letter, you described your building plan and asked that one of our attorneys advise you on how to proceed.

I studied the plan and found it attractive. However, the drawings show that the east edge of the proposed deck would extend within six feet of your side property line, thereby violating Article X in the city's building code. That article requires ten feet between a building and a side property line.

Given this restriction, you could proceed with your building plan in one of two ways: (1) present your plan to the Planning and Zoning Commission and ask for a variance to Article X, or (2) adapt the plan so that it conforms to the code.

Please call me at 555-0654 to discuss this matter.

Yours sincerely,

Sydney George

Ms. Sydney George
Attorney-at-Law

SG/mbb
Enc.: Article X
cc: Leah Theodore

SIMPLIFIED

R & J Law Office
105 East Bay Road, Bar Harbor, ME 04609-6327
207-555-0665   rjlawoffice.com

August 5, 2003

Ref. A. Bruins #2

CONFIDENTIAL

Abigail Bruins
Paul Meyer
Rena's Restaurant
Box 248
Bar Harbor, ME 04609-3427

BUILDING PERMIT

Early last week, we received your letter, along with drawings of the deck that you want to add to the east side of your restaurant. In that letter, you described your building plan and asked that one of our attorneys advise you on how to proceed.

I studied the plan and found it attractive. However, the drawings show that the east edge of the proposed deck would extend within six feet of your side property line, thereby violating Article X in the city's building code. That article requires ten feet between a building and a side property line.

Given this restriction, you could proceed with your building plan in one of two ways: (1) present your plan to the Planning and Zoning Commission and ask for a variance to Article X, or (2) adapt the plan so that it conforms to the code.

Please call me at 555-0654 to discuss this matter.

Sydney George

MS. SYDNEY GEORGE—ATTORNEY-AT-LAW

SG/mbb
Enc.: Article X
cc: Leah Theodore

Letters and Envelopes

FOLDING LETTERS

A Standard Fold: To put a letter in its matching envelope, place the letter face up and follow these steps:

1 Fold the bottom edge up so that the paper is divided into thirds. Use your thumbnail to create a clean crease.

2 Fold the top third down over the bottom third, leaving 1/4 inch for easy unfolding, and crease firmly.

3 Insert the letter (with the open end at the top) into the envelope.

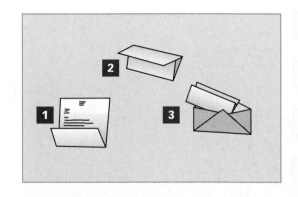

A Large Sheet in a Small Envelope: If you must place a letter in a small envelope, follow these steps:

1 Fold the bottom edge up so that the paper is divided in half, and create a clean crease.

2 Fold the right side to the left so that the sheet is divided into thirds; crease firmly.

3 Fold the left third over the right third and crease firmly.

4 Turn the letter sideways and insert it (with the open end at the top) into the envelope.

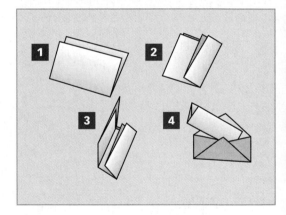

A Window Envelope: Position the inside address on the letter so that it will show through the window. Then place the letter face up and fold it as follows:

1 Fold the bottom edge up so that the paper is divided into thirds, and create a clean crease.

2 Turn the letter face down with the top edge toward you and fold the top third of the letter back.

3 Insert the letter in the envelope and make sure that the whole address shows through the window.

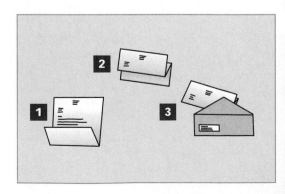

U.S. Postal Service (USPS) Envelope Guidelines

To be sure that your letters are delivered quickly and correctly, follow all United States Postal Service (USPS) guidelines when you address an envelope. See the envelope and helpful guidelines below.

MS ABIGAIL BRUINS
RENAS RESTAURANT
BOX 248
BAR HARBOR ME 04609-3427

CONFIDENTIAL

2 3/8" maximum from bottom

MS ELIZABETH MOIZE
ASSOCIATE EDITOR
NATIONAL GEOGRAPHIC SOCIETY
1145 17TH ST NW RM 14
WASHINGTON DC 20036-4701

1" minimum
left and right

5/8" minimum from bottom

1. Type the receiver's name and address in black ink on a light-colored envelope. Use an all-cap style for everything in the address. Make sure all lines are horizontal and lined up flush left. Leave out all punctuation except the hyphen in the zip code.

2. Type the receiver's address—including the type of street (ST, AVE), compass points (NE, SW), and full ZIP code—in the order pictured. Place the suite, room, or apartment number on the address line, after the street address.

3. Use USPS abbreviations for states and other words in the address. Use numerals rather than words for numbered streets (9TH AVE). Add ZIP+4 codes. (Go to **www.usps.com** to get the ZIP code for any street address in the country.)

TIPS FOR INTERNATIONAL MAIL

When sending international mail, print the country name alone on the last line. As long as the country, city, and state or province are in English, the name and address may be in the language of the country listed.

Pattern: *Name of Receiver*
Street Address or PO Box
City, State/Province, Code
Country (Caps, English)

Examples:

MR BRUCE WARNER
2431 EDEN WAY
LONDON W1P 4HQ
ENGLAND

MS TAMARA BEALS
56 METCALFE CRES
MONTREAL QC J7V 8P2
CANADA

Standard Postal Abbreviations

STATES, PROVINCES, AND TERRITORIES

U.S. States						Canadian Provinces, Territories	
Alabama	AL	Kansas	KS	Ohio	OH		
Alaska	AK	Kentucky	KY	Oklahoma	OK	Alberta	AB
Arizona	AZ	Louisiana	LA	Oregon	OR	British Columbia	BC
Arkansas	AR	Maine	ME	Pennsylvania	PA	Manitoba	MB
California	CA	Maryland	MD	Puerto Rico	PR	New Brunswick	NB
Colorado	CO	Massachusetts	MA	Rhode Island	RI	Newfoundland	
Connecticut	CT	Michigan	MI	South Carolina	SC	and Labrador	NL
Delaware	DE	Minnesota	MN	South Dakota	SD	Northwest	
District of		Mississippi	MS	Tennessee	TN	Territories	NT
Columbia	DC	Missouri	MO	Texas	TX	Nova Scotia	NS
Florida	FL	Montana	MT	Utah	UT	Nunavut	NU
Georgia	GA	Nebraska	NE	Vermont	VT	Ontario	ON
Guam	GU	Nevada	NV	Virginia	VA	Prince Edward	
Hawaii	HI	New Hampshire	NH	Virgin Islands	VI	Island	PE
Idaho	ID	New Jersey	NJ	Washington	WA	Quebec	QC
Illinois	IL	New Mexico	NM	West Virginia	WV	Saskatchewan	SK
Indiana	IN	New York	NY	Wisconsin	WI	Yukon Territory	YT
Iowa	IA	North Carolina	NC	Wyoming	WY		
		North Dakota	ND				

ABBREVIATIONS FOR USE ON ENVELOPES

FYI For mass mailings, check the Postal Service's bar-coding and mailing-list services for speed and savings. Go to **www.usps.com**.

Annex	ANX	Lake	LK	Route	RTE
Apartment	APT	Lakes	LKS	Rural	R
Avenue	AVE	Lane	LN	Rural Route	RR
Boulevard	BLVD	Meadows	MDWS	Shore	SH
Building	BLDG	North	N	South	S
Causeway	CSWY	Northeast	NE	Southeast	SE
Circle	CIR	Northwest	NW	Southwest	SW
Court	CT	Office	OFC	Square	SQ
Drive	DR	Palms	PLMS	Station	STA
East	E	Park	PARK	Street	ST
Expressway	EXPY	Parkway	PKWY	Suite	STE
Floor	FL	Place	PL	Terrace	TER
Fort	FT	Plaza	PLZ	Throughway	TRWY
Freeway	FWY	Port	PRT	Turnpike	TPKE
Harbor	HBR	Post Office Box	PO BOX	Union	UN
Heights	HTS	Ridge	RDG	Viaduct	VIA
Highway	HWY	River	RIV	View	VW
Hospital	HOSP	Road	RD	Village	VLG
Junction	JCT	Room	RM	West	W

Faxing Documents

Fax machines send and receive documents quickly and cheaply. When sending a fax, use your organization's cover sheet. If no cover sheet is available, create your own using some or all of the items below. (Most software programs include templates for cover sheets.)

Your company's letterhead

The receiver's name, title, company, phone number, and fax number

Your name, telephone number, and fax number

The date

Message: a subject line or brief direction

The number of pages sent

A trouble-shooting statement asking the receiver to call if a transmission problem occurs

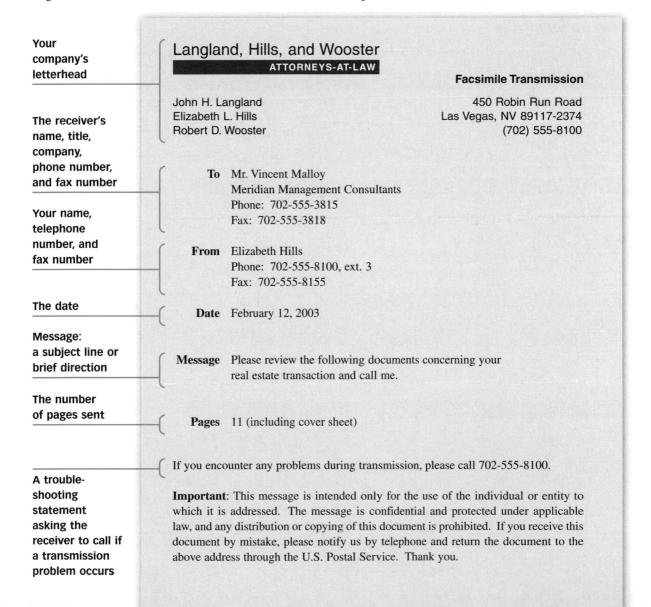

Langland, Hills, and Wooster
ATTORNEYS-AT-LAW

John H. Langland
Elizabeth L. Hills
Robert D. Wooster

Facsimile Transmission

450 Robin Run Road
Las Vegas, NV 89117-2374
(702) 555-8100

To   Mr. Vincent Malloy
Meridian Management Consultants
Phone: 702-555-3815
Fax: 702-555-3818

From   Elizabeth Hills
Phone: 702-555-8100, ext. 3
Fax: 702-555-8155

Date   February 12, 2003

Message   Please review the following documents concerning your real estate transaction and call me.

Pages   11 (including cover sheet)

If you encounter any problems during transmission, please call 702-555-8100.

Important: This message is intended only for the use of the individual or entity to which it is addressed. The message is confidential and protected under applicable law, and any distribution or copying of this document is prohibited. If you receive this document by mistake, please notify us by telephone and return the document to the above address through the U.S. Postal Service. Thank you.

Forms of Address

Usually, you can rely on common sense to tell you how to address your reader with respect. When you're unsure, use the guidelines below and on the following pages to find a fitting title, salutation, and complimentary closing.

Professional Titles

	Titles in Address	Salutations
Business		
CEO	Ms. Sarah Falwell Chief Executive Officer	Dear Ms. Falwell:
Vice President	Dr. David Levengood Vice President	Dear Dr. Levengood:
Company Official	Ms. Susan Cook, Comptroller	Dear Ms. Cook:
Education		
President or Chancellor of University (Ph.D.)	Dr. Joe Smith, President	Dear Dr. Smith: (or) Dear President Smith:
Dean of a School or College (Ph.D.)	Dr. Marjorie Stone, Dean School of Life Sciences	Dear Dr. Stone: (or) Dear Dean Stone:
Professor (Ph.D.)	Dr. Patricia Monk Professor of Psychology	Dear Dr. Monk: (or) Dear Professor Monk:
Instructor (no Ph.D.)	Mr. Art Linkman Instructor of Physics	Dear Mr. Linkman:
Legal		
Lawyer	Mr. Daniel Walker Attorney-at-Law	Dear Mr. Walker:
	Daniel Walker, Esq.	Dear Daniel Walker, Esq.:
Medical		
Physician	Dr. Sarah McDonald	Dear Dr. McDonald:
	Sarah McDonald, M.D.	
Registered Nurse	Nurse John Seguin	Dear Nurse Seguin:
	John Seguin, R.N.	
Dentist	Dr. Leslie Matheson	Dear Dr. Matheson:
	Leslie Matheson, D.D.S.	
Veterinarian	Dr. Manuel Ortega	Dear Dr. Ortega:
	Manuel Ortega, D.V.M.	

Professional Titles

- Avoid writing to positions, titles, or departments. Call the organization (or visit its Web site) for names.

- Spell out all professional titles except **Dr.**

- Avoid using two professional titles that mean the same thing: *Dr. Paula Felch, M.D.*

Male, Female, Multiple, and Unnamed Readers

	Titles in Address	Salutations
One Woman (avoid showing marital status)		
Preferred	**Ms. Barbara Jordan**	**Dear Ms. Jordan:**
Married or Widowed	**Mrs. Lorene Frost**	**Dear Mrs. Frost:**
Single	**Miss Adriana Langille**	**Dear Miss Langille:**
Two or More Women (alphabetical)		
Standard	**Ms. Bethany Jergens Ms. Shavonn Mitchell**	**Dear Ms. Jergens and Ms. Mitchell:**
Formal	**Mmes. Bethany Jergens and Shavonn Mitchell**	**Dear Mmes. Jergens and Mitchell:**
One Man		
Standard	**Mr. Hugh Knight**	**Dear Mr. Knight:**
With Jr., Sr., or Roman Numeral	**Mr. Brian Boswell, Jr. Mr. Brian Boswell III**	**Dear Mr. Boswell:**
Two or More Men (alphabetical)		
Standard	**Mr. Alex Fernandez Mr. Nate Shaw**	**Dear Mr. Fernandez and Mr. Shaw:**
Formal	**Messrs. Alex Fernandez and Nate Shaw**	**Dear Messrs. Fernandez and Shaw:**
One Man and One Woman (alphabetical)		
	Ms. Paula Trunhope Mr. Joe Williams	**Dear Ms. Trunhope and Mr. Williams:**
Married Couple		
Same Last Name	**Mr. William and Mrs. Susan Lui**	**Dear Mr. and Mrs. Lui:**
Different Last Names	**Mr. William Bentley Ms. Sinead Sweeney**	**Dear Mr. Bentley and Ms. Sweeney:**
One Reader (gender unknown)		
	M. Robin Leeds Robin Leeds	**Dear M. Leeds: Dear Robin Leeds:**
Mixed Group		
Company, Department, Job Title, or Unknown Reader	**Acme Corporation Human Resources Dept.**	Formal **Dear Sir or Madam:** Informal **Dear Manager:**

Courtesy Titles

- Choose "standard" or "formal" titles and salutations based on your relationship with the reader and the seriousness of the message.

- Abbreviate all courtesy titles: **Mr., Ms., Mrs.**

- Never guess your reader's gender (*Robin, Pat, Chris*).

Government Officials and Representatives

To properly address government officials (national, state, local, judicial, and so on), follow this pattern:

Title in Inside Address:	The Honorable *(full name)*
	(full title on second line)

Formal Salutation:	**Dear Sir/Madam:** or **Dear Mr./Madam** *(position)***:**
Informal Salutation:	**Dear Mr./Ms.** *(last name)***:** or **Dear** *(position) (last name)***:**

	Titles in Address	Salutations
National		
President	**The President**	**Dear Mr./Madam President:**
Vice President	**The Vice President**	**Dear Mr. Vice President:**
Speaker of the House	**The Honorable Steven Kudo**	**Dear Mr. Speaker:**
Cabinet Members, Undersecretaries, etc.	**The Honorable Jane Doe**	**Dear Madam:**
		Dear Attorney General Doe:
Senators (U.S. or State)	**The Honorable Bill Johnson**	**Dear Senator Johnson:**
Representatives (U.S. or State)	**The Honorable Joan Walker**	**Dear Ms. Walker:**
		Dear Representative Walker:
Heads of Offices and Agencies	**The Honorable John Hillman** **Postmaster General**	**Dear Mr. Postmaster General:**
		Dear Mr. Hillman:
Chief Justice (U.S. or State)	**The Honorable Shelby Woo** **Chief Justice of California**	**Dear Madam Chief Justice:**
U.S. Ambassador	**The Honorable Francis del Verda**	**Dear Madam Ambassador:**
		Dear Ambassador del Verda:
State/Local		
Governor	**The Honorable Mary Lee**	**Dear Governor Lee:**
Mayor	**The Honorable Mark Barne**	**Dear Mayor Barne:**
Council Member	**The Honorable Corey Springs**	**Dear Mr. Springs:**
Judge	**The Honorable Grace Kim**	**Dear Judge Kim:**
Military		
General	**Major General Karl P. Bastion, USAF**	**Sir: (formal)** **Dear General Bastion:**
Lieutenant	**Lieutenant Jane Evans, USMC**	**Dear Ms. Evans:**

Official Titles

- Use a formal title (**Senator, General**) rather than a standard courtesy title (*Mr., Ms.*).

- Avoid outdated courtesy forms (*Gentlemen, To Whom It May Concern*).

Religious Titles

To address religious leaders from any faith with titles that fit their positions, follow these guidelines.

	Titles in Address	Salutations
Roman Catholic Clergy		
Cardinal	His Eminence, Edward Cardinal Romero	Your Eminence:
		Dear Cardinal Romero:
Archbishop and Bishop	The Most Reverend Henri Crétien	Your Excellency:
		Dear Bishop/Archbishop Crétien:
Priest	The Reverend Morris Franklin	Reverend Sir:
		Dear Father Franklin:
Nun	Sister Mary Jennsen	Dear Sister Mary:
		Dear Sister Jennsen:
Monk	Brother Atticus Bartholemew	Dear Brother Atticus:
		Dear Brother Bartholemew:
Protestant Clergy		
Bishop (Anglican, Episcopal, Methodist)	The Right Reverend Samuel Wolfe	Right Reverend Sir:
		Reverend Sir:
		Dear Bishop Wolfe:
Dean (Head of Cathedral or Seminary)	The Very Reverend Nicholas Cameron	Very Reverend Sir:
		Dear Dean Cameron:
Minister or Priest	The Reverend Susan Edwards	Dear Reverend Edwards:
	Pastor Edwards	Dear Pastor Edwards:
Chaplain	Chaplain Adam Carp Captain, USMC	Dear Chaplain Carp:
Jewish Clergy		
Rabbi	Rabbi Joshua Gould	Dear Rabbi Gould:
Rabbi with Doctor of Divinity Degree	Rabbi Joshua Gould, D.D.	Dear Dr. Gould:

Religious Titles

- The use of *The* before *Reverend* differs from church to church. Follow the organization's preference.

- In some religious orders, the title in the salutation is followed by the reader's first name. Other orders prefer the last name.

- If the person has a Doctor of Divinity degree, add a comma and *D.D.* after his or her name in the address (not the salutation).

CHECKLIST The Memo, E-Mail Message, or Letter . . .

STRONG IDEAS 140

- ☐ is strong, clear, and accurate.
- ☐ has answered the reader's questions: Why are you writing me? What needs to be done?

LOGICAL ORGANIZATION 142

- ☐ is appropriately direct or indirect, based on the reader's likely response.
- ☐ contains an informative subject line (especially an e-mail message or a memo).
- ☐ follows a fitting opening, middle, closing structure.

CONVERSATIONAL VOICE 144

- ☐ is courteous throughout, from salutation to complimentary closing.
- ☐ uses an appropriate voice and focuses on the reader's needs.

CLEAR WORDS 148

- ☐ uses plain English—precise, clear, and simple words.
- ☐ uses and defines technical terms carefully.
- ☐ uses names and personal pronouns, especially "you," effectively.

SMOOTH SENTENCES 152

- ☐ has short- to medium-length sentences that pass the "read aloud" test.
- ☐ uses transition words to link ideas.

CORRECT COPY 156

- ☐ follows all punctuation and capitalization rules for memos and letters.
- ☐ uses correct abbreviations, titles, and spelling throughout.
- ☐ contains no grammar or typing errors.

READER-FRIENDLY DESIGN 158

- ☐ follows all the rules of the format—spacing, margins, alignment, and so on.
- ☐ contains short paragraphs—with no indenting, single-spacing within, and double-spacing between.
- ☐ uses headings and bulleted or numbered lists wherever helpful.
- ☐ has a polished look—white space, clean typography, and good stationery.
- ☐ includes initials, signatures, and attachments, if appropriate.

LESSON

Writing Good-News and Neutral Messages

There's no news like good news. That's as true in the workplace as it is in the rest of life. Readers are happy to receive good-news letters, memos, and e-mail messages. They usually respond, "It's good to know this!" or "It's my job to deal with this, so I'll take care of it."

When you believe that your reader will respond positively, draft a message that gets right to the main point. You may also want to state why the message is good news and how it may benefit the reader. If a response is expected, be sure to advise the reader that you are looking forward to hearing from him or her again, and clarify what it is you need to know.

Guidelines for Good-News and Neutral Messages

1 PREWRITE
Consider your audience and purpose.
- Ask yourself what you want your message to do.
- Think about the person you are writing to, what he or she already knows, and what he or she needs to know.

2 **Prepare to draft.**
- Find and list details that describe, explain, and clarify your main point.
- Jot down a brief outline to organize the message.

3 DRAFT
Present your message clearly.

[opening] Identify the topic and explain why you are writing. Present your key point as either a statement, a question, or a request.
[middle] Support your main point with details that clarify the situation, news, and implications. If appropriate, focus on benefits.
[closing] Note any action the reader should take; include steps that may be taken; and add contact information. Indicate *who* should do *what, when, where, why,* and *how.* If action is unnecessary, simply end the message positively and politely.

4 REVISE
Review your draft for ideas, organization, and voice.
- Have you included accurate details—in the best order?
- Have you used a businesslike tone with polite attention to the reader's needs and benefits?

5 REFINE
Check your writing line by line for the following:
- ☐ clear, concise wording.
- ☐ readable sentences and helpful transitions.
- ☐ correct grammar, punctuation, and spelling.
- ☐ effective format (spacing, type size, fonts, and so on).

"Good words are worth much, and cost little."
—George Herbert

TEMPLATE

ANNOUNCEMENT OR NOTICE

MEMO

Date: March 24, 2003

To: All Rankin Employees

From: Brittany Elias

Subject: New Policy for Air-Travel Arrangements

[opening]
State the main point up front.

Starting April 1, please make all your company-related flight arrangements through The Travel Center. This change will require some adjustments, but it will actually benefit both you and the company.

[middle]
Provide details to explain the main point.

Present information from the reader's point of view.

The business office is implementing the change because The Travel Center is now offering several options for its corporate customers. In checking out the options, we found an attractive reservation and payment plan. Here are some details:

- If you personally book a flight with The Travel Center, you will accumulate bonus miles in your name.

- If the company books the flight, as in the past, the company will receive the bonus miles.

- The company will have a more efficient way to track travel costs.

[closing]
Explain what the reader should do. Close the message by inviting feedback.

Please follow the procedure below for all future company flights:

1. Book flights through The Travel Center (262-555-8898) and charge them to Rankin.

2. When Sherri Pomerenki forwards the invoice to you, specify the account to be charged, sign the invoice, and return it to her.

If you have any questions, please contact me by phone (ext. 9721) or e-mail (belias@rnkn.com).

APOLOGY

∾MAGNOLIA GRAND∾
2580 Peach Tree Court
Memphis, TN 64301
901-555-5400 maggrand@hytp.com

July 7, 2003

Ms. Joan Meyer
605 Appleton Avenue
Green Bay, WI 53401

Dear Ms. Meyer:

[opening]
Use a positive tone.

Welcome to Magnolia Grand! We are pleased to host your stay in Memphis.

[middle]
Apologize and explain what you are doing to make amends.

We apologize that your confirmed room was unavailable last night, and we are sorry for the inconvenience this may have caused you. Because several guests did not depart as scheduled, we were forced to change your accommodations. For your trouble, there will be no charge for last night's lodging.

As always, our goal is to offer you outstanding service and genuine hospitality. To that end, we have upgraded your room at no expense to you.

[closing]
Stress further assistance and continued satisfaction.

Should you need any assistance, please call the front desk or contact me directly at extension 408. We hope you enjoy the remainder of your stay with us. Thank you for your patience, understanding, and patronage.

Yours sincerely,

Mary-Lee Preston

Mary-Lee Preston
Front Office Manager

MP/am

COVER MESSAGE

MEMO

Date: June 19, 2003

To: Department Heads

From: Melissa St. James, Human Resources (ext. 89) MS

Subject: New-Employee Orientation Checklist

[opening]
Announce the attachment and its purpose.

To help new employees become familiar with day-to-day procedures, Human Resources has revised the New-Employee Orientation Checklist (attached). The revised checklist should shorten the time it takes for new employees to learn their assignments, company policies, and department procedures.

[middle]
Use a numbered list to provide details the reader needs to understand.

You will receive the checklist on the first day that a new employee starts work in your department. As before, please use the form for 30 days and then return it to Human Resources. Note the following details:

1. While the form does not cite all topics addressed during orientation, the form does list the key topics that need to be covered.

2. The form lists the topics Human Resources will address and the topics that department heads will need to cover.

3. The last section of the form covers how new employees are reviewed. The review process is broken into four time periods: after day one, at the end of week one, at the end of week two, and after 30 days.

[closing]
Request feedback.

Because the updated checklist includes more information, it will take more time to complete. However, we believe this checklist will help all new employees learn their jobs more quickly. Please review the checklist. If you have questions about it, call me at extension 89, or e-mail me (mstjames@dliver.com) with any questions.

Attachment 1

CREDIT APPROVAL

GREENHOUSE AND FLORIST SUPPLY

Rural Route 2 • Macon, GA 31220-2339
Phone 655-555-3321 • Fax 655-555-1440
www.cottonwoodhills.com

March 3, 2003

Mr. Grant Bostwick, President
Dale's Garden Center
484 Leeward Avenue, SE
Tuscaloosa, AL 35406-3770

Dear Mr. Bostwick:

[opening]
State the approval positively.

Thank you for requesting a credit account at Cottonwood Hills Greenhouse and Florist Supply. We are pleased to extend you $100,000 in credit based on Dale's Garden Center's strong financial condition. Congratulations!

[middle]
To avoid future problems, spell out details of credit terms.

Here are some details concerning your account:
1. You will be billed the first day of the month.
2. The balance is due within 30 days, interest free.
3. Any balance owed beyond 30 days will be subject to a 15 percent annual finance charge.

I have enclosed a brochure describing our credit policies and procedures in more detail. Please call me (655-555-3321) if you have any questions.

[closing]
Include sales material and anticipate a positive future.

Because you indicated that you plan to expand your sales of bedding plants and silk flowers, I have also enclosed our spring catalog with these sections flagged. Mr. Bostwick, we look forward to filling your orders and satisfying your customers. Count on us to help Dale's flourish!

Yours sincerely,

Salome Nguru

Salome Nguru
Sales Manager

Enclosures 2

INFORMATION REQUEST

Wilson & Wilson *Attorneys-at-Law*

626 State Street, Halifax, NS B3J 3A5 ■ 613-555-7500 ■ wilsnandwilsn.com

February 21, 2003

Planning & Development Services
Halifax Regional Municipality
P.O. Box 1749
Halifax, NS B3J 3A5
CANADA

SUBJECT: ZONING INQUIRY FOR 219 WELLS ST., HALIFAX, NS

[opening]
Put key details up front so that the request makes sense.

I represent the purchaser, Hector Coyote, in a transaction for the property noted above, presently owned by Diana Elbach.

[middle]
Make your requests politely.

List your questions in a logical order.

Please send me the following information:

1. According to the owner, the building on the property is being used as a residence with a second unit (an attic apartment). Does this use conform with the current zoning code?

2. Were building and occupancy permits issued for this property? If so, when was each issued? Were conditions attached? If so, what?

3. Does the property meet municipal standards for side- and front-yard clearance? (Please refer to the enclosed survey.)

[closing]
Give clear, simple response directions and close politely.

Because of the purchase agreement between Ms. Elbach and Mr. Coyote, I need this information by March 3. Please feel free to fax (613-555-7501) or mail your answers on the enclosed form.

Thank you for your assistance.

David S. Wilson

DAVID S. WILSON

DSW/bbk
Enclosures 2

INVITATION

R_T **Rankin Technologies**
401 South Manheim Road ❖ Albany, NY 12236 ❖ Phone 708.555.1980 ❖ Fax 708.555.0056

May 30, 2003

Ms. Lorraine Scott
Sales Representative
206 West Dundee Street
Chicago, IL 60614

Dear Lorraine:

[opening]
**State the
invitation politely.**

Welcome to the Sales Seminar! I hope that you will have a productive week. While you are here, please help us celebrate Rankin's 20th anniversary.

[middle]
**Provide the
context.**

**Give all necessary
details of the
event.**

This year, we have a lot to celebrate. Our office expansion is finished, and sales grew by 16 percent. On Wednesday, June 4, we would like you to be our guest at the following events:

- an open house from 8:30 a.m. to 4:00 p.m. with hourly tours of the new office, engineering, and manufacturing facilities.

- a ribbon-cutting ceremony at 4:00 p.m. on the west lawn, with refreshments served at 4:30 p.m.

[closing]
**Anticipate
participation
and offer help.**

You are a big part of Rankin's success, Lorraine. I hope that you can take a break from your busy seminar schedule and join us. If you need directions, transportation, or other information, please speak with Rebecca Wright or call Matthew Nicolai at 555-1980, extension 4, or send him an e-mail at mnicolai@rnkn.com.

Sincerely,

Robert Hershey

Robert Hershey
Vice President of Sales

RH/svw

POSITIVE ADJUSTMENT

1400 NW Academy Drive
Phone 412/555-0900

Atlanta, GA 30425
Fax 412/555-0054

July 8, 2003

Mr. Jamaal Ellison
Southeast Electric
1976 Boulder Road, Suite 1214
Charlotte, NC 28216-1203

Dear Mr. Ellison:

[opening]
Provide
necessary
background,
apologize, and
offer solutions.

Thank you for your patience and understanding as we investigated the malfunction of the ATV16 drives that you had installed for American Linc Company. I apologize for the inconvenience caused to both your company and American Linc. Below is a description of the problem, along with our solution.

[middle]
Explain causes
and solutions
clearly in neutral
language.

Problem: Serial-link failure. In response to your report on the malfunction, AC Drives sent a technician to American Linc Company. He determined the cause of the failure to be a defective voltage regulator in the serial-link box.

Solution: Our technician replaced the voltage regulator and apologized to Jean Snow, plant manager. This morning I wrote a letter to Ms. Snow in which I acknowledged that the problem was ours (not yours), and I apologized for the inconvenience.

[closing]
Express
appreciation
and focus on
future business.

Thanks again for alerting us to the problem. With your help, it was resolved promptly. I look forward to future business with Southeast Electric.

Yours sincerely,

Elaine Hoffman

Elaine Hoffman
Product Manager

TEMPLATE

POSITIVE REPLY TO AN INQUIRY

Aspen State Bank
4554 Ridgemount Boulevard, Aspen, CO 81225-0064, PHONE 459-555-0098, FAX 459 555 5886
contact@aspenstatebank.com

February 24, 2003

Christine and Dale Shepherd
1026 11th Avenue, NE
Aspen, CO 81212-3219

Dear Christine and Dale:

[opening]
State the reason for your response and your appreciation for the inquiry.

Thank you for your inquiry yesterday about financing your resort project. I enjoyed discussing your project and appreciated your frankness about your current loan with Boulder National Bank.

[middle]
Provide the reader with the desired information and stress its value.

Although you commented that you will seek an extension of your loan from Boulder National, I have enclosed Aspen State Bank's commitment letter, subject to the terms we discussed. Perhaps you will consider our package. Rates available are as follows:

5-year fixed rate	4.5%
10-year fixed rate	4.875%
20-year fixed rate	5.375%

In case you do not proceed with the Boulder loan, this commitment will be good for 60 business days from today (February 24). If lower rates are available at closing, you will receive the benefit of that reduction.

[closing]
Anticipate and invite future contact.

Thank you for your interest. I hope that your project goes well. If we can't work together on this project, please keep us in mind for future credit needs.

Yours sincerely,

Cara Harrison

Cara Harrison
Loan Officer

Enclosure: Commitment Letter

REQUEST OR PROPOSAL ACCEPTANCE

Juanita Guiverra, Computer Consultant

368 Palm Palace Boulevard
Miami, FL 33166-0064
Telephone: 313.555.0010
FAX: 313.555.0500
E-Mail: jguiverra@cnsult.com

March 21, 2003

Mr. Gavin Farnsworth
Miami Computer Enterprises
1202 South Benton
Miami, FL 33166-1217

Dear Mr. Farnsworth:

[opening]
State your acceptance positively.

I have reviewed your letter of March 14. In response to your proposal, I am happy to offer my consulting services to Miami Computer customers.

[middle]
Stress the benefits of the decision and cover details that need to be clarified or recorded.

This arrangement will benefit all parties involved. Together, we will be able to offer your clients "one-stop shopping" for all their computer needs— hardware, software, training, and support. And I will be able to work with your established customer base without having to generate my own.

Therefore, I accept your proposed rate of $45 per hour (minimum of 20 hours per week) as indicated in the amended agreement (outline enclosed). Please note that the bold items on the outline indicate additions to the original proposal. I simply added the items covered in your letter.

[closing]
Explore the next step and anticipate a positive outcome.

Please let me know of any specific information or documentation that you need to see on my invoices. I look forward to a productive partnership in which we will serve each other and your clients.

Yours sincerely,

Juanita Guiverra

Juanita Guiverra

Enc.: Agreement Outline

THANK-YOU MESSAGE

Hope Services *Child Development Center*

2141 South Fifth Place, Seattle, WA 90761 • Telephone 436-555-1400
www.hopeserv.org

May 16, 2003

Mr. Donald Keebler
Keebler Electronics
466 Hanover Boulevard
Penticton, BC V2A 5S1
CANADA

Dear Mr. Keebler:

[opening]
State your thanks directly.

On behalf of the entire staff at Hope Services, I want to thank you for helping us choose a sound system that fits both our needs and our budget. Thanks, too, for working around our schedule during installation.

[middle]
Provide clear, specific details.

Be personal and professional in tone.

We have found that the system meets all our needs. Being able to adjust sound input and output for different uses in different rooms has been wonderful. The system helps staff in the family room with play-based assessment, and team members are tuning in to different conversations as if they were in the room themselves. As a result, children who might feel overwhelmed with too many people in the room can relax and play naturally.

In addition, parents also use the sound system to listen in on sessions in the therapy room as therapists model constructive one-on-one communication methods with children.

[closing]
Use the reader's name and stress cooperation and future contact.

Thanks again, Donald, for your cooperation and excellent work. I would be happy to recommend your services to anyone needing sound equipment.

Yours sincerely,

Barbara Talbot

Barbara Talbot
Executive Director

UPDATE

MEMO

Date: June 10, 2003

To: Randall Poole

From: Melissa St. James, Human Resources (ext. 89) *MS*

Subject: Update on New-Employee Orientation Process

[opening]

Announce your purpose and subject.

Randall, here's an update on the new-employee orientation program.

[middle]

Organize your points clearly, logically, and completely.

Present information in lists.

First, I developed a new checklist by combining two forms into one and by adding several items. The new form is attached, with additions highlighted.

Second, I fine-tuned the orientation procedure to work with the new form. Here's an overview:

1. Human Resources will enclose this checklist in each new employee's orientation packet.

2. Rebecca will cover items one through six during her new-employee presentation.

3. The employee's supervisor will confirm that the employee understands items one through six, and then cover the remaining items.

4. The supervisor will fill out the performance reviews on the reverse side of the form following this schedule: after day one, at the end of week one, at the end of week two, and after 30 days.

5. After the final review, the supervisor and the new employee will sign the form, and the supervisor will return it to Human Resources.

[closing]

Anticipate the next step.

Please look at the attached form and evaluate the procedure. With your approval, we will present this information to area supervisors at their next meeting.

Attachment 1

CHECKLIST The Good-News or Neutral Message . . .

STRONG IDEAS 140

- ☐ has a main point, and all supporting points are clear, precise, and accurate.
- ☐ supplies readers with all the necessary information.

LOGICAL ORGANIZATION 142

- ☐ has an opening that provides necessary background and presents the key point as either a statement, a question, or a request.
- ☐ has a middle that expands the main point by adding supporting details while explaining benefits to the reader.
- ☐ has a closing that calls for action, stresses continued contact, offers help, and/or focuses positively on the future by answering *who* should do *what, when, where, why,* and *how.*

CONVERSATIONAL VOICE 144

- ☐ uses a businesslike and polite voice that is not rushed or abrupt.

CLEAR WORDS 148

- ☐ uses everyday language (plain English) as much as possible.
- ☐ defines words unfamiliar to readers.

SMOOTH SENTENCES 152

- ☐ states the main point in a clear sentence.
- ☐ contains helpful transitions and reads well aloud.

CORRECT COPY 156

- ☐ is free of errors in grammar, spelling, punctuation, and typing.

READER-FRIENDLY DESIGN 158

- ☐ uses correct format for a letter, a memo, or an e-mail message.
- ☐ includes white space and easy-to-read type.
- ☐ organizes ideas, points, and details using numbers, bullets, or graphics.

Writing Bad-News Messages

It used to be dangerous to be the bearer of bad news. In ancient times, people often killed the messenger if they disliked the message! While today business may be more civilized, the fact remains that a bad-news message is one that your reader doesn't want to receive.

To deliver bad news, you have two choices: (1) state the bad news right away, or (2) soften it by leading up to it with an explanation. If the bad news is minor, or if your reader expects it, go ahead and be direct. But in most cases, the second approach is best.

In this chapter

"Tact is the art of making a point without making an enemy."

—Howard H. Newton

Guidelines for Bad-News Messages

1 PREWRITE

Consider your audience and purpose.
- Aim to convince the reader that your news is necessary and fair.
- Strive to continue a good relationship with the reader.

2 **Prepare to draft.**
- Consider what your reader wants or expects.
- Gather work-related reasons for your news.
- If appropriate, explore other options for the reader.

3 DRAFT

Present your thoughts with the reader in mind.

[opening] Begin with a buffer: a neutral statement like thanking the reader for past business, agreeing on a point, or expressing understanding.

[middle] Build up to the bad news.
- Be brief. One good reason is preferable to several weak ones.
- If helpful, explain company policy.
- State the bad news in the middle or at the end of a paragraph. If possible, follow with an alternative.

[closing] Express regret (without apologizing) and end politely.

4 REVISE

Review your draft for ideas, organization, and voice.
- Have you supplied a clear, sensitive explanation that helps the reader say, "I understand"?
- Have you used a sincere, gracious tone that avoids a "we" versus "you" attitude?

5 REFINE

Check your writing line by line for the following:
- ☐ neutral, exact, and sensitive wording.
- ☐ easy-to-read sentences with smooth transitions.
- ☐ correct names, data, grammar, punctuation, and spelling.
- ☐ effective format (spacing, type, and so on).

BID REJECTION

EVERSON CITY PLANNING AND DEVELOPMENT COMMITTEE

Everson City Council • Everson, WA 98247-2311 • 306/555-2134 • www.eversonpdc.org

February 12, 2003

Mr. Felix Grove
Sea-to-Mountain Landscapers
8900 Coast Road
Seattle, WA 98134-6508

Dear Mr. Grove:

[opening]

Buffer: Specify the bid and thank the bidder.

SUBJECT: Bid 4459 Everson City Park

Thank you for your bid to design and develop Everson's eight-acre city park adjacent to Kingston Elementary School and the Nooksack River.

[middle]

Highlight the reader's strengths objectively, but specify why another bid won.

Your bid was competitive for several of the criteria outlined in our original Request for Proposals (RFP). Your cost estimates, experience, and references were as strong as those from other bidders. However, Earth-Scape Design's overall plan tipped the bid in their favor. By including a variety of native plant species, Earth-Scape's natural, sustainable landscape will require less long-term care and create less stress on the Nooksack watershed. Because their plan contained a variety of plants, it also offered added educational value.

[closing]

If appropriate, encourage bidding on future projects.

The Planning and Development Committee appreciates the work that you put into your proposal. We look forward to your interest in future Everson projects.

Yours sincerely,

Alice Potter

Alice Potter
Development Committee Chair

CLAIM DENIAL

1400 NW Academy Drive
Phone 412/555-0900

Atlanta, GA 30425
Fax 412/555-0054

June 16, 2003

Mr. Jamaal Ellison
Southeast Electric
1976 Boulder Road, Suite 1214
Charlotte, NC 28261-1203

Dear Mr. Ellison:

[opening]

Buffer: Restate the problem and show concern.

We have finished investigating your concerns about the ATV16 drives that you installed for American Linc Company. We do understand that the drive and serial-link failures have inconvenienced both you and American Linc.

[middle]

Use sound evidence and state the rejection clearly.

Offer helpful alternatives.

After testing the drives you returned, our line engineer determined that they failed because the temperatures in the cabinet exceeded the maximum operating temperature of the drives, leading to electronic-component failure. As noted in the ATV16 manual, the drive may malfunction under such conditions. For this reason, we cannot repair the drives without charge. We would be happy, however, to consider the following solutions:

1. We could remove the drive's plastic cover and install a stirring fan in the enclosure to moderate the temperature.

2. We could replace the ATV16 drives with the ATV18 model, a model more suitable for the machine you are using. (If you choose this option, we would give you a 15 percent discount on the ATV18s.)

[closing]

Focus on the next step and on future business.

Please let me know how you would like to proceed. I look forward to hearing from you and to continuing our partnership.

Yours sincerely,

Elaine Hoffman

Elaine Hoffman
Product Manager

COMPLAINT (BASIC)

brunewald systems design   5690 Brantley Boulevard, P. O. Box 6094
Trenton, NJ 08561-4221
451.555.0900

February 26, 2003

BHC Office Supply Company
39 Davis Street
Pittsburgh, PA 15209-1334

ATTENTION: Shipping Manager

[opening]

Buffer: Establish the claim's context.

I'm writing about a problem with the purchase order #07-1201. Copies of the original PO plus two invoices are enclosed.

[middle]

Tactfully spell out the facts.

Here is the sequence of events concerning PO 07-1201:

Dec. 16, 2002: I faxed the original purchase order.

Jan. 8, 2003:   Because I hadn't heard from your office, I spoke with Kim in customer service. Then I re-sent the PO because she could not find the original in your system.

Jan. 16, 2003: I received a partial shipment, with the remaining items back-ordered (invoice 0151498).

Jan. 21, 2003: I then received a second shipment that was complete (invoice 0151511). Noting the duplication, I contacted Kim, and she cancelled the back-ordered items.

Point out results of the problem in a neutral tone.

Specify the adjustment that you want.

I am returning the partial order (duplicate items) by UPS. Please credit our account for the following: (1) the duplicate items listed on invoice 0151498 ($563.85), (2) the shipping costs of the partial order ($69.20), and (3) the UPS costs to return the duplicate items ($58.10). The total credit comes to $691.15.

[closing]

Anticipate future business.

I look forward to receiving an adjusted statement and to continued cooperation in the future.

Gary Sheridan

GARY SHERIDAN—OFFICE MANAGER

GS/mc
Enclosures 3

COMPLAINT (SERIOUS)

Ŗ Rankin Technologies
1595 Rosa Plaza SE ❖ Albuquerque, NM 87105-1029 ❖ Phone 507.555.9000 ❖ Fax 507.555.9002 ❖ www.rnkn.com

January 15, 2003

Mr. Steven Grinnel
Director of Operations
Industrial Aggregate Equipment Company
4018 Tower Road
Albuquerque, NM 87105-3443

Dear Mr. Grinnel:

[opening]

Buffer: Specify the problem and the reason for concern.

I am very concerned about the 40-foot Snorkel Lift that we contracted with you to rebuild when we traded in our old Marklift. Continued delays in the rebuilding schedule and subsequent problems with the lift itself leave me uncertain about Industrial Aggregate's ability to provide Rankin Technologies with continued service.

[middle]

Provide a detailed outline of the problem and its history.

Keep your tone neutral.

Be specific and factual.

Here is an overview of the problem:

1. We ordered the Snorkel Lift in April 2002, and you promised delivery in July. We did not receive the lift until September.

2. When the lift arrived, we noticed several key parts had not been replaced, and the boom did not operate correctly. Your project supervisor, Nick Luther, assured us that the parts would be fixed in a timely manner, and he provided a substitute lift free of charge.

3. Two months later, Mr. Luther called to say that everything was fixed. However, when we visited your facility on December 18, the gauges and tires on the lift had not been replaced, and the dual fuel unit had not been installed.

4. When we finally received the Snorkel Lift on December 22, several items we noticed on December 18 still had not been fixed. In fact, the lift still had these deficiencies:
   - several oil leaks
   - missing "on/off" switch in the basket
   - no dual fuel capabilities
   - boom vibration when retracted after full extension

Page 2
Steven Grinnel
January 15, 2003

[middle]

Give needed background and attach relevant support.

We have been extremely disappointed with the lift's condition and overall performance. Your original promise of a fully operational Snorkel Lift in "like new" condition by July 2002 (agreement copy enclosed) has not been met.

In the past, we have appreciated your service and assistance. From our experience of the past six months, however, we can only conclude that you are experiencing problems that make it difficult for you to provide the service Rankin Technologies needs.

[closing]

State the proposed solution clearly and firmly.

We want to resolve this issue. By February 14, please provide us with a lift that meets all the specifications agreed to and that has no operational deficiencies. If you are unable to provide the lift by that date, we will cancel our order and seek reimbursement for the used Marklift we traded in April 2002.

Sincerely,

Jane Ballentine

Jane Ballentine
Maintenance Project Engineer

JB/rd
Enc.: copy of agreement
cc: Andrew Longfellow
        President, Industrial Aggregate Equipment Company

TEMPLATE

CREDIT OR LOAN APPLICATION DENIAL

LONE STAR BANK
5550 North Adeline Road, Houston, TX 77022
Phone 547.555.0100, FAX 547.555.7024, E-Mail contact@loanestar.com

May 5, 2003

Ms. Mary-Lou Twain
780 East 41st Street, Apartment 712
Houston, TX 77022-1183

Dear Ms. Twain:

[opening]

Buffer: Express appreciation for the application.

Thank you for meeting with loan officer Jean Olms last Friday and applying for a loan to open your gift shop.

[middle]

Provide objective reasons for the rejection and offer suggestions.

When we review an application, one of the factors that we consider is the applicant's credit history. A good credit history shows a pattern of paying obligations. At this time, because you have not established a credit history, we cannot approve your request to borrow $95,000. However, you can establish a good credit history in one of two ways:

- Apply for, use, and make prompt payments on a credit card.
- Take out and repay a smaller loan at Lone Star Bank. Just a $5,000 loan successfully repaid would establish a positive financial record.

[closing]

If appropriate, encourage applying when conditions change.

We hope that these suggestions will help you begin to establish a good credit history. Then you may reapply for the loan that you requested.

Sincerely,

Rodney Thayer

Rodney Thayer
President

RT/bjh

P.S. Please see the reverse side of this letter for information about your rights under the Federal Equal Credit Opportunity Act and other relevant laws.

CRISIS MANAGEMENT

MEMO

Date: July 18, 2003
To: All Staff
From: Lawrence Durante, President
Subject: Recent FDA Plant Inspection

As you know, this past Monday, July 14, the FDA came to our plant for a spot inspection. I'm writing to share the inspection results and our response.

The good news is that the FDA inspectors did not find problems warranting a shutdown of Premium Meats. However, the bad news is that the inspectors cited us for three major violations resulting in a fine of $90,000.

The FDA is sending us a clear message. We must take immediate steps to protect our customers, our jobs, and our company. To that end, I have taken the following steps:

1. The Executive Committee met with me to review the FDA report and determine the problem areas in our production process.

2. I have directed the Production Management Team to review quality-control procedures and conduct two retraining sessions immediately.

3. I have appointed a Quality Task Force of both management and production staff to study the production process and make further recommendations.

4. I have briefed Sales and Public-Relations staff and directed them to contact customers and the media.

With short-term solutions and long-term cooperation, we will keep Premium Meats operating and prospering.

If you have any suggestions or questions, please speak to your immediate supervisor or a member of the Quality Task Force. (The Task Force membership, mandate, and time line are listed on the back.)

[opening]

Use a neutral subject line.

Buffer: State your reason for writing.

[middle]

State the bad news factually and calmly.

Focus on solutions: what has been done and what needs to be done.

[closing]

Stress a positive future, but be realistic.
Ask for feedback, if appropriate.

NEGATIVE CHANGE ANNOUNCEMENT

Wright Insurance Agency

3406 Capitol Boulevard, Suite 588
Washington, DC 20037-1124
Phone 612-555-0020
wright@insre.com

January 15, 2003

Policy 46759

Ms. Virginia Beloit
72 Elias Street
Washington, DC 20018-8262

Dear Ms. Beloit:

[opening]
Buffer: Introduce the topic and its context.

Periodically, insurance companies review their policies, assess the cost of offering the policies, and make changes where needed. When that happens, it's my responsibility as an insurance agent to inform my clients and help them make necessary adjustments.

[middle]
Give rationale for the change.

State the change. If possible, offer help.

Last week Hawkeye Casualty, the company with whom you have your auto insurance policy, discontinued all policies for drivers considered "high risk." Because you have had a traffic accident within the past 12 months, and have received two speeding tickets during the same period, the company has re-labeled your status as "high risk." As a result, Hawkeye Casualty has cancelled your auto-insurance policy effective January 31, 2003. However, I have found another company that will offer you auto insurance. While the cost of this new policy is somewhat higher than your present policy, the coverage is comparable, and the company is reliable.

[closing]
Explain what the reader should do.

Please call me at 612-489-0020 within the next week so we can discuss the situation and decide how to proceed.

Sincerely,

Eric Wright

Eric Wright

EW/rn

TEMPLATE

POOR RESULTS EXPLANATION

Heading
Send a copy to
the appropriate
people.

Use a neutral
subject line.

File Edit View Insert Format Tools Message Help	
Send Cut Copy Paste Undo Check Spelling Attach Priority Sign Encrypt Offline	

From:	Bernice Gardener <bg@vgouto.com>
To:	Sales Managers <laurie@vgouto.com> <julie@vgouto.com> <mark@vgouto.com>
Cc:	micah@vgouto.com
Bc:	jake@vgouto.com
Subject:	Van Gorp Automotive 2002 Sales Report and Customer Survey
Attach:	Salesreport2002.doc., Surveysummary2002.doc

Laurie, Julie, and Mark:

[opening]
Buffer: Explain
the context and
give some good
news.

Last week, Jesse Cam from marketing sent me the 2002 sales report, along with a summary of our customer survey (copies attached). As the report shows, we had another good year: annual receipts in our three stores increased 9 percent. In addition, the survey shows that customers' satisfaction with our Maintenance Departments continues to be high: 74 percent, Excellent; 18 percent, Good; 6 percent, Fair; and 2 percent, Poor. That's great news—and our employees deserve the credit!

[middle]
Explain the
problem, focusing
on issues and
solutions,
not individuals.

However, the survey also shows that our sales personnel can improve. During your next meetings with them, please read through customers' comments listed in Jesse's summary. Note statements like those listed below, identify the problems, and discuss how we can improve:

1. "Nobody greeted me when I walked in."

2. "The sales guy talked to me and two other customers—all at the same time."

3. "Your salesman knew his stuff—but he seemed to push a sunroof, and I didn't want one."

4. "Leah was great, but she was your ONLY female salesperson!"

[closing]
Politely explain
follow-up.

After reviewing the attachments and then meeting with your sales staffs, please write a report on your findings and send copies to Jim N., Jamie, and me.

Thanks,
Bernice Gardener

PROPOSAL REJECTION

Juanita Guiverra, Computer Consultant

368 Palm Palace Boulevard
Miami, FL 33166-0064
Telephone: 313.555.0010
Fax: 313.555-0500
E-Mail: jguiverra@cnsult.com

March 24, 2003

Mr. Gavin Farnsworth
Miami Computer Enterprises
Box 115
South Benton Mall
Miami, FL 33166-1217

Dear Gavin:

[opening]
Buffer: Show appreciation.

Thank you for your proposal that I join your Customer Training Department. I appreciate your confidence in my ability to provide Miami Computer Enterprises' clients with instruction and technical support.

[middle]
Give your reasons objectively, stress positives in the proposal, state the rejection tactfully, and explore other options.

While considering your proposal, I reflected on the reasons that I started my own computer-consulting service two years ago. One of the reasons was flexibility. As an independent consultant, I could regulate my work activities around family demands. Although your proposal was financially attractive, I must turn down your offer, at least for now.

In 17 months (August 2004), my youngest child will enter grade school. If you are still interested in me at that time, I would be happy to reconsider your proposal. Until then, I hope you will want me to continue doing contract projects for MCE, especially with your Spanish-speaking clients.

[closing]
End positively.

Thanks again for your generous proposal. I wish MCE continued growth and success.

Yours sincerely,

Juanita Guiverra

Juanita Guiverra

TEMPLATE

DONATION-REQUEST DENIAL

RT **Rankin Technologies**
401 Manheim Road ❖ Albany, NY 12236 ❖ Phone 708.555.1980 ❖ Fax 708.555.0056 ❖ www.rnkn.com

April 18, 2003

Ms. Marlis DeQuincey
Executive Director
Family First Center
468 Provis Way
Fairfield, NY 12377-2089

Dear Ms. DeQuincey:

[opening]
Buffer: Express interest in the reader's cause.

I read with interest your letter about Family First Center's project. I commend your efforts to build a shelter for women and children victimized by domestic violence.

[middle]
Provide clear reasons for not participating. State the refusal tactfully. If possible, offer an alternative.

I am honored that you have invited Rankin Technologies to participate in your project. Rankin seeks to be a good corporate citizen and a positive force in the community. To that end, we have already committed ourselves to partnerships with nonprofit organizations that mesh with Rankin's interests in the environment, in urban renewal, and in Third-World development. For this reason, we cannot participate in your project at this time.

Rankin employees will, however, be encouraged to continue to support your work in the community campaign. In fact, I will distribute materials about your project to our employees so that individuals may choose to get involved.

[closing]
Affirm the reader.

I wish you well, Ms. DeQuincey, in your important work of helping the victims of physical and emotional violence in this community.

Yours sincerely,

Barbara Reinholdt

Barbara Reinholdt
Office Manager

BR/dn

FUNDING-REQUEST DENIAL

MEMORANDUM

Date: July 2, 2003

To: Oscar Nunez, Sales Manager

From: Jim Musial, Training Manager *JM*

Subject: Netscape Training for Sales Staff

[opening]

Buffer: Restate the request and offer a point of agreement.

I've reviewed your request to send all the sales reps to the Netscape training seminar in Cincinnati. Oscar, I agree that this training would help your staff be more productive.

[middle]

State your reasons briefly, clearly, and objectively. If possible, explore alternatives.

With your request in mind, I reviewed our training budget to see if we could afford the seminar. A large portion of our budget has already been used to upgrade design software for the engineering staff. In addition, we have some prior commitments for training office staff in August. Therefore, there is not enough money available to send all sales reps to Cincinnati.

Perhaps there's another way. If we sent two of your key staff to the seminar, they could then train others in your department. Or we could plan an extensive in-house training session for your entire group.

[closing]

End on a note of encouragement.

I'd be happy to explore these or other options with you. With a little creativity, I think that we could get your reps the training they need. Just call or e-mail me (ext. 3957 or jmusial@rnkn.com).

Headings can be single- or double-spaced.

Avoid the following words and phrases when rejecting a request:

I am surprised
company policy prohibits
are not able to
must refuse/reject
you claim/complain
has never happened before
misinformed

I question/take issue with
you apparently overlooked
you obviously failed to
I cannot understand your
contrary to what you say
unjustified
I trust you will agree

SUGGESTION REJECTION

MEMO

Date: September 16, 2003

To: Duane Bolton

From: Arthur Mellencamp   *AM*

Subject: Offering Telecommuting to Employees

[opening]

Buffer: Restate the suggestion and show appreciation.

Thanks for suggesting that Rankin create work-at-home possibilities for staff. I've been intrigued with this work concept for some time.

[middle]

Explain how you reviewed the suggestion and why it won't work. Explore other options.

I asked Melissa St. James in Human Resources about the costs and benefits of telecommuting. She said that her department conducted a feasibility study on telecommuting three years ago and concluded that it would not benefit the company for these reasons: (1) employees could become isolated, (2) few tasks could be efficiently performed away from the plant, and (3) home offices could prove too costly. Perhaps the situation has changed since that study. Melissa said that she would be willing to discuss the idea with you.

[closing]

Affirm the reader and invite further suggestions.

Please follow up on that offer, Duane. In addition, please continue to submit suggestions for improving operations here at Rankin.

CHECKLIST The Bad-News Message . . .

STRONG IDEAS 140

☐ is clear yet tactful.
☐ presents all the facts accurately and focuses on solutions.

LOGICAL ORGANIZATION 142

☐ begins with a buffer statement that
  • explains the message's purpose.
  • establishes common ground by offering agreement or understanding.
  • builds sensitively (indirectly) to the bad-news statement.
☐ develops a middle that
  • provides well-supported reasons without overexplaining.
  • states the bad news tactfully in the middle of a paragraph.
  • offers the reader a compromise or an alternative, if possible.
☐ closes in a manner that
  • clarifies steps needed for an alternative solution.
  • refers to the problem again without ending apologetically.
  • looks forward to future work or contact, without sounding too upbeat.

CONVERSATIONAL VOICE 144

☐ uses an understanding yet firm voice that is not defensive or angry.

CLEAR WORDS 148

☐ conveys the bad news clearly but tactfully.
☐ avoids the pronoun "you" if it sounds accusatory.
☐ uses neutral or mildly positive language.

SMOOTH SENTENCES 152

☐ reads well aloud; sentences aren't awkward or wordy.
☐ uses passive voice to soften negative or difficult statements.

CORRECT COPY 156

☐ is free of grammar, spelling, punctuation, and typing errors.

READER-FRIENDLY DESIGN 158

☐ features an attractive layout with ample white space.
☐ organizes points and details with numbers, bullets, or graphics.

LESSON

Writing Persuasive Messages

All persuasive messages are sales pitches—whether you're selling an idea, a product, a service, or a special request. However, even though you may have a great idea, a dynamite product, or a noble cause, your readers won't necessarily see that. They may be indifferent or even resistant to your message.

So how, exactly, do you persuade readers to accept your point of view? How do you sell the value of your idea, product, service, or request without resorting to a hard sell or an overly aggressive manner? If you can speak to your readers' needs and focus on how they will benefit, then your letter, memo, or e-mail may well produce the results you want.

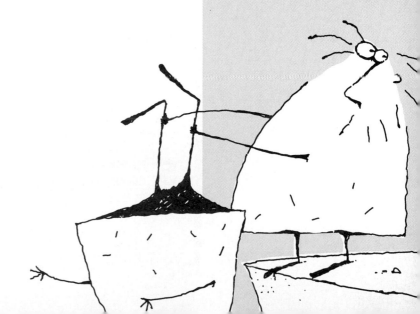

Guidelines for Persuasive Messages

1 PREWRITE
Consider your audience.
- What motivates your reader and what does he or she need?
- What benefits (publicity, contacts, or satisfaction) might the reader gain from supporting your cause?

2 Consider your purpose and clarify your cause.
- What outcome do you want or realistically expect?
- What exactly is your idea, cause, or product?
- What are the social or economic benefits of your cause?

3 DRAFT
Organize your thoughts with the reader in mind.

[opening] Get your reader's attention and present your idea, cause, or product.

[middle] Explain its value and show how your reader will benefit.
- Use facts, quotations, and examples to help the reader understand and appreciate what you're promoting.
- Address obstacles and counter any objections if possible.

[closing] Confidently ask for a reasonable action. Supply response cards, e-mail addresses, Web sites, or other easy-response options.

4 REVISE
Review your draft for ideas, organization, and voice.
- Have you provided a complete explanation that speaks to your reader's motivations?
- Have you used a sincere tone that avoids pressure tactics, flattery, and exaggeration?
- Does the message follow a clear, logical pattern?

5 REFINE
Check your writing line by line for
- ☐ exact, fresh phrasing and easy-to-read sentences.
- ☐ correct grammar, punctuation, spelling, and mechanics.
- ☐ consistent and correct use of headings, lists, boldface, and other format and design strategies.

YOUR GOAL When writing persuasive messages, your goal is to convince the reader to do something (buy a product, pay a bill) by showing the value of the action.

"The best argument is that which sounds like merely an explanation."
— Dale Carnegie

COLLECTION LETTER (FIRST NOTICE)

TEMPLATE

HANFORD BUILDING SUPPLY COMPANY, INC.

5821 North Fairheights Road, Milsap, CA 94218, Phone 567-555-1908

June 1, 2003

Account: 4879003

Mr. Robert Burnside, Controller
Circuit Electronics Company
4900 Gorham Road
Mountain View, CA 94040-1093

Dear Mr. Burnside:

[opening]

State the account's status.

This letter is a reminder that your account is past due (presently 60 days).

[middle]

Review the account's history. Focus on keeping a positive relationship.

As of today, we have not yet received your payment of $1,806.00, originally due March 31. A copy of the March 1 invoice #QR483928 is enclosed. It refers to your January 10, 2003, order #S95832 for 3,000 mitered flanges that we shipped January 28.

Hanford appreciates your business, Mr. Burnside. Please give this matter your prompt attention so that Hanford Building Supply Company and Circuit Electronics can continue their good relationship. Your check for $1,828.58 (past due amount, plus 1.25 percent interest) will keep your account in good standing and avoid further interest charges and penalties. We have enclosed a postage-paid envelope for your convenience.

[closing]

Urge the reader to contact you with any problems.

If there are any problems, please call (567-555-1908, ext. 227) or e-mail me (marta@hanford.com). As always, we look forward to serving you.

Sincerely,

Marta Ramones

Marta Ramones
Billing Department

Enclosures 2

COLLECTION LETTER (SECOND NOTICE)

HANFORD BUILDING SUPPLY COMPANY, INC.
5821 North Fairheights Road, Milsap, CA 94218, Phone 567-555-1908

July 2, 2003

Account: 4879003

Mr. Robert Burnside, Controller
Circuit Electronics Company
4900 Gorham Road
Mountain View, CA 94040-1093

Dear Mr. Burnside:

[opening]

Express concern about the account.

Despite the reminder we sent on June 1, your account is now 90 days past due.

[middle]

Review the account's history.

Outline benefits of good credit and offer to help.

As of today, your payment of $1,828.58 has not arrived. A copy of your March 1 invoice #QR483928 is enclosed. It refers to your January 10, 2003, order #S95832 for 3,000 mitered flanges that we shipped January 28.

Because of your excellent credit rating, you have enjoyed substantial discounts, convenient payment terms, and positive credit references from us. If you wish to maintain your good credit rating, we need your payment.

Circuit Electronics has been one of Hanford's most valued customers for more than five years. You have always paid your bills promptly. We are concerned about this uncharacteristic tardiness. Is there a problem we can help solve?

[closing]

Request payment or contact; stress cooperation.

Please send your payment of $1,851.44 today (includes 1.25 percent interest) or contact me at 567-555-1908, ext. 227 so that we can resolve this matter.

Sincerely,

Marta Ramones

Marta Ramones
Billing Department

Enclosure 1

COLLECTION LETTER (FINAL NOTICE)

HANFORD BUILDING SUPPLY COMPANY, INC.
5821 North Fairheights Road, Milsap, CA 94218, Phone 567-555-1908

August 1, 2003

Account: 4879003

Mr. Robert Burnside, Controller
Circuit Electronics Company
4900 Gorham Road
Mountain View, CA 94040-1093

Dear Mr. Burnside:

[opening]
Recap the facts.

On January 28, 2003, we shipped you the 3,000 mitered flanges you ordered (#S95832). On March 1, we sent you the invoice for $1,806.00 (#QR483928). Copies of your purchase order and our invoice are enclosed.

[middle]
Outline the steps taken. State the next step in clear, neutral terms.

Each month since then, Hanford has sent Circuit Electronics a reminder urging payment, and asking you to contact us. We have not heard from you, and your account is now 120 days past due with a balance of $1,874.58 (includes 1.25 percent interest per month). Consequently, we must begin collection proceedings.

[closing]
Offer one final way to cooperate by a specific date.

However, you can still resolve this matter, Mr. Burnside. Either call me now to discuss this problem (ext. 240 at the number above), or send a check by August 15 for the balance owed. By choosing either option, you can prevent this account from being turned over to a collection agency.

Sincerely,

Floyd Kovic

Floyd Kovic
Vice President
Finance Division

Enclosures 2

CREDIT APPLICATION

484 Leeward Avenue, SE, Tuscaloosa, AL 35406-3770
Phone 908/555-8900 FAX 908/555-1600
E-mail grant@garden.com

January 3, 2003

Ms. Salome Nguru, Manager
Cottonwood Hills Greenhouse and Florist Supply
R.R. 2
Macon, GA 31220-2339

Dear Ms. Nguru:

[opening]

Stress positive aspects of the current relationship.

For the past nine months, Dale's has been ordering fresh, dried, and silk flowers from Cottonwood Hills. We have been impressed with the quality of your products, most recently with those we sold for the Christmas holidays.

[middle]

Explain the need for credit.

Stress benefits for the reader.

Establish your credit record.

We are now planning to expand our product offerings, particularly of silk flowers and bedding plants. For this reason, we expect to make larger orders more frequently. However, before we can submit the orders, we need Cottonwood Hills to set up an account for us with a $100,000 line of credit.

Dale's Garden Center has been in business for almost a year and is on solid financial footing. The attached references and financial statements show that we are strong and growing.

[closing]

Ask for reasonable action and suggest further benefits.

By January 24, we hope that you will be able to check our statements and references, send information about your credit terms, and confirm a credit line of $100,000. Dale's will then submit an order for spring plants.

Thank you for considering our request.

Yours sincerely,

Grant Bostwick

Grant Bostwick
President

Enclosures 4

FUND-RAISING MESSAGE

TEMPLATE

NATIONAL CAMPAIGN FOR LITERACY
1516 West Elizabeth Terrace, Wadsworth, IL 60421
Phone 431-555-9000, Fax 431-555-1066, Web Site ncl.org

November 12, 2003

Mr. Cecil Featherstone
Words, Words, Words, Inc.
541 West 34th Street
New York, NY 10001-7352

Dear Mr. Featherstone:

[opening]
Use attention-getting facts.

More than 20 percent of adults in this country cannot read at a third-grade level. Each year, more than a million students leave high school functionally illiterate (some with diplomas).

[middle]
Sell your cause with key details.

Create a sense of urgency.

Request a donation politely.

List benefits for both giver and receiver.

As you know, the National Campaign for Literacy has spent 14 years helping millions of citizens learn to read. We work with more than 300 schools, neighborhood groups, and government agencies to combat illiteracy. Yet, illiteracy remains an enormous problem. To address this need, we plan to fund 29 new programs this year, as well as to expand existing ones.

We appreciate your past generosity and hope we can count on your continued support. In addition, to enable us to help more people, we are asking that you please consider raising your donation level.

Of course, your gift will bring you recognition, including a personal acknowledgment of your generosity in more than 100,000 promotional brochures. However, the greatest benefit comes as you help millions of people get better jobs and earn personal dignity.

[closing]
Make donating simple.

Please continue supporting our effort to promote adult reading. You may make out your check to National Campaign for Literacy and return it to me, or you may call me at 431-555-9000, ext. 0786.

Sincerely,

Gail Goldstein

Gail Goldstein
Associate Director

REQUEST FOR ASSISTANCE

MEMO

Date: August 11, 2003

To: Felton Engineering Staff

From: Jilliane Seaforth

Subject: Ideas for Open House Displays

[opening]

Create a sense of shared purpose.

As you know, we will be moving to our new location on August 18, and we have scheduled an open house for September 1. To help visitors at that event learn what Felton Engineering does, I plan to set up displays showing samples of your unique heater designs and interesting product applications.

[middle]

Give any needed background information.

Ask for specific help.

As you pack for the move, please help me by doing the following: (1) identify products that would interest visitors, and (2) look for blueprints, sketches, or small models that illustrate those products. (Remember that visitors may understand commercial applications more easily than technical military or aerospace designs.)

Then, list below (1) your name, (2) the name of the product, (3) the product number, and (4) the type of display materials that you have.

[closing]

Set a deadline, make cooperation simple, and be positive.

Please return this memo to me no later than August 22. I will pick up your materials, set up the displays, and return the materials to you after the open house. I look forward to turning your ideas and samples into great displays!

1. Your Name:_____

2. Product Name   3. Product Number   4. Display Materials

_____   _____   _____

_____   _____   _____

_____   _____   _____

_____   _____   _____

_____   _____   _____

TEMPLATE

SALES LETTER: FIRST CONTACT

Juanita Guiverra, Computer Consultant

368 Palm Palace Boulevard
Miami, FL 33166-0064
Telephone: 313.555.0010
Fax: 313.555.0500
E-mail: jguiverra@cnsult.com

November 19, 2003

Mr. Alexander Bennitez
Nova Advertising
664 Helene Boulevard, Suite 200
Miami, FL 33135-0493

Dear Mr. Bennitez:

[opening]
Show that you understand the reader's situation.

Do you have numerous projects on hold because your staff is too busy? Consider getting your important projects back on schedule by outsourcing.

[middle]
Create interest by relating your services to the reader's needs.

Sell your credibility.

My areas of expertise include the following:
- writing, editing, and keyboarding documents.
- processing mailings from start to finish.
- developing spreadsheets or flyers.

Outsourcing with me offers the following advantages:
- no long-term employment commitment.
- satisfaction guaranteed (most reworking at no charge).
- confidentiality.

You can put my 10 years of experience in the advertising business to work for you. The enclosed pamphlet describes my services, equipment, and rates. I have also enclosed samples of my work.

[closing]
Call for action.

Mr. Bennitez, I can help Nova Advertising complete its projects in a timely and professional manner. I would be available for an interview at your convenience.

Sincerely,

Juanita Guiverra

Juanita Guiverra

Enclosures 4

[postscript]
Offer an incentive.

P.S. As a new client, your first in-office consultation would be free.

SALES LETTER: FOLLOWING A CONTACT

R *Rankin Technologies*
T *1595 Rosa Plaza SE* ❖ *Albuquerque, NM 87105-1029* ❖ *Phone 507.555.9000* ❖ *Fax 507.555.9002* ❖ *www.rankin.com*

April 28, 2003

Mr. Henry Danburn
Construction Manager
Titan Industrial Construction, Inc.
P.O. Box 2112
Phoenix, AZ 85009-3887

Dear Mr. Danburn:

[opening]

Mention previous
positive contact.

Thank you for meeting with me last week at the national convention in Las Vegas. I want to follow up on our discussion of ways that Rankin Technologies could work with Titan Industrial Construction.

[middle]

Provide details
the reader needs.

Build credibility.

Enclosed is the information that you requested: Rankin's corporate brochure, past and current job lists, recommendation letters, and more. I believe this material demonstrates that Rankin Technologies would be a solid match for your projects in western Illinois.

You mentioned that you will be the construction manager for the Arrow Mills renovation project in California. Rankin did the electrical installation on that project initially, and we would be very interested in working with you on the renovation. Someone who is familiar with our work at Arrow Mills is Mitch Knowlan, Plant Manager. He can be reached at 606-555-6328 or at mknowlan@arrowmills.com.

[closing]

Stress
cooperation
and the key
selling point.

Henry, here at Rankin, we're excited about the possibility of working with you on any future project, and the Arrow Mills project, in particular. Please call me with any questions (507-555-9011).

Sincerely,

James Gabriel

James Gabriel
Vice President

Enclosures 5

SALES LETTER: FOLLOWING A SALE

Dale's Garden Center

484 Leeward Avenue, SE, Tuscaloosa, AL 35406-3770
Phone 908/555-8900   FAX 908/555-1600
E-mail bryce@grdon.com

December 6, 2003

Ms. Taryn Dionne
93 Claremont Crescent
Tuscaloosa, AL 35401-1553

Dear Ms. Dionne:

[opening]
Thank the reader for previous business.

Thank you for your recent order of a Southern Charm Bouquet. We hope you were pleased with the arrangement.

[middle]
Introduce other products without high-pressure tactics. Stress value and benefits.

Because this was your first order with Dale's, we're sending you the enclosed *2004 Occasions Diary* as a gift. The diary will help you remember important events in the lives of people you care about. You'll find room for birthdays, anniversaries, graduations, and more.

Flowers are a thoughtful gift for any occasion. That's why we've listed appropriate arrangements at the back of your diary. On the first page of each month, you'll also notice our monthly specials at the low price of $29.95 (plus delivery and tax).

[closing]
Invite action.

So keep your *2004 Occasions Diary* handy throughout the year. Then just call our toll-free number on the inside front cover (or visit our Web site), and we'll gladly make all the arrangements!

Best wishes,

Bryce Calahan

Bryce Calahan
Customer-Service Manager

[postscript]
Emphasize a special offer.

P.S. I've also enclosed a *2004 Christmas Floral Selection Guide* filled with gift-giving ideas for friends and family.

CHECKLIST The Persuasive Message . . .

STRONG IDEAS 140

- ☐ states the main point clearly and convincingly.
- ☐ uses accurate and persuasive details.
- ☐ connects with the reader's needs and concerns.

LOGICAL ORGANIZATION 142

- ☐ uses an opening that
  - gains the reader's attention.
  - identifies a benefit to the reader and supplies the necessary context.
- ☐ offers a strong argument in the middle that
  - establishes a need and shows how to meet it.
  - uses clear, convincing evidence to "sell" the idea or product.
  - anticipates and answers objections.
- ☐ ends with a closing that
  - asks the reader to take a specific, realistic next step.
  - encourages a prompt response with an appropriate incentive.

CONVERSATIONAL VOICE 144

- ☐ uses a polite and personal voice that is not hesitant, apologetic, or aggressive.
- ☐ demonstrates a "you attitude"—a sensitivity to the reader's needs and concerns.

CLEAR WORDS 148

- ☐ avoids cliches, jargon, flowery phrases, and "business English."
- ☐ uses precise nouns, vivid modifiers, and energetic verbs.

SMOOTH SENTENCES 152

- ☐ uses transitions to tie ideas together and reads well out loud.
- ☐ uses generally short- to medium-length sentences.

CORRECT COPY 156

- ☐ is free of grammar, spelling, punctuation, and typing errors.

READER-FRIENDLY DESIGN 158

- ☐ uses page layout, white space, and type style to make content accessible.
- ☐ organizes points and details with headings, numbers, bullets, and graphics.

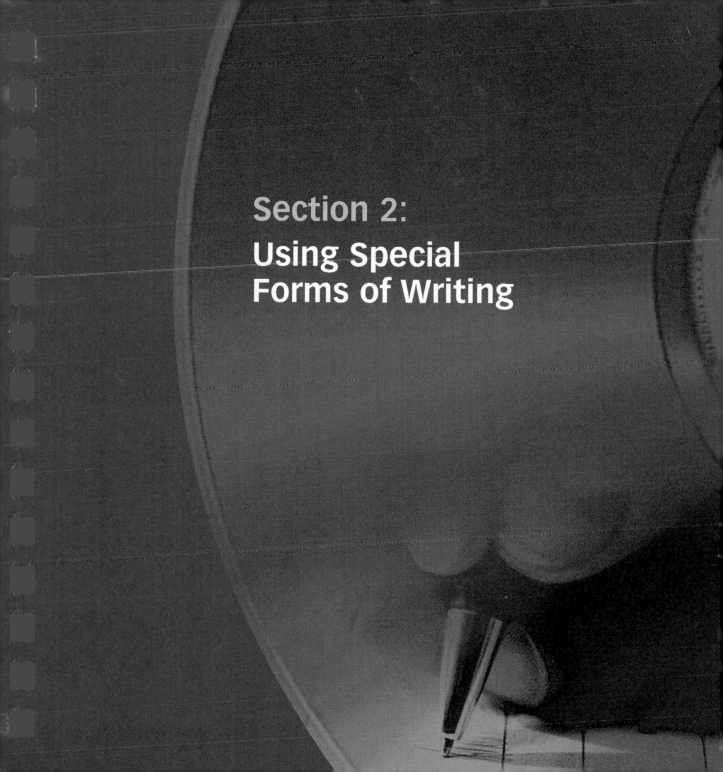

Section 2:
Using Special Forms of Writing

In this section

LESSON

Writing Reports

Good reports deliver. They deliver essential information that people need in order to understand experiments, complete projects, evaluate outcomes, and advance the company's goals in a safe, efficient manner.

Specifically, reports can

- answer questions about what's happening in your company so that readers can check results, monitor progress, keep work on track, evaluate options, and make decisions.
- get to the point quickly with a factual, no-nonsense style.
- range from two pages to hundreds of pages.
- be presented as memos, letters, filled-out forms, on-line documents, or bound documents.

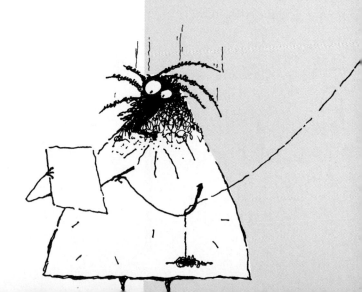

"This report, by its very length, defends itself against the risk of being read."
—Winston Churchill

Guidelines for Reports

1 PREWRITE
Consider your purpose and your audience.
- Know your purpose: Is it to supply information only, or to share conclusions as well? What outcome do you want?
- Know your readers: What are their needs? What is their knowledge of the topic and expected use of the report? What will be their likely response? Do different readers have different needs?
- Consider the big picture: Why is the report important? What effects might it have within and beyond your organization?

2 Prepare to draft.
- Carefully study the topic and gather accurate data.
- Review previous reports or related documents. Consult with colleagues and experts as needed.
- Outline your report using an appropriate method of organization.

3 DRAFT
Organize your report into three parts.
[opening] Introduce the topic and provide a context. To be direct, summarize key points; to be indirect, exclude the summary and simply give appropriate background information.
[middle] Supply, organize, and explain your findings, including all essential details.
[closing] Offer conclusions and, if expected, recommendations.

4 REVISE
Check your draft for ideas, organization, and voice.
- Have you supplied the facts objectively?
- Have you used effective transitions and summaries?
- Is your tone businesslike, but not stuffy or impersonal?

5 REFINE
Check your writing and design for
- ☐ a natural, condensed style: crisp, clear words and smooth sentences.
- ☐ correct grammar, punctuation, spelling, and mechanics.
- ☐ helpful headings, lists, and numbering.
- ☐ use of graphics, white space, boldface type, and color.

Organizing Reports

Organized reports deliver information in manageable pieces. You can organize your reports by following the three-part structure outlined below.

[opening]

- **Label** the report with a title, your name, your reader's name, the date, a subject line indicating the topic, and any identifying information such as a reference number.
- **Introduce** the report's purpose, provide background information, and preview topics covered.
- **Summarize** your main points, conclusions, and recommendations if you want to be direct.

[middle]

Organize findings according to one or more of these patterns:

- **Time**—in a step-by-step sequence.
- **Space location**—from top to bottom, left to right, near to far.
- **Order of importance**—from most to least, or least to most.
- **Categories**—by similarities and differences.
- **Alphabetical order**—by key terms.
- **Cause-effect**—by examining the forces that brought about a result or examining the results growing out of a specific force.
- **Compare-contrast**—by weighing and balancing alternatives against each other.
- **Hypothesis testing**—by suggesting possible conclusions, testing each, and selecting the best one.

Note: Present your data with the help of headings, lists, tables, spreadsheets, and other graphics.

[closing]

- For an informative report, summarize the main points.
- For an analytical report, supply conclusions.
- For a persuasive report, include recommendations.

INCIDENT REPORT

1 of 2

Maintainer Corporation of New Mexico

Date: March 25, 2003

To: Alice Jenkins, General Manager
          Roger Smythe, Safety Committee Chair

From: Gwen Vos, Supervisor
          Truck Finishing Department

[opening]

Identify the type
of incident.

Preview the
report.

Subject: Undercoating Safety Incident on March 20, 2003

This report details a recent event in the undercoating bay. You will find
(A) a description of the incident, (B) conclusions about the causes, and
(C) recommendations for fixing the problem.

[middle]

Divide the report
into logical
sections with
clear headings.

Provide context,
describe the
incident, and
explain what
followed.

List and number
the events in
the order they
happened.

A. The Incident: Tangled Air Hose

During a routine inspection of work on Thursday, March 20, at 10:45 a.m.,
I found undercoater Bob Irving struggling to breathe underneath the truck
he was working on. While spraying liquid-rubber sealant on the undercarriage, he had rolled his dolly over his air hose, cutting off the air supply.
I immediately pulled him out, untangled him, and took the following steps:

1. I checked Bob for injuries and determined that he was unharmed.
2. I asked him what had happened. He explained that he couldn't free
   himself because (a) he became tangled in the spray-gun cords, (b) his
   air hose was locked into his oxygen suit, and (c) he was lying down
   in a cramped space.
3. I discussed the incident with the undercoating crew. They confirmed
   that similar problems had developed before, but they hadn't filed
   reports because no one had actually been injured.
4. I inspected thoroughly all undercoating equipment.
5. As a short-term solution, I bought airhorn alarms to attach to the
   undercoaters' dollies.

2 of 2

[middle]
Develop clear cause-effect thinking.

Use strong transitional words.

Be precise and objective.

B. Conclusions: Probable Causes

Presently, undercoaters maneuver under trucks and spray liquid-rubber sealant on the undercarriage while lying on their backs. Maintainer provides oxygen suits to protect their skin and oxygen supply from this sealant that (a) produces noxious fumes, (b) causes choking if swallowed, and (c) injures skin upon contact. However, this incident shows that our safeguards are inadequate:

- Ten-year-old oxygen-suit meters and air tubes frequently malfunction. Masks and hoses are beginning to crack.
- The practice of lying on a dolly while spraying can cause undercoaters to get tangled in cords and hoses or roll over their air hoses.
- Spraying from a prone position allows liquid rubber to drip onto undercoaters' masks. This dripping obscures vision and makes it more likely that workers will get entangled and more difficult for them to get untangled.

[closing]
Suggest solutions that clearly match the problem.

Be realistic.

Stress benefits of action.

C. Recommendations: New Safety Measures

To further protect undercoaters from these hazards, I recommend the following actions:

1. Replace oxygen suits and equipment to meet the 2002 OSHA oxygen-safety standards (air-hose locks with emergency-release latches).
2. Put trucks on lifts so that undercoaters can work standing up.
3. Have two undercoaters work together on the same truck in order to monitor each other.
4. Purchase No-Drip Sealant Applicators to eliminate dripping liquid rubber.

With these measures, undercoating incidents such as the one with Bob Irving should not happen again. Please contact me at 692-555-1222 (extension 2422) with any questions and with your response to these recommendations.

PERIODIC REPORT

STEWART PLASTICS, INC.
JOLIET ANNUAL REPORT

[opening]

**Identify
the report,
the time period,
the writer, and
the reader.**

Date Submitted: November 15, 2002
Period Covered: November 1, 2001, to October 31, 2002
Prepared By: Denzel Irving
Prepared For: Senior Management

**State the
purpose of
the report and
what it covers.**

The following report reviews 2001-2002 activities at Stewart Plastics' Joliet facility. Topics covered include manufacturing, safety, and quality. Based on this review, the report projects sales and production needs for 2002-2003.

**Provide main
points in a
summary. (The
summary may
be placed at
the end.)**

Summary

Major projects involved plastite screws for Fimco, spray-on graphics for Newland, Kelch steel clamps on EcoLab molds, and soda blasting to clean molds. Safety remained a priority through consultation with Liberty Mutual. First-Time Quality improved from 96.8 to 97.5 percent. Anticipated sales should be $5.1 million. To reach maximum output of $6 million, purchase a 5-Axis Router and hire a Process Engineer.

[middle]

**Divide
information
into logical
categories with
clear headings.**

Year-End Operations Report

Manufacturing and Process Engineering

- Evaluated using thread-forming plastite screws to replace aluminum T-inserts on standard spot tank. Submitted samples to Fimco for testing.
- Completed testing of spray-on graphics and submitted samples to Newland. Though test parts looked good, the masking process proved time-consuming and costly. Alternate technology (Mark-It Company's post-molding graphic application) looked promising.
- Tested stainless steel clamps from Kelch on EcoLab molds. Clamps reduced maintenance downtime 50 percent.

**Use a
"telegraphic"
style (short
clauses).**

Use short lists and parallel structure.

Safety and Maintenance

- Tessa Swann, Loss Prevention Consultant from Liberty Mutual, continued to identify safety issues and to implement solutions.
- Safety Committee facilitated improvements.
- Crews completed annual maintenance on all machines.

Quality

- Thermo King Quality System assessment gave us a 53.7 rating.
- Awarded Newland Quality Award in 2001.
- First-Time Quality for 2002 was 97.5 percent, up from 96.8 percent.

2002-2003 Goals

[middle]

Shift from looking back to looking forward.

Sales Overview

Anticipated production output is $5.1 million, based on the following:

- Newland: anticipate sales to go from $1.4 to $1.6 million.
- Fermont: release of 5, 10, 15, 30, and 60KW parts for production should mean $150,000 increase in sales.
- Fimco: anticipate sales to go from $950,000 to $1.1 million.

Manufacturing Goals and Production Needs

- Combine the 800 and 160 work areas into a cell and analyze the effects on through-put and overall machine efficiencies.
- Consider purchasing a 5-Axis Router for custom-job applications requiring exact-trim procedures.
- Hire a Process Engineer by March 2003: crucial to success of custom-job applications and implementing 5-Axis Router technology.

[closing]

Summarize the report and the suggested follow-up.

Conclusions and Recommendations

The Joliet Plant is capable of $6 million in sales. Roadblocks include the lack of a 5-Axis Router for custom-trimmed products and training for the use of this router. Therefore, I recommend the following:

1. Purchase a 5-Axis Router.
2. Hire a Process Engineer who can use the 5-Axis Router and conduct training.

PROGRESS REPORT

Hope Services *Development Center*

199 Myrtle Avenue, Reading, PA 19606-5464 • Telephone 610-555-6577

July 16, 2003

Mr. Anthony Jenson
Contract Compliance Officer
Community Planning and Development
473 Maple Street
Reading, PA 19608-3361

Dear Anthony:

[opening]

Give a title and a reference number if appropriate.

Clarify the period and preview the report.

Subject: Hope Services Annual Progress Report (CDBG 2368-02)

Please accept this Annual Progress Report concerning Hope Services' work with minorities for fiscal year July 1, 2002, through June 30, 2003.

I have included these statistics: (1) total number of minority persons assisted, (2) the number of households and their ethnic origin, and (3) their status as low- or moderate-income households. In addition, I have included a narrative describing highlights of culturally specific services for the past fiscal year.

[middle]

Provide precise project data.

Client Numbers (July 1, 2002 - June 30, 2003)

The following is client information for the minority households served by the Hope Services' staff through the Cultural Diversity Program at the shelter:
1. 178 minorities served, including 102 children.
2. 76 households served, 100 percent female-headed (36 African American, 10 Asian, 23 Hispanic, 7 Native American).
3. 96 percent of households served had incomes below the poverty level, while the remaining 4 percent of households were at low-income levels.

2 of 2

[middle]

Explain key developments.

Use lists where appropriate.

[closing]

Summarize the project's status, and look forward to the next stages.

Anticipate further contact.

Outreach Highlights of the Cultural Diversity Program

In addition to the previous statistics, here are two illustrations of our progress on cultural-diversity issues:

- In January, Jasmine Michaels joined Hope Services to develop the Cultural Diversity Program, including (a) services for victims of sexual or domestic assault, and (b) community outreach to minority populations.
- In April, representatives from the following organizations formed Project SART (Sexual Abuse Response Team): Hope Services, Reading Hospital, Berks County Attorney's Office, Reading Police Department, and Penn State University.

Conclusions and Projections

As shown above, Hope Services (HS) continues to improve its services to minority clients and communities in Reading.

- Numbers indicate that HS is helping its target clientele (low-income minority households headed by women).
- Hiring a Cultural Diversity Specialist has given HS a strong presence in the community.
- In the coming year, HS will focus on strengthening its outreach to minority communities and increasing its training of staff and volunteers in cultural-diversity issues.

Thank you for supporting our work with minorities through Hope Services. If you need additional information, please contact me at 555-6577, ext. 427.

Yours sincerely,

Melissa S. Drummond

Melissa S. Drummond
Resource Development Director

TRIP REPORT

PACIFIC PIPELINE CORPORATION
REPAIR REPORT

Date: February 3, 2003

To: Ralph Arnoldson
         Pasco District Supervisor

From: Chris Waterford, Crew Chief

Repair: Leak Clamp Installation
Location: Camas Eugene Lateral near the city of Mollala, Oregon
Date: January 30, 2003
Crew: #3 (Brad Drenton, Lena Harold, John Baldritch,
            Laura Postit, Jill Reynaldo, Chris Waterford)

Crew #3 and I (Chris Waterford, Crew Chief) responded to a call from the Eugene District crew asking for help on repairing a leak. Based on their request, we took the emergency trailer and a 24-inch Plidco clamp. Our response time was 6.5 hours (2 hours loading, 4.5 hours driving). We arrived about 2:30 p.m.

Assessment of Problem

The Eugene crew had exposed the leak area on the pipe. Then Crew #3 and I assessed damage and conditions:
- Mud covered the work area and the ramps in the ditch.
- Water in the ditch came up to the bottom of the pipe.
- Rain was falling.
- The leak came from two quarter-inch cracks on a seam (at 10 o'clock looking south).
- A power generator was on site.
- Three bolt-on leak clamps and one hydraulic leak clamp were on hand.
- Space for a hydro crane and an emergency trailer was limited.

[opening]
Identify the job.

Provide trip background.

[middle]
Divide trip activities into logical categories.

Use headings, subheadings, and lists.

Repair Plan and Decisions

[middle]

Condense key trip events and issues.

With conditions in mind, we considered three issues: the possibility of more leaks, clamp selection, and safety precautions.

Highlight decisions and developments.

More Leaks? Eugene crew members probed three-foot sections of pipe on each side of the two quarter-inch cracks and found no more leaks.

Best Clamp? Laura indicated that the clamp would not need to be welded, so we decided to use the 24-inch bolt-on clamp.

Safety Precautions? We decided not to use the air systems for these reasons:
- The gas leak was minor (detectable only with a detecting agent).
- Safer installation of the clamp in daylight would be delayed by using air systems.
- Suits and breathing systems limit visibility, add weight, and create fatigue that could cause errors and injuries.

Based on these considerations, we installed the 24-inch bolt-on clamp in 1.5 hours. The Eugene crew took responsibility for site cleanup. We packed up, returned home in 4.5 hours, and unloaded in 1 hour.

Summary

[closing]

Summarize work done.

Stress costs and benefits.

The January 30, 2003, repair trip for Crew #3 aimed to help the Eugene District crew repair two leaks on the Camas Eugene Lateral near Mollala. Based on the small leak size, the muddy site, and the poor weather (rain), we decided to repair the leak without using protective air systems while installing a 24-inch bolt-on clamp. As a result, we completed the repair with these benefits:
- A less-expensive clamp was used.
- A time savings of approximately two hours was realized.

Total time spent on this repair was 13.5 hours, including travel, repair, loading, and unloading.

CHECKLIST The Report . . .

STRONG IDEAS 140

- ☐ has a clear purpose: to answer questions, monitor work, move something forward, create a record, and so on.
- ☐ spells out its purpose.
- ☐ provides complete, accurate data.
- ☐ offers conclusions and recommendations that follow logically from the information.
- ☐ uses tables, charts (lists, graphics) to communicate information clearly.

LOGICAL ORGANIZATION 142

- ☐ is organized logically into three parts: (1) introduction, (2) findings, and (3) conclusions and recommendations.
- ☐ presents a summary up front if the news is good or neutral; presents conclusions at the end in bad-news or persuasive situations.
- ☐ arranges findings in a pattern: order of importance, time or space, cause-effect, problem-solution, comparison-contrast, and so on.
- ☐ has informative, parallel headings that divide the report.

CONVERSATIONAL VOICE 144

- ☐ has a matter-of-fact but positive tone.

CLEAR WORDS 148

- ☐ uses words that fit the reader: the right level of formality and technical complexity.

SMOOTH SENTENCES 152

- ☐ uses brief, parallel phrases or sentences in lists.

CORRECT COPY 156

- ☐ uses correct grammar, punctuation, spelling, and mechanics.
- ☐ is free of typing errors.

READER-FRIENDLY DESIGN 158

- ☐ has a format and presentation that follow company guidelines.
- ☐ uses white space, boldface type, and graphics effectively.

LESSON

Writing Proposals

A proposal can be as simple as a suggestion-box memo or as complex as a book-length bid. Either way, a proposal identifies a need or a problem and lays out a convincing plan for meeting that need or solving that problem. A proposal can tackle issues like these:

- fixing inefficient operating practices;
- winning contracts and selling products or services;
- developing new markets, products, or services;
- improving current products or services; and
- meeting legal and ethical requirements.

A well-written proposal, whether it is designed to sell a service, fix a problem, or establish a relationship, offers you a force for positive change.

"In good writing, words become one with things."
— Ralph Waldo Emerson

Guidelines for Proposals

1 PREWRITE
Consider your audience and your purpose.
- To whom are you making this proposal? What are your reader's needs, attitudes, and concerns in relation to the issue?
- Exactly what are you proposing? Why?
- What outcome do you want?

2 Study the need or problem and possible solutions.
- Research the problem's background and history.
- Break the problem into parts, noting causes and effects.
- Review any solutions attempted in the past, noting their successes and failures.
- Identify other solutions and choose the best one.

3 DRAFT
Organize your proposal into three parts:

[opening] Provide context, as well as a summary, if appropriate.
[middle] Present the problem or need and your solution.
- Explain what the problem is and why it should be corrected.
- Map out the solution and stress its value.
[closing] Summarize your conclusions and recommendations.

4 REVISE
Review your draft for ideas, organization, and voice.
- Have you provided all the details readers need?
- Does the proposal address alternatives, stress benefits, consider ripple effects (who will be affected and how), and show your ability to implement the solution?
- Is your tone confident and positive, but not aggressive?

5 REFINE
Check your writing line by line for
- ☐ precise words, easy-to-read sentences, and strong transitions.
- ☐ correct grammar, punctuation, and spelling.
- ☐ document design that follows specifications, creates a good impression, and makes information accessible.

Organizing Proposals

[opening]

- **Label** your proposal with the following: a title or a subject line that promises productive change, your name, your reader's name, the date, and any reference numbers.
- **Introduce** your proposal by providing background, and establishing the theme—the need to be met, the problem to be solved, and the benefits to be gained.
- **Summarize** your proposal if you want to be direct. To be indirect, do not include the summary.

[middle]

- **Define** the problem or need. Explain its importance, limits, causes, effects, history, and connection with larger issues. Review any past attempts to solve the problem, noting their successes and failures. *Note:* If the reader is aware of the need or problem, be brief and informative. If the reader is unaware or resistant, build a persuasive case about the problem or need and its importance.
- **List** criteria for a solution. What should a solution accomplish?
- **Compare** alternative solutions. Then promote the best one.
- **Prove** the solution's workability by highlighting the following:
  - outcomes of the solution.
  - requirements (facilities, equipment, material, personnel, and so on).
  - schedules for start-up, stages, finishing dates, and follow-up.
  - cost breakdowns (services, equipment, materials, travel, and so on).
  - methods of monitoring costs and quality.
  - your qualifications for undertaking the task.

[closing]

- **Summarize** the problem or need and alternative solutions.
- **Provide conclusions** about the best solution—results and benefits.
- **Review your recommendations** for implementing the solution.

SALES PROPOSAL (BID FORM)

ASPHALT SPECIALISTS

605 CHERRY STREET   SIOUX FALLS, SOUTH DAKOTA 57103   (605) 555-2402

PROPOSAL

[opening]

Provide details to identify the bid.

PROPOSAL SUBMITTED TO: Agnes Lead, Superintendent
Clark Elementary School
1206 Missouri Avenue South
Vermillion, SD 57701

PHONE: (605) 555-0800
FAX: (605) 555-0848
DATE: April 4, 2003
E-MAIL: alead@clarkelementary.edu

[middle]

Outline the products and services to be provided.

State prices and delivery schedules.

JOB DESCRIPTION:
South Parking Lot
1. Clean existing asphalt.
2. Overlay existing asphalt using SS-1 tack oil.
3. Apply two inches of hot-mix asphalt.
4. Compact asphalt with steel-wheel vibratory roller.
5. Re-stripe entire lot.
6. Clean up work area and dispose of all debris.

COST:
252,100 square feet @ $.45 per SF = $113,445.00

SCHEDULE:
Work will begin July 14, 2003, and be completed by July 18, 2003.

[closing]

Summarize the bid and its conditions.

Sign the bid and indicate a place for customer's signature.

TERMS:
We shall furnish material and labor as specified above for the sum of $113,445.00.
Payment is due 30 days after the date shown on the invoice.

All material is guaranteed to be as specified. All work is to be completed in a professional manner according to standard practices. Any changes to the specifications and estimates listed above will be executed only after receiving your written agreement. All agreements are contingent upon strikes, accidents, or delays beyond our control.

AUTHORIZED SIGNATURE _James Dolan_____
Note: This proposal may be withdrawn by us if not accepted within ___30___ days.

ACCEPTANCE OF PROPOSAL
We accept the prices, specifications, and conditions listed above.

Signature _____

SALES PROPOSAL (LETTER)

BONIFACE SANITATION, INC.
846 Watson Way   Tallahassee, FL 32308
302•555•2356   www.bonif.com

February 26, 2003

Ms. Agnes Grey
Millwood Pharmaceuticals
2211 Green Valley Road
Tallahassee, FL 32303-5122

Dear Ms. Grey:

[opening]
Be positive
and polite.

Thank you for the opportunity to bid on Millwood's waste removal and recycling needs.

[middle]
Provide a precise
bid with the
necessary details.

Promote your
company.

Based on the bid requirements, we are submitting the following proposal:
- One eight-cubic-yard container for regular refuse, serviced twice a week.
- One eight-cubic-yard container for cardboard, serviced once a week.
- Total cost per month: $169.00.
- Extra pick-ups: $30.00 per trip.

As Tallahassee's leading waste collector, Boniface serves more than 300 organizations. References and brochures are enclosed for your review.

[closing]
Anticipate a
positive reply.

Ms. Grey, I look forward to your response. Please call me if you have questions.

Sincerely,

Robert Estavez

Robert Estavez
Sales Representative

Enclosures 3

Major Sales Proposal or Bid

A major bid is usually a response to an RFP (Request for Proposals) published by a company or a government agency. While the bid must follow the RFP specifications, a common pattern is outlined below:

[opening]

- **Include** some or all of the following "front matter":
  — a title page with the title, writer, reader, and submission date
  — a cover letter that introduces the proposal, sells its strengths, notes the key players, and thanks the reader
  — a copy of the RFP or the letter of authorization
  — a table of contents and a list of illustrations
  — an executive summary in nontechnical language

[middle]

- **Review** the reader's need as indicated in the RFP.
- **Explain** the solution—your product or service.
- **Describe** implementation, focusing on the following:
  — products and services to be delivered
  — methods of delivery and a schedule of delivery
  — costs, fees, budget breakdowns
  — evaluation plans for checking progress and results
  — personnel requirements
  — a statement of responsibilities (yours and the company's)
- **Outline** the bid's benefits for the client (results, efficiency, reliability, value, and so on).

[closing]

- **Describe** your company and its resources; list relevant past and current jobs; and provide references, testimonial letters, and résumés of key personnel.
- **Summarize** your proposal, focusing on the reader's need, your solution, the results you can deliver, and the advantages.

TROUBLESHOOTING PROPOSAL

1 of 3

Rankin Manufacturing
PROPOSAL

Date: June 19, 2003

To: John Cameron

From: Nick Jeffries

Subject: Reducing Carbon Monoxide Levels

As you requested, I have investigated the high levels of carbon monoxide in the main warehouse. The following proposal (A) explains the source of the problem, (B) proposes a solution, and (C) details an implementation plan.

A. Problem: Emissions from Lift Trucks

From November 2002 through March 2003, Rankin has been registering high carbon monoxide (CO) levels in Area 3 of the warehouse. General CO levels in the area have exceeded 35 ppm, and many office spaces show levels of 40-80 ppm (OSHA recommends 25 ppm).

These CO levels are a concern for three reasons:

1. High CO levels cause sickness and lower productivity.
2. Using summer exhaust fans in winter to reduce CO results in low humidity that shrinks wood used for manufacturing.
3. High CO levels can result in a substantial OSHA fine.

To determine the cause of the high CO levels, I investigated all sources of combustion in the warehouse. I concluded that the excess CO was caused by lift trucks operating in Area 3.

I then checked all lift trucks. They were in good working condition and were being properly used and maintained.

[opening]

Focus on positive change in the subject line and introduction.

[middle]

Define the problem and detail its impact.

Be objective.

Show clear understanding of the causes.

B. Proposal: Phase Out Internal-Combustion Lifts

[middle]

List solution criteria.

In order to correct the CO emissions problem, the ideal solution should accomplish the following in a timely and cost-effective manner:

1. Bring CO levels within OSHA limits.

2. Maintain relative humidity to ensure product quality.

Show that you considered alternatives.

To do this, Rankin could continue using the exhaust fans and install humidifying equipment at a cost of $32,000. (See attached estimate.) Or Rankin could replace all internal-combustion lift trucks in Area 3 with electric lift trucks for $195,000.

Offer your solution and provide a clear rationale.

Instead, I propose gradual replacement of the internal-combustion lifts in shipping with electric lift trucks, for these reasons:

- Shipping (Area 3) has 14 lift trucks that operate almost 24 hours per day.

- The shipping area is well-suited for electric lift trucks (no long-distance travel or use of ramps is required).

- While electric lifts cost more initially, they have lower operating and maintenance costs. A five-year cost analysis shows that the cost of operating the two types of lift trucks is similar. (See attachment.) In fact, after five years, electric lift trucks save money.

C. Implementation: Phase In Electric Lifts

Show that the solution will work.

Because Rankin buys an average of four lift trucks annually, the plans below will complete the changeover in the shipping area within the next four years.

1. When an area requests replacement of an existing lift truck, management approves purchase of a new electric lift truck.

2. The new electric lift truck goes to the Shipping Department.

3. The newest internal-combustion lift truck in Shipping is transferred to the area that requested a new lift truck.

By beginning this plan in January 2004, we could replace all internal-combustion lift trucks in Shipping by December 31, 2007.

[closing]

**Restate your
solution and
its benefits.**

Cite attachments.

Conclusion

Gradual replacement of internal-combustion lift trucks in Shipping with electric lift trucks will involve a higher initial cost but will reap two important benefits: (1) CO levels will fall below OSHA's 25 ppm, enhancing the safety of Rankin employees and guarding product quality; (2) the electric lift trucks will prove less costly to own and operate in the long run.

Therefore, I recommend that Rankin management approve this plan, and phase it in over the next four years as outlined. Improved safety, increased product quality, and lower total long-term operating costs outweigh higher initial costs.

If you wish to discuss this proposal, please call me at extension 1449.

Attachments: Renovation Estimate
                 Five-Year Cost Analysis

JUSTIFICATION PROPOSAL

1 of 2

Heartland Veterinary Services, Inc.
MEMO

Date: March 14, 2003

To: Drs. Hom-Kuh Kao, Arnold Shaffer, and Adrie Markus

From: Chris Tanyel

Subject: Improving Cleanup with a Power Washer

[opening]
Present your idea and stress its benefits.

I'm writing to recommend that Heartland buy a power washer for the cattle-processing department. A power washer will (1) save time, (2) cut costs, (3) clean effectively, and (4) improve the work environment.

[middle]
Give the reason for your proposal.

Review the present situation in detail.

Current Cleaning Practices

The current cleanup procedure in cattle processing is labor-intensive, costly, ineffective, and unsanitary.

Presently, we use a large fire hose, a garden hose, and a hand brush to clean the manure, dirt, and grease off equipment in the cattle-processing room. Cleanup involves spraying an area with water; letting the water soak into the floor; scrubbing with Rocal D; and rinsing. Here are some of the problems with this method:

1. Doing the process thoroughly takes about two hours. (If time is limited, things get missed.)

2. This procedure uses 1/2 gallon of Rocal D ($48.50 per gallon).

3. The fire hose washes the floor effectively, but lacks the high pressure needed for walls and equipment. It uses 600 gallons per cleanup.

4. Metal surfaces, especially those in hard-to-reach areas, often appear dirty and unsanitary even after the process.

Power Washer Benefits

[middle]

**Justify an
expenditure
by stressing
benefits.**

Detail costs.

Replacing the current cleaning equipment with a power washer would
supply pressure to remove even the driest material from both flat and hard-
to-reach surfaces, would eliminate brush streaks, and would cut costs:

- Cleanup time would be reduced to 30 minutes.

- A 2000 psi washer would use 75-80 gallons of water per cleanup.

- Only 1 pint of Rocal D disinfectant would be needed per cleanup.

Savings realized by a power washer would pay for the washer in less than
two months. While the current method costs $53.15 per day, a power
washer would reduce that figure to $13.05 per day. (See attached cost
analysis.)

Purchase Options and Recommendation

[closing]

**State recom-
mendations
clearly
and positively.**

**Summarize
the benefits.**

**Anticipate a
positive reply.**

Cite attachments.

After checking with several retailers, I recommend that HVS purchase a
Douser power washer. The Douser by Hancock is available for $1,499
(including delivery and installation). It has a pressure rating of 2200 psi
and comes with 100 feet of pressure hose and three nozzles.

The Douser power washer will keep the cattle-processing room cleaner and
will recoup the initial investment in less than two months through savings
on water, labor, disinfectant, and repairs.

If you need more information or wish to discuss this proposal, please call
me at ext. 366.

Attachment 1

CHECKLIST The Proposal . . .

STRONG IDEAS   140

- ☐ shows a thorough understanding of the problem, alternative solutions, the reader's needs, and your own resources.
- ☐ offers a clear, persuasive line of thinking from beginning to end.
- ☐ contains accurate and realistic details, figures, and estimates.
- ☐ includes supporting graphics such as tables and charts.
  (See pages 161-172.)

LOGICAL ORGANIZATION   142

- ☐ explains the problem (nature, importance, history, and so on).
- ☐ states the solution, stresses benefits, and shows how this solution addresses the problem better than the alternatives do.
- ☐ presents an implementation plan in terms of time, money, and personnel.
- ☐ includes measures for checking progress and testing the outcome.

CONVERSATIONAL VOICE   144

- ☐ has a positive and confident, but objective tone.
- ☐ shows "you attitude"—careful attention to the reader's perspective.

CLEAR WORDS   148

- ☐ uses language at an appropriate level of formality.
- ☐ uses technical terms carefully, defining any unfamiliar terms.

SMOOTH SENTENCES   152

- ☐ passes the "read-aloud" test for smoothness and logical transitions.
- ☐ states main points, conclusions, and recommendations in clear sentences.

CORRECT COPY   156

- ☐ contains no errors in grammar, punctuation, usage, and spelling.

READER-FRIENDLY DESIGN   158

- ☐ follows the format expected by the company.
- ☐ uses consistent, parallel, informative headings.
- ☐ uses white space, underlining, boldface, and other layout features.

Writing Instructions

Instructions are how-to documents that both organizations and customers need to reach their goals. Organizations need instructions that help employees produce goods and services efficiently and safely, and customers need them in order to use those goods and services productively. When these documents are well written, they help organizations run smoothly and successfully. On the other hand, poorly written instructions can lead to frustrated customers, expensive errors, personal injuries, and even lawsuits.

This chapter will help you write effective instructions. Guidelines and models will show you how to use tools such as lists, numbered steps, and photographs or drawings to get your message across. At the end of the chapter, a checklist will identify areas for special attention and suggest ways to refine your document.

YOUR GOAL When writing instructions, your goal is to break down a task into logical steps and describe those steps so clearly that a reader can do the task.

"Nothing is particularly hard if you divide it into small jobs."
—Henry Ford

Guidelines for Instructions

1 PREWRITE
Think about the task.
Make sure that you know your subject well: the materials needed to do the task, the number of people required to complete the task, starting and finishing times, and the steps in the process.

2 **Think about your reader.**
Is she or he familiar with the setting, the process, the equipment, the personnel needed, technical terminology, and the English language?

3 DRAFT
Organize the message into three parts:
[opening] Introduce the process by
- describing it briefly, explaining its importance, and stating its goal.
- listing materials, equipment, and tools needed to get the job done.

[middle] Tell the reader what to do by
- giving numbered, step-by-step instructions that use command verbs, short sentences, and precise terms for materials, tools, and measurements.
- stating clear *warnings* (potential for danger or injury), *cautions* (possible error or damage to equipment), and *notes* (tips or clarification on how to do the task).
- including clear, well-placed photos, drawings, or diagrams.

[closing] State the desired outcome and any final reminders.

4 REVISE
Carefully check your draft.
- Make sure you've used numbered steps to help the reader move back and forth easily between the task and the instructions.
- Check that specific, closely related actions are grouped together.
- Test the instructions by reading them to a listener who completes the task. Check the clarity of any pronouns used.

5 REFINE
Proofread for clarity and correctness by checking that
- ☐ *WARNINGS* are in boldface and caps; *cautions* are in boldface.
- ☐ spelling, labels, numbers, and terms are accurate.
- ☐ graphics, photos, and drawings enhance the message.

INSTRUCTIONS WITH A LIST OF MATERIALS

[opening]
Identify the task by using a clear title.

List materials and/or tools.

[middle]
Present steps in a chronological order.

Use short sentences with command verbs.

Use few (if any) pronouns.

Place *warnings* in boldface and caps; place *cautions* in boldface only.

Put closely related actions in a single step.

[closing]
Review a key point.

Instructions for Closing Off the Cash Register

Follow the steps below in order to (1) close off the cash register and (2) account for the day's receipts.

Materials needed: Daily Account Form, deposit bag, adding machine, pen, and paper

Steps:

1. **MAKE SURE THE STORE'S DOORS ARE LOCKED.** Then take the cash tray out of the register drawer and place the tray on the counter. (Leave the empty drawer open to deter thieves.)

2. Turn the cash-register key to the X setting and press the X key. The machine will print the X reading: the total amount of receipts for the day.

3. Turn the key to the Z setting and press the Z key. The machine will print the Z reading: itemized, department-by-department subtotals.

4. Count out $100.00 and place the bills in the envelope marked "FLOAT"; currency amounts are shown on the envelope. (The float is the $100.00 of cash placed in each cash register when the store opens.) The remaining cash, checks, and credit-card slips make up the day's receipts. **Do not place the float back in the drawer.**

5. Total the day's receipts using an adding machine, and check the total against the X reading. If the totals differ, count the receipts a second time and a third time if necessary. Write a note indicating any difference and attach the note to the receipts.

6. Fill out the Daily Account Form by entering the X reading total and the Z reading total and then the totals of the day's receipts. Place the day's receipts in the deposit bag.

7. Lock the following in the safe: (1) the deposit bag, (2) the Daily Account Form, (3) the X and Z printouts, and (4) the envelope marked "FLOAT."

DOUBLE-CHECK THE SAFE DOOR TO MAKE SURE IT'S LOCKED.

INSTRUCTIONS FOR A PROCEDURE

[opening]

Identify the task.

Explain when to do the procedure and how to prepare to do it.

[middle]

List steps in chronological order.

State *warnings* in boldface and in caps.

State *cautions* in boldface without full caps.

State *notes* in regular type.

[closing]

End with a final point.

Regis City Hospital
HAND-WASHING PROCEDURE

Perform this procedure whenever you report for duty and before and after providing care for a patient. Also use this procedure after bathroom use, eating, coughing, or sneezing, and before and after using sterile gloves, gowns, and masks. **Whenever in doubt, wash your hands.**

Caution: Rings and other jewelry harbor bacteria and are difficult to clean. Before reporting for work, remove all jewelry.

Steps in the Procedure:

1. Remove the first paper towel, and place that towel in the wastebasket.

2. Take the next paper towel and use it to turn the water on to a comfortable temperature. **DO NOT TOUCH THE CONTROLS WITH YOUR HANDS.**

3. Put your hands and wrists under the running water, keeping your fingertips pointed downward. Allow the water to flow gently.

4. Once your hands and wrists are completely wet, apply antiseptic solution.

5. Bring your hands together and create a heavy lather. Wash at least three inches above the wrists, and get soap under your fingernails and between your fingers. **Wash well for one full minute.**

6. With the fingertips of your opposite hand, circle each finger on the other hand with a rotary motion from base to tip. Pay careful attention to the area between your fingers, around nail beds, and under your fingernails.

7. Rinse your hands well under running water. **Hold your hands down** so that the direction of the water flow is from the wrist to your fingertips.

8. Pat your hands dry with a clean paper towel, and turn off the water with the towel. Discard the paper towel into the wastebasket.

Note: If your hands touch the sink, faucet, or spout, repeat the entire procedure.

INSTRUCTIONS FOR A POLICY PROCEDURE

[opening]
Identify the topic.

State and
summarize
the policy.

[middle]
Use clear
headings
throughout.

Note: The
passive voice
may be used to
emphasize key
points.

List steps
clearly,
including which
documents
to complete
and submit.

[closing]
Close with a
fitting summary
or restatement.

Family and Children Coalition
Confidentiality Procedures

The Family and Children Coalition Confidentiality Policy states that all clients have the right to confidentiality. Conduct your work in keeping with this policy by following the procedures below.

Client Intakes:

During the client intake, the Coalition counselor should discuss the conditions of confidentiality with the client. These conditions include the following:

1. Information will never be shared unless the client has given written permission using the Consent to Release Form.
2. Confidentiality may be limited or canceled if Coalition staff have serious concerns about child abuse or neglect, or if the client is a danger to herself or himself, or to others.

Outside Requests for Information:

Coalition counselors will handle outside requests for client information.

1. No client information will be shared without the client's written permission.
2. Clients will be notified of any outside requests for information. If the client gives permission, he or she must sign the Consent to Release Form and specifically indicate what information may be released and to whom. A Coalition counselor must also sign the release form.

Breaches of Confidentiality:

If a client believes that Coalition staff have not observed the confidentiality policy and procedures, the client should be directed to follow the Client-Grievance Process.

By carefully following the procedures above, the Coalition staff can help their clients while also respecting the clients' rights to confidentiality.

INSTRUCTIONS CONTAINING PHOTOGRAPHS

[opening]

Use a descriptive title. Note or list materials needed.

[middle]

Give steps and photos in chronological order.

Add graphics (such as the arrow) to create a quick visual cue.

To show an object's size, use a reference (such as the fingers).

Boldface words that need special attention.

Use only well-focused photographs.

Downloading Photographs from the MC-150 Digital Camera

Note: MC-150 software must be loaded on your computer to download photographs from the camera.

1. Turn your computer on.

2. Plug the camera's USB cable into your computer.

3. Turn the camera's mode dial to the **data transfer setting** (Figure 1).

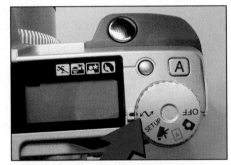

Figure 1: Data Transfer Setting

4. Open the camera's flash-card door and plug the other end of the USB cable into the **camera port** (Figure 2).

5. Select USB transfer from the camera screen menu. The MC-150 software will then launch onto your computer.

6. Follow the instructions on the computer screen to download all of your photos or specific photos.

Figure 2: Camera Port

7. When your download is complete, turn the camera off and unplug the USB cable from the camera and the computer.

[closing]

Note common problems that are easily solved.

Note: If MC-150 software doesn't launch, disconnect the camera (step 7), and then restart the computer and continue on from step 2.

INSTRUCTIONS WITH DRAWINGS

[opening]
Identify topic.

Instructions for Replacing Auger Bearing on Bale-Press 64-D

Use the instructions below to replace the right, rear auger bearing on the Bale-Press 64-D.

Parts Needed:

List the parts needed in a table format. If helpful, add illustrations.

Item No.	Quantity	Part No.	Description
1	1	RRAB20024	right, rear auger bearing
2	1	RRASP20007	right, rear auger-support post
3	2	BLT5/8X3.5HX	5/8" x 3 1/2" hex bolt
4	2	NUT5/8HX	5/8" hex nut
5	2	CP1/8X2	1/8" x 2" cotter pin

[middle]

Indicate danger with a warning message in caps and in bold print. Use an icon, if helpful.

Give steps in chronological order.

Use the same terms in the steps as were used in the parts list.

Place the illustration next to the steps.

WARNING: SHUT OFF ENGINE AND REMOVE KEY!

Steps:

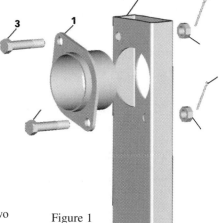

Figure 1

1. Take out the existing bearing by removing the two 1/8" cotter pins, two 5/8" nuts, and two 5/8" bolts. (See Figure 1.)

2. Insert the new bearing (item #1) into the 4 3/8" hole on the post (item #2).

3. Fasten the bearing to the post with two 5/8" bolts (item #3), two 5/8" nuts (item #4), and two 1/8" cotter pins (item #5).

Note: For ease of installation, insert both bolts before tightening the nuts.

[closing]

Use *cautions* (boldface without caps) to warn of damage.

Caution: For safer installation, fasten the replacement bearing with the new bolts, nuts, and cotter pins included with the replacement kit.

CHECKLIST The Instructions . . .

STRONG IDEAS 140

- ☐ identify the task and list all the parts, materials, and tools needed.
- ☐ explain step-by-step what to do and how to do it.
- ☐ use accurate measurements of time, distance, length, height, and so on.
- ☐ include clear and appropriate *warnings, cautions,* and *notes.*

LOGICAL ORGANIZATION 142

- ☐ open with a clear title and short introduction that identify the procedure and set the context.
- ☐ have a middle with numbered steps: each step has a single, clear action.
- ☐ include a conclusion, if needed, that summarizes the process or clarifies the task's context or importance.

CONVERSATIONAL VOICE 144

- ☐ speak clearly and confidently about the subject.
- ☐ address sensitive issues directly, but tactfully.

CLEAR WORDS 148

- ☐ use words—including technical terms—appropriate for the task, the situation, and the readers' abilities.
- ☐ identify parts using the same terms in lists, steps, and illustrations.
- ☐ state *notes, cautions,* and *warnings* clearly, without alarm.

SMOOTH SENTENCES 152

- ☐ state steps in crisp phrases or sentences using command verbs.
- ☐ include clear transitions where needed.

CORRECT COPY 156

- ☐ cite accurate specifications, names, titles, quotations, and figures.
- ☐ include error-free grammar, punctuation, capitalization, and spelling.

READER-FRIENDLY DESIGN 158

- ☐ use headings, numbers, and graphics to identify and organize information.
- ☐ include illustrations that are labeled, readable, and set off with white space.
- ☐ use correct format for *notes* (regular type), **cautions** (boldface), and ***WARNINGS*** (boldface and caps).

Writing Application-Related Documents

Whether you're a job applicant, a manager, or an employer, writing application-related documents is just part of doing business. If you're a job applicant, you have to write application documents that stand out in what may be a sea of competing applications. And even after you get that job, at some point you may want to apply for a new position within your organization, or for a special project or training program. Each situation will require a well-written application letter and an updated résumé.

If you're a manager or an employer, you also will write application documents—particularly follow-up letters to applicants. If a candidate is weak, you will want to deliver the bad news diplomatically. If the candidate is strong, you will want to encourage the person to remain interested in your organization until the selection process ends, and you can, perhaps, send a job-offer letter.

"Choose a job you love, and you will never have to work a day in your life."
—Confucius

Guidelines for Application Letters

1 **PREWRITE**
Consider your audience and purpose.
- What does the employer or company do?
- Which of your skills, academic degrees, or work experiences match the job requirements?

2 **Prepare to draft.**
- Find the name, title, and address of the person you are writing to.
- Review the job description and your résumé.

3 **DRAFT**
Organize your letter into three parts:

[opening] Use a courteous but confident voice.
- Refer to the job and tell how you learned about it.
- State your main qualification.

[middle] Show that you're qualified.
- Tell how your education, experience, and skills fit the job. (Refer to your résumé.)
- Communicate your interest in and knowledge of the job and the company.

[closing] Close by encouraging contact.
- Explain when and where you may be reached.
- Request an interview.

4 **REVISE**
Check your draft for ideas, organization, and voice.
- Have you explained why you can do the job well?
- Have you delivered your message in clear, well-organized paragraphs?
- Have you used a courteous, confident, businesslike tone?

5 **REFINE**
Edit and proofread your letter carefully.
- ☐ Double-check names, titles, and addresses.
- ☐ Run a spell check, and then read carefully for additional spelling and usage errors.
- ☐ Print your letter on quality paper that matches the résumé.

TEMPLATE

APPLICATION LETTER

3041 45th Avenue
Lake City, WA 98125-3722
November 17, 2003

Ms. Marla Tamor
Human-Resources Director
Evergreen Medical Center
812 University Street
Seattle, WA 98105-6152

Dear Ms. Tamor:

[opening]
Name the job and the source of the ad. Introduce your qualifications.

In response to your advertisement in the *Seattle Times* on November 12, I am writing to apply for the position of Software-Training Specialist. For the past seven years, I have worked as a trainer in the health-care system at Pacific Way Hospital.

[middle]
List specific training, experience, and skills.

I have instructed individuals and groups on how to use the following systems/software: Microsoft Office, WordPerfect Office, Lotus Millennium, as well as mainframe/business-specific programs. I am also trained to instruct clients in CorelDRAW and Pagemaker products.

In addition to my work with software systems, I have developed job descriptions, recruited technical employees, and trained human-resources personnel. I believe this experience would help me address the needs of a growing health-care facility such as Evergreen Medical Center.

[closing]
Invite follow-up, provide contact information, and close politely.

Enclosed is my résumé, which further details my qualifications. I look forward to hearing from you and can be reached at (206) 555-0242 or at <jmvrtz@aol.com>. Thank you for your consideration.

Sincerely,

Jamie Vertz

Jamie Vertz

Enc.: Résumé

"Information is pretty thin stuff, unless mixed with experience."
—Clarence Day

Guidelines for Employer's Follow-Up Letters

1 PREWRITE
Consider your audience and purpose.
- What are the applicant's strengths and weaknesses?
- How does this applicant compare with others?

2 Gather details and prepare to write.
- Reread the job description and list the applicant's strengths.
- Review the application for key (or missing) information.
- Note the person's current job situation and availability.

3 DRAFT
Organize the letter into three parts:

[opening] Use a formal but conversational voice.
- Express appreciation for the person's interest in the job.
- Mention when and how you received the person's application.

[middle] Explain the selection process.
- State how and when applications will be evaluated.
- For strong candidates, list additional information needed and due dates; list the time and place for interviews; and note when and how the reader will learn of the outcome. For weak candidates, state objectively—but courteously—why the person does not meet the job requirements.

[closing] Thank the applicant.
- Restate your appreciation for the application.
- Encourage strong candidates to complete the process.

4 REVISE
Check your draft for ideas, organization, and voice.
- Are your details correct and in the best order?
- Is the voice confident, professional, and positive?

5 REFINE
Check your writing line by line for the following:
- ☐ clear wording and correct spelling, punctuation, and usage.
- ☐ effective format (parts, spacing, typography, and so forth).

EMPLOYER'S FOLLOW-UP LETTER (Strong Candidate)

 TRIPLEX TECHNOLOGIES, INC.

3020 Gore Road ● Imlay City, MI 48444-0981 ● 616-555-8069

June 25, 2003

Mr. Marvin Greenfield
1554 Bastian Street
Lapeer, MI 48446-1601

Dear Mr. Greenfield:

[opening]

Maintain a formal tone and acknowledge the application.

Thank you for submitting your application and résumé for the position of Chief Microbiologist at Triplex Technologies, Inc. Your academic research on environmental hazards with the University of Michigan's Biology Department and your subsequent work as a microbiologist for the EPA indicate that you have much to offer our company.

[middle]

Describe the current status of the process and request information.

Evaluation of all applications is nearly complete, and we will begin interviewing in two weeks. To help us gain a clearer view of your qualifications, please send us a detailed summary of your current work responsibilities.

[closing]

Express thanks and encourage the applicant.

Thank you again for your interest in Triplex Technologies. Your résumé and credentials show you to be a deserving candidate for the position of Chief Microbiologist. Please send the requested materials to our Human Resources Department by Monday, July 7.

Sincerely,

Keith Ryster

Keith Ryster
Human Resources Manager

EMPLOYER'S FOLLOW-UP LETTER (Unqualified Candidate)

 400 Talbot Avenue, NE, Oakland, CA 94623-1412

May 14, 2003

Mr. Frederick O'Brien
1525 Montgomery Street
Oakland, CA 94612-6315

Dear Mr. O'Brien:

[opening]

Express appreciation for the application.

Thank you for submitting your application and résumé for the accounting position at Levinsky and Gring. We have reviewed your academic achievements and experience.

[middle]

State your disinterest in the application courteously.

You are probably aware that the competition is formidable for staff accounting positions in large firms. Although your background is commendable, it does not match our current needs. Experience working at a smaller firm could strengthen your résumé and increase your chances of employment in a large firm.

[closing]

Encourage the reader.

We do appreciate your interest and wish you success in securing a position.

Sincerely,

Ruby Unger
Director of Recruiting

EMPLOYER'S JOB-OFFER LETTER

 TRIPLEX TECHNOLOGIES, INC.

3020 Gore Road ● Imlay City, MI 48444-0981 ● 616-555-8069

July 24, 2003

Mr. Marvin Greenfield
1554 Bastian Street
Lapeer, MI 48446-1601

Dear Mr. Greenfield:

[opening]
Offer congratulations.

I am pleased to offer to you the position of Chief Microbiologist at Triplex Technologies. Our selection committee noted that your enthusiasm and range of experience set you apart from the other applicants whom we considered.

[middle]
Affirm the person's strengths and state contract details.

Following are further details regarding this position:
1. Your salary will be $85,000, with a review based on your yearly performance appraisal.
2. The starting date is Monday, August 18, 2003, with a three-month probationary period.
3. An overview of employee benefits is enclosed. If you have questions, please call Judy Owen, Human Resources Assistant (616-555-8911).

Mr. Greenfield, we sincerely hope that you will accept our offer. We are eager to work with you and believe that our relationship will be mutually beneficial.

[closing]
Encourage acceptance and note the date for the reader's decision.

Please inform me of your decision by August 1, 2003. You may call my office at 616-555-8948. Thank you again for your interest in Triplex Technologies, and I look forward to your reply.

Sincerely,

Keith Ryster

Keith Ryster
Human Resources Manager

Enc.: Employee Benefits

YOUR GOAL When writing a résumé, your goal is to show that your skills, knowledge, and experience match the requirements for a specific job. Each style of résumé presents that information differently.

"A résumé is a balance sheet with no liabilities."
—Robert Half

Guidelines for Résumés

1 PREWRITE
Review your goals.
- Show that your skills and experience match the job requirements.
- Choose the style of résumé that best highlights your qualifications (*chronological* features experience; *functional* features skills).
- Choose the format (paper or electronic) that the employer prefers.

2 Gather details about the following:
- your career objective, worded to match the job description.
- your educational experiences (schools, degrees, certification).
- your work experiences (employers and dates; responsibilities, skills, and titles; special projects, leadership roles, and awards).
- activities and interests directly or indirectly related to the job.
- responsible people who are willing to recommend you.

3 DRAFT
Organize the résumé into three parts.

[opening] List your contact information and job objective.
[middle] Write appropriate headings, and list educational and work experiences in parallel phrases or clauses. Refer to your training and skills with key words that match the job description (terms that could be identified by an employer's scanner).
[closing] List names, job titles, and contact information for your references; or state that references are available upon request.

4 REVISE
Review your résumé for ideas, organization, and voice.
- Check for skills, training, and key words listed in the job description.
- Check for clear organization, correct details, and a professional tone.

5 REFINE
Check your résumé line by line for the following:
- ☐ strong verbs, precise nouns, and parallel phrases.
- ☐ correct names, dates, grammar, and punctuation.
- ☐ appropriate format (divisions, headings, lists, spacing).

CHRONOLOGICAL RÉSUMÉ

[opening]

Present contact information.

State your employment objective.

[middle]

List experiences, skills, and training (most recent first).

Use periods after clauses— including those with understood subjects.

Do not use periods after headings or phrases.

Keep all phrases and clauses parallel.

List awards and honors in order of importance.

[closing]

Offer references.

LLOYD A. CLARK
1913 Linden Street
Charlotte, NC 28205-5611
(704) 555-2422
lloydac@erthlk.net

EMPLOYMENT OBJECTIVE
Law enforcement position that calls for technical skills, military experience, self-discipline, reliability, and people skills.

WORK EXPERIENCE
Positions held in the United States Marine Corps:
- Guard Supervisor—Sasebo Naval Base, Japan, 1999-2003
  Scheduled and supervised 24 guards.
- Marksmanship Instructor—Sasebo Naval Base, Japan, 1997-1999
  Trained personnel in small-arms marksmanship techniques.
- Company Clerk—Okinawa, Japan, 1996-1997
  Handled correspondence; prepared training schedules and assignments.

SKILLS AND QUALIFICATIONS
- In-depth knowledge of laws and regulations concerning apprehension, search and seizure, rules of evidence, and use of deadly force
- Knowledge of security-management principles, training methods, and countermeasures
- Experience in physical-training management, marksmanship, and weaponry
- Computer word-processing and database skills on an IBM-compatible system
- Excellent one-on-one skills and communication abilities

EDUCATION
- Arrest, Apprehension, and Riot Control Course, Sasebo, Japan, 1998
- Marksmanship Instructor Course, Okinawa, Japan, 1997
- Sexual-Harassment Sensitivity Training, Camp Lejeune, NC, 1996
- School of Infantry, Camp Pendleton, CA, 1996

AWARDS AND HONORS
- Promoted meritoriously from Private (E-1) to Lance Corporal (E-3); promoted meritoriously to final rank of Corporal (E-4) in less than 2 years.
- Achieved "Expert" rating for pistol at annual marksmanship qualifications (3 years).
- Represented Marine Barracks, Japan, in division shooting matches (placed in top half).

References available upon request

TEMPLATE

FUNCTIONAL RÉSUMÉ

[opening]

Present contact information and your employment objective.

MICHELLE MOORE
3448 Skyway Drive
Missoula, MT 59801-2883
(406) 555-2166
E-mail: mimoore@erthlk.net

EMPLOYMENT OBJECTIVE   Electrical Engineer—designing or developing digital and/or microprocessor systems.

[middle]

Feature skills by referring to educational and work experiences.

Put the most important skills first.

Use periods after clauses— including those with understood subjects—but not after phrases.

Format for paper only:
• boldface
• underlining
• bulleted lists
• two columns

QUALIFICATIONS AND SKILLS

Design
• Wrote two "C" programs to increase production-lab efficiency.
• Built, tested, and modified prototypes in digital and analog circuit design.
• Designed and worked with CMOS components.
• Wrote code for specific set of requirements.
• Helped implement circuitry and hardware for a "bed-of-nails" test.

Troubleshooting and Repair
• Repaired circuit boards of peripheral computer products.
• Helped maintain equipment using circuit-board testing.
• Improved product quality by correcting recurring problems.
• Debugged IBM-XT/Fox Kit Microprocessor Trainer (Z80).

Management
• Trained and supervised production technicians.
• Facilitated smooth operation of production lab.
• Assisted in lab teaching for Microprocessors and Digital Circuits class.

EDUCATION
Montana State University, Bozeman, MT
• Bachelor of Science in Engineering, 2002
• Major: Electrical Engineering
• Independent Study: C programming, DOS and BIOS interrupts

EXPERIENCE
October 2002 to present   Production Engineer (full-time)
                                 Big Sky Computer Products, Inc., Missoula, MT

June 2002 to September 2002   Engineer (part-time)
                                 Western Labs, Missoula, MT

September 2001 to May 2002   Engineering Assistant
                                 Montana State University, Bozeman, MT

May 2000 to September 2001   Engineering Intern
                                 Montana State University, Bozeman, MT

[closing]

Offer references.

References available upon request

TEMPLATE

ELECTRONIC RÉSUMÉ

[opening]

Present contact information and employment objectives.

Jonathan L. Greenlind
806 5th Avenue
Waterloo, IA 50701-9351
Phone: 319.555.6955
E-mail: grnlnd@aol.com

OBJECTIVE
Position as hydraulics supervisor that calls for hydraulics expertise, technical skills, mechanical knowledge, reliability, and enthusiasm.

[middle]

List skills, experiences, and education using many key words.

Format for e-mail, scanner, and Web site:
- **one column**
- **asterisks as bullets**
- **simple sans-serif typeface**
- **flush left margin**
- **no italics, boldface, or underlining**
- **ASCII or RTF text (readable by all computers)**

SKILLS
Operation and repair specialist in main and auxiliary power systems, subsystems, landing gears, brakes and pneumatic systems, hydraulic motors, reservoirs, actuators, pumps, and cylinders from six types of hydraulic systems
Dependable, resourceful, strong leader, team worker

EXPERIENCE
Aviation Hydraulics Technician
United States Navy (1990-present)
* Repair, test, and maintain basic hydraulics, distribution systems, and aircraft structural hydraulics systems.
* Manufacture low-, medium-, and high-pressure rubber and Teflon hydraulic hoses.
* Perform preflight, postflight, and other periodic aircraft inspections.
* Supervise personnel.
Aircraft Mechanic
Sioux Falls International Airport (1988-1990)
Sioux Falls, South Dakota
* Performed fueling, engine overhauls, minor repairs, and tire and oil changes of various aircraft.

EDUCATION
United States Navy (1990-1994)
Certificate in Hydraulic Technical School; GPA 3.8/4.0
Certificate in Hydraulic, Pneumatic Test Stand School; GPA 3.9/4.0
Courses in Corrosion Control, Hydraulic Tube Bender, Aviation Structural Mechanics
Equivalent of 10 semester hours in Hydraulic Systems Maintenance and Structural Repair

[closing]

Offer references.

References available upon request

CHECKLIST The Résumé . . .

STRONG IDEAS 140

- ☐ shows that I understand the prospective job and am qualified for it.
- ☐ includes accurate and honest details about training, skills, awards, and experiences matched to the job requirements.

LOGICAL ORGANIZATION 142

- ☐ begins with my name, contact information, and employment objective.
- ☐ follows with specific details starting with most recent (chronological) or most important (functional) and groups details under appropriate headings.
- ☐ concludes with how the reader can access my references.

CONVERSATIONAL VOICE 144

- ☐ is confident and knowledgeable, but not arrogant.

CLEAR WORDS 148

- ☐ includes key words from the job description as well as related terms.
- ☐ uses accurate terms for academic degrees, training programs, professional certifications, job titles, and tasks.
- ☐ uses strong verbs, especially for a paper-only résumé.

SMOOTH SENTENCES 152

- ☐ provides information in parallel lists, phrases, and clauses.
- ☐ uses complete sentences only when needed to make a point.

CORRECT COPY 156

- ☐ uses correct terms, names, dates, and titles.
- ☐ includes no errors in grammar, punctuation, capitalization, and spelling.
- ☐ uses periods after clauses (including those with understood subjects).

READER-FRIENDLY DESIGN 158

- ☐ (*paper only*) uses bulleted lists, boldface, underlining, and business typeface.
- ☐ (*electronic*) uses ASCII or RTF text (readable by all computers), simple sans-serif typeface, single-column format, and wide margins—but no boldface or underlining.

Section 3:
Writing and
Presenting Skills

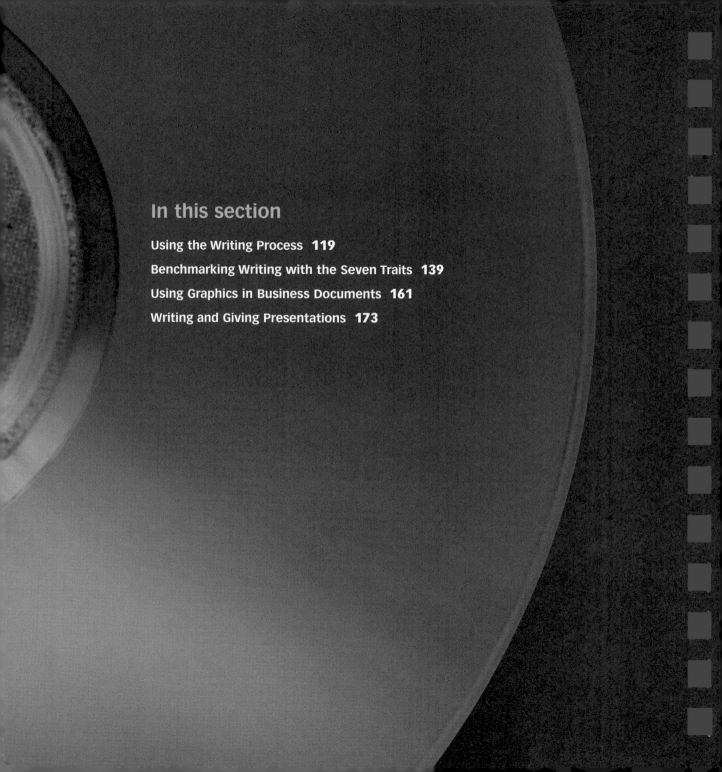

In this section

Using the Writing Process

Effective writing seldom, if ever, "hatches" on the spot. In point of fact, the best writing is most often the product of much planning, writing, and rewriting. This is why writing is called a process; it must go through a series of steps before it is clear and complete.

This chapter explains each step in the writing process: prewriting, drafting, revising, and refining. Whatever type of writing you're doing, these steps will carry you from start to finish. Use the explanations, techniques, and tips in this chapter to strengthen your writing process as a whole, or to refine a specific step you would like to improve.

In this chapter

The Process of Writing:
An Overview

It's easy to feel overwhelmed about a writing project—especially if the form of writing is new to you, or the topic is complex. However, using the writing process will relieve some of that pressure by breaking down the task into manageable steps: **Prewriting, Drafting, Revising,** and **Refining**.

> **FYI**
> The diagram on this page shows how the writing process works. The diagram indicates the usual order of the steps in the process; the arrows show that writers commonly move back and forth between steps.

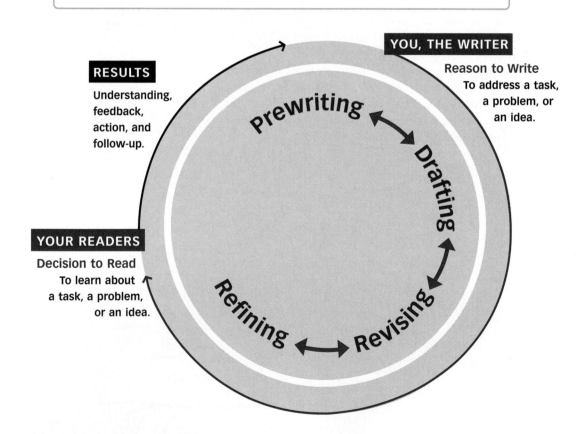

RESULTS

Understanding, feedback, action, and follow-up.

YOU, THE WRITER

Reason to Write
To address a task, a problem, or an idea.

Prewriting

Drafting

Refining

Revising

YOUR READERS

Decision to Read
To learn about a task, a problem, or an idea.

Top 10 Tips for Business Writing

You can develop successful workplace documents if you make the writing process work for you. Follow the tips below.

1 **Be committed.** Care about your writing. It is a clear reflection of both you and your company.

2 **Be conversational.** Write as if you were speaking to your reader. Test your writing for effective tone by reading it out loud. (See pages 144-147.)

3 **Be considerate.** Know your reader and his or her needs in order to make recommendations or referrals.

4 **Be connected.** Understand your subject well by consulting customers, coworkers, and company records to gather information.

5 **Be consistent.** Make your point and stick to it. Keep your thoughts organized, and don't wander off the subject.

6 **Be clear.** First, be clear in your thinking. Then, write with common words, avoiding jargon or inflated language. (See pages 148-151.)

7 **Be concrete.** Always use specific names, numbers, and examples. (*Eight* is concrete; *some* is abstract.)

8 **Be concise.** Get to the point. You need not cover everything or try to include every detail.

9 **Be complete.** Tell the reader how to respond. Include all the names, dates, and numbers the reader might need.

10 **Be correct.** Check your facts for accuracy and your language for appropriateness. Always double-check names of people and companies for correct spelling.

THE PROCESS UP CLOSE

Each of the steps in the writing process has a specific goal that can be achieved with a variety of activities.

Prewriting

Goal: Find your focus and prepare to draft.

Activities: Clarify your purpose, think about your reader, choose a format, and list the information you need to share. Then do any necessary research, review models, and develop an outline.

Drafting

Goal: Get your thoughts on paper.

Activities: Expand your outline with sentences and paragraphs that use a fitting tone.

Revising

Goal: Fix any content problems in the first draft.

Activities: Test the quality and clarity of the ideas, organization, and voice. Add, cut, and clarify as needed.

Refining

Goal: Fine-tune the piece before sending it out.

Activities: Review format and design. Edit and proofread by checking word choice, sentence structure, grammar, punctuation, spelling, and mechanics.

Prewriting

Using prewriting strategies can jump-start your writing. Techniques from brainstorming to free-writing get you ready to draft by helping you collect information and focus your thinking. Before you begin, you need to consider your purpose, the readers, the context, and your desired result.

TIPS & TECHNIQUES

1. Clarify your purpose.

Consider your overall purpose and your specific goal.

- What specific result do you want to see from your writing?
- Is the desired goal or outcome realistic and measurable?
- Do you need to inform or persuade to achieve results?

  Informing tasks: state, clarify, outline, list, record, report, analyze, compare, describe, define, explain

  Persuading tasks: request, sell, recommend, convince, apologize, evaluate, complain, turn down, promote

2. Profile your readers.

Consider who your reader is in relation to your goal.

- Is your reader within or outside your organization?
- How well do you know your reader?
- How much does your reader know about the topic?
- What are your reader's values, needs, and priorities? Is your message likely to be received positively or negatively?
- Will your reader be making a decision or doing something? What authority and responsibility does your reader have?
- Will there be a number of readers? If so, are they diverse in age, occupation, gender, education, culture, and language skills?

3. Know the context.

Consider requirements related to format, deadline, or follow-up.

- What type of document are you writing? What are its design requirements? How will you create, send, and store this document?
- When must the document be finished and sent?
- What information do you have available? What additional information do you need to gather?
- What future contact or action might be needed by you, the reader, others?

GATHERING AND ORGANIZING INFORMATION

You can identify key ideas, gather reliable material, and organize information by using a variety of prewriting techniques like those below and on the next two pages. Remember, you should not be overly concerned with grammar or mechanics at this stage in the process.

Using a Planner

Consider using a planner similar to the one below to help you clarify your audience, purpose, and time frame. Planners can be especially helpful for longer projects such as reports or proposals.

Prewriting Planner

1. Why am I writing? _____

_____

2. Who is my reader? _____

_____

3. What do I want the reader to think or do? _____

_____

4. What are her or his needs, biases, questions?_____

_____

5. How can I get the desired results? _____

_____

6. What information do I need? _____

_____

7. Where can I find this information?_____

_____

8. What form of writing should I use? _____

_____

9. When and where do I need to send or submit this? _____

_____

FYI A prewriting planner similar to the one shown here can help you better understand the writing situation by focusing your attention on the 5 W's and H: *who, what, when, where, why,* and *how.*

Freewriting

Writing whatever comes to mind on a particular topic is called *freewriting*. Freewriting is really brainstorming on paper (or on the computer). It helps you record, develop, and understand your thinking.

1 Write nonstop about your subject or project, *following* rather than *directing* your thoughts.

2 Resist the temptation to stop and judge or edit what you write.

3 If you get stuck, switch directions and follow a different line of thinking.

4 When you finish, reread your material and highlight passages you think might be useful.

Clustering

Clustering creates a web of connections between a general topic and specific subtopics. A cluster allows you to see the structure of your topic and plan your writing.

1 Write a key word or phrase in the middle of your page.

2 Record or "cluster" related words and phrases around this key word.

3 Circle each idea and link it to related ideas in your cluster.

4 Continue recording related ideas until you have covered the topic.

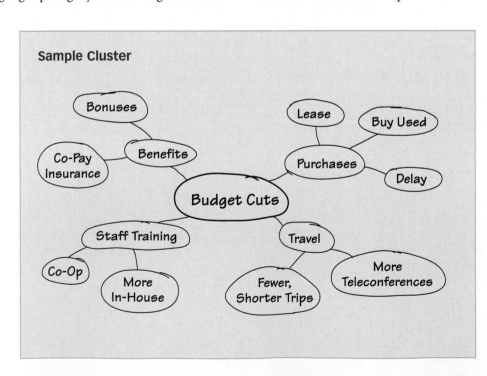

Sample Cluster

Using a Diagram

Diagrams can be used to help you record and organize information graphically. The diagrams below are two of the most useful.

1 | **Use a Venn diagram.** Use a Venn diagram to compare and contrast two things.

2 | **Use a problem/solution diagram.** Use this diagram to help you understand a problem, break it into parts, specify its causes, list its effects, and develop solutions.

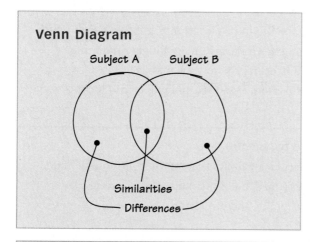

Venn Diagram

Subject A   Subject B

Similarities

Differences

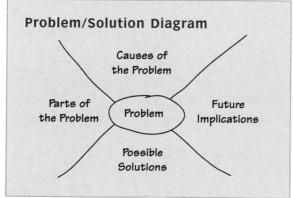

Problem/Solution Diagram

Causes of
the Problem

Parts of
the Problem

Problem

Future
Implications

Possible
Solutions

Using an Outline

One way to organize the information you've collected is to construct an outline or a detailed list. Follow the guidelines below to get started.

1 | **Find your focus.** Clarify the main point or controlling idea of your writing project.

2 | **Develop your outline.** A good outline provides a plan for developing your main point:

- Highlight the key ideas you'll want to use to develop your main point.
- Connect your supporting details to these key ideas. Add ideas and details as needed, and number them appropriately.
- Arrange your information into the best possible order. Consider your reader's likely response, and select a sequence that best advances your main point. You may use your own method of development or one of these approaches:

cause/effect	question/answer
chronological order	classification
compare/contrast	order of importance
partitioning	problem/solution

Outline

I. Introduction
II. Body
   A. Main point
      1. Supporting details
      2. Supporting details
   B. Main point
      1. Supporting details
      2. Supporting details
III. Closing

Drafting

When you draft, you convert raw material into coherent sentences and paragraphs. Drafting involves your best first effort to state your ideas clearly.

Computer Link: Drafting on a computer helps you concentrate on ideas and share your work easily with coworkers and colleagues.

TIPS & TECHNIQUES

1. **Create productive conditions.**	**Before you begin drafting, gather your materials.** ● Make your writing area efficient and comfortable. ● Set aside a block of uninterrupted time if possible. ● Place your writing tools and prewriting material within easy reach.
2. **Use your prewriting material.**	**Look to your notes for the information and approach you need.** ● Draw on your planning, clustering, freewriting, or outlining. ● Review other documents related to your message. ● Highlight statements, facts, examples, and graphics to include in your draft.
3. **Focus on ideas, organization, and voice.**	**Concentrate on the big picture.** ● Expand and connect ideas, always keeping your purpose in mind. ● Use your outline as a map, but remain open to new ideas. ● Maintain a natural, polite, and professional voice or tone.
4. **Develop a logical flow.**	**Determine the best way to present your information.** ● Common approaches include moving from overview to close-up, background to discussion, problem to solution, main idea to explanation, or familiar topic to new information.
5. **Think paragraphs.**	**Group similar thoughts together on the page.** ● Present each main idea in a single sentence, and then support that idea in a single paragraph. ● Consider possible closings or conclusions. Doing so can help focus and direct your drafting.

DRAFTING OPENINGS

Your opening should quickly set a clear direction for your writing. Use the guidelines and models below to help you do that.

FYI In many documents, the subject line opens your message. Your reader should be able to "get the point" at a glance, so subject lines should be direct and precise, not vague or confusing.

An effective opening should

- indicate the document type (report, proposal, instructions).
- state your topic, your reason for writing, and your main point (if appropriate).
- get the reader's attention and interest.
- establish a tone or voice.
- provide background and context.
- preview the content.
- provide a summary (if appropriate).

Sample Openings

Simple Opening (letter)

context

main point → Thank you for requesting a credit account at Cottonwood Hills Greenhouse and Florist Supply. We are pleased to extend you $100,000 in credit based on Dale's Garden Center's strong financial condition. Congratulations!

positive tone

Complex Opening (report, proposal)

writing form and topic

Subject: Report on Investigation of Cockroach Infestation at 5690 Cherryhill

background

During the month of July 2003, 26 tenants from the 400-unit building at 5690 Cherryhill informed the building superintendent that they had found cockroaches in their units. On August 8, the Management-Tenant Committee authorized our group to investigate these questions:

1. How extensive is the cockroach infestation?
2. How can the cockroach population best be controlled?

objective tone

We investigated this problem from August 9 to September 11, 2003. This report contains (1) a summary, (2) an overview of our research methods and findings, (3) conclusions, and (4) recommendations.

preview of content

DRAFTING THE MIDDLE

In the middle part of your message, you need to develop strong, clear paragraphs that advance the main idea presented in your introduction. Follow your outline and tackle one paragraph at a time. If necessary, go back to your prewriting material or rework your outline.

An effective middle should

(1) link back to the opening through a clear transition,
(2) provide readers with necessary information, and
(3) include well-written paragraphs that have strong opening sentences.

To achieve the goals above, follow these guidelines:

- Develop each main point in a separate paragraph.
- Keep each paragraph fairly short, 3 to 8 lines in length.
- Use a topic sentence to signal each paragraph's direction.
- Expand and connect ideas, always keeping your reader in mind.
- Incorporate headings, lists, and graphics when appropriate.
- Maintain the tone established in the opening.
- Prepare readers for the closing.

> "The art of writing is the art of applying the seat of the pants to the seat of the chair."
> —Mary Heaton Vorse

Sample Middle Paragraphs (Letter)

clear topic sentences

As you requested, I have enclosed a list of Home Builders' affiliates in Missouri. Each affiliate schedules and handles its own work groups. Call or write directly to any of them for more information about local offerings.

Because you are in college, I have also enclosed some information on Home Builders' Campus Chapters. The pamphlet explains how to join or start a Campus Chapter and discusses service learning for academic credit. Feel free to contact Ben Abramson, the Campus Outreach Coordinator for your area, at the address on the enclosed material.

helpful tone throughout

prepare reader for closing

DRAFTING CLOSINGS

Close your writing logically and naturally by recalling your goal and main point. Your closing should help the reader understand and act on the message.

An effective closing should

- restate your main point and offer conclusions.
- provide recommendations, propose the next step, or offer help.
- focus on appreciation, cooperation, and future contact.
- include all details needed for follow-up and action.
- end with energy by using clear, strong verbs.

Note: Avoid stating the obvious in your closing, or rambling on and on.

FYI If appropriate, present possible outcomes or long-term implications of what has been discussed. In other words, what's the real bottom line?

Sample Closings

Simple Closing (memo, e-mail, letter)

— *focus on cooperation*

With short-term solutions and long-term cooperation, together we will keep Premium Meats operating and prospering.

recommendation and follow-up

If you have any questions or suggestions, please speak to your immediate supervisor or a member of the Quality Task Force. (Task Force information is supplied in the attachment.)

Complex Closing (report, proposal)

restatement of main point

Our proposal is to replace our internal-combustion forklifts with electric lifts. This change will involve a higher initial cost but will reap two important benefits: (1) CO levels will drop below OSHA's recommended 25 ppm, ensuring employee safety and product quality; (2) in the long run, the electric lifts will prove less costly to own and operate.

— *focus on outcomes*

recommendation

Therefore, I recommend that Rankin management approve this plan, to be phased in over the next four years as outlined above. Improved safety and product quality, combined with total operating costs over the long run, outweigh the plan's initial costs. If you wish to discuss this proposal, please call me at extension 1449.

— *action, future contact*

Revising

Your focus while revising is to step back and look at the big picture. Keep reworking your draft until it says exactly what you want it to say.

Computer Link: Computers make it easy to delete, copy, and paste, but revising still requires careful thought. As always, take the time to do it right.

TIPS & TECHNIQUES

1. Set aside the draft.	**Gain some objectivity by letting your draft sit.** • Let your draft sit for a few minutes if it's a simple e-mail. • Let your draft sit for a day or two if it's a major report.
2. Print a hard copy.	**See your message in total on paper.** • Assess the overall effectiveness of your writing and map out changes as you review the entire document.
3. Review your purpose.	**Test to see if you've done what you set out to do.** • Check to see that your message stays focused. • Make sure you address your reader's potential questions: Why did I receive this? What's the point? Why is it important?
4. Read the draft aloud.	**Listen to your writing from your reader's perspective.** • Identify problems in content and tone.
5. Go through your draft with pencil in hand.	**Test your draft's ideas, organization, and voice.** • Add comments in the margins about the focus, details, and overall flow of your draft. • Try the cut-clarify-condense system: [Bracket] material that could be cut. <u>Underline</u> material that needs to be clarified. Put (parentheses) around material that needs to be condensed. • Transfer changes to your electronic draft.
6. Get input from others.	**Share your draft with a colleague or a potential reader.** • Get a fresh view of your writing from an objective perspective.

REVISING FOR IDEAS

If your first draft lacks focus, substance, or clarity, you need to revise your content. The following guidelines and models should help you assess the ideas in your draft.

Focus

Check the focus of the whole document and each paragraph. Try cutting or moving material that rambles or is unrelated to the point being developed.

Original Passage

Thursdays are generally light days for truck undercoating. However, during a routine inspection, I found an undercoater struggling to breathe under a truck. It was March 21 around 10:45 a.m. because it was the same date that we received our long-overdue order of oil filters.

Revised Version

During a routine inspection of work on Thursday, March 21, at 10:45 a.m., I found undercoater Bob Irving struggling to breathe underneath the truck he was working on.

Content

Strengthen the content in your draft where necessary by expanding explanations, offering examples, and adding concrete details.

Original Passage

Maintainer Corporation provides suits to protect undercoaters from this dangerous sealant. However, this isn't good enough.

Revised Version

Maintainer Corporation provides oxygen suits to protect undercoaters' skin and oxygen supply from sealants that (a) produce noxious fumes, (b) cause choking if swallowed, and (c) injure skin upon contact. However, the incident shows that our safeguards are inadequate. First, because the oxygen suits are 10 years old, the meters and air tubes frequently malfunction. . . .

Clarity

Check your writing for clarity and ease of reading. Where necessary, add background and context, define terms, and rewrite confusing passages.

Original Passage

We should do something about the problem. The facts point toward an investment in new equipment and in undercoaters working together.

Revised Version

To further protect undercoaters from sealant hazards, I recommend the following actions:

1. **Purchase oxygen suits and equipment that meet the 2003 OSHA oxygen-safety standards. In particular, air-hose locks should have emergency-release latches.**
2. **Raise trucks on a lift so that undercoaters may stand.**

REVISING FOR ORGANIZATION

To make sure the reader is able to follow and understand your writing, test your draft's organization and flow from start to finish. (See pages 130-131.)

The Opening

Does the opening clearly announce your purpose, provide background information, and then point forward?

Original Passage

As you know, insurance is important when accidents happen. How are you doing with coverage?

Revised Version

Periodically, insurance companies review the cost of offering their policies and then make changes where needed. When changes are made, it's my responsibility as an agent to inform my clients and help them make necessary adjustments.

The Middle

Does the middle cover your key points in a smooth, logical way?

- Does each point follow logically from the previous one?
- Are transitions used between sentences and paragraphs?
- Does the information flow at a steady pace?

Original Passage

Hawkeye Casualty has chosen not to renew you. In order to keep their premiums low, some insurance companies will not cover high-risk drivers. In the past two years, you have had an at-fault accident and four moving violations. Your present coverage will cease January 31, 2003. A nonstandard auto insurance company is willing to provide you coverage.

Revised Version

Last week Hawkeye Casualty, your auto insurance carrier, discontinued all policies for "high-risk" drivers. Your at-fault accident and four moving violations put you in that category. As a result, Hawkeye Casualty has cancelled your auto insurance policy effective January 31, 2003. However, I have found another company that will cover you. While the cost of the new policy is somewhat higher than your present policy, the coverage is comparable, and the company is reliable.

The Closing

Do you pull your message together? Have you summarized points, recommended steps, and specified action to be taken?

Original Passage

This coverage issue needs attention soon.

Revised Version

Please call me at 555-0020 before the end of the month so that we can discuss the situation and decide how to proceed.

REVISING FOR VOICE

Respect your reader by writing in a natural but professional voice. Fine-tune your writing voice as necessary so that it fits your purpose, your topic, and your audience. (See pages 144-147).

Attitude

Keep attention focused on the topic and the reader. In most business writing, avoid putting yourself in the spotlight.

Original Passage

We at Birks Cleaners are motivated to provide the best dry cleaning around. We're in our third generation of quality-minded dry cleaners. Our quality speaks for itself.

Revised Version

At Birks Cleaners, you'll find services to meet all your dry cleaning needs. For three generations, our goal has been to treat your clothes as if they were our own.

Transparency

Create an invisible style that lets the reader focus on content, not fancy phrases. Rewrite passages that say, "Look at these words!"

Original Passage

From the starting pistol of this pivotal project, Janice worked with superhuman strength to maneuver the company ship through the turbulent waters of this transition.

Revised Version

From start to finish, Janice worked hard to help us manage during this often difficult transition.

Level

Maintain a consistent tone. Test your draft for a positive attitude, an appropriate seriousness, and the correct level of technical discussion.

Original Passage

Even though your being inconvenienced wasn't entirely our fault, we're obviously sorry about it.

Revised Version

We apologize that your confirmed room was unavailable last night, and we are sorry for the inconvenience this may have caused you.

Energy

Show that you really care about the topic. If your voice drags, reenergize it by rewriting the passage as needed.

Original Passage

There is very little doubt that the multiple organizational changes designed to meet our business challenges create uncertainty and anxiety for employees at all levels.

Revised Version

We know that change creates concern for all employees, but we are looking for creative ways to meet these challenges.

Refining

To develop quality writing and impress your readers, you need to pay close attention to details. Take time to make the line-by-line changes that ensure your document is clean, clear, and correct.

TIPS & TECHNIQUES

1. Determine if you're ready to refine.	**Make sure you've finished revising for overall meaning.** ● If possible, let the draft sit for a while. ● Get mentally prepared to check your draft word by word.
2. Gather your tools.	**Have writing aids at hand.** ● Use the models and the "Proofreader's Guide" in this handbook. ● Keep a dictionary, thesaurus, and company style sheet handy. ● Utilize computer tools (spell check, on-line thesaurus, grammar check, templates, cut-and-paste, find-and-replace).
3. Set limits.	**Decide how much time and effort to put into refining.** ● Consider the overall importance of the document. ● The wider the distribution, the higher the reader's status, or the more complex the content—the more refining you should do.
4. Focus on details.	**Follow logical steps.** ● First, edit for effective word choice and sentence smoothness. ● Second, proofread for errors in grammar, usage, and mechanics. ● Third, check the document's format and design for correctness, readability, and consistency with similar documents. ● Finally, address details related to distributing the document.
5. Ask for help.	**Find an objective reader.** ● Turn to a coworker with good editing skills. ● Share documents with managers, experts, and legal counsel as needed.
6. Use your computer wisely.	**Remember that computer tools aren't foolproof.** ● Run a final grammar check and spell check to catch basic errors. ● Print out your document and proofread it carefully.

EDITING FOR WORD CHOICE

In *effective* business messages, each word is necessary, clear, and appropriate. To achieve these qualities, edit your writing with the following guidelines in mind. (See pages 148-151.)

Wordiness

Cut repetitive words, and replace vague words or phrases. *Don't* use too many words in making your point.

Original Passage

The committee has been organized and set up in order to provide leadership in our effort to improve our abilities to communicate in and between departmental structures.

Revised Version

The committee's goal is to improve communication between all departments.

Unclear Words

Replace cliches, jargon, and flowery phrases with clear, simple words. *Don't* use big words when simple words will do.

Original Passage

Pursuant to his request, I analyzed Bob's physiological constitution and determined that his physical state of being was unimpaired.

Revised Version

I checked Bob for injuries and determined that he was unharmed.

Negative Words

Replace negative words with neutral or positive ones. *Don't* use insensitive or derogatory phrasing. (See page 147.)

Original Passage

I read your memo requesting that all sales reps be given a whole day off for training in Cincinnati. While that stuff is important, Oscar, the bottom line is no less important! So I have no choice but to say, "No."

Revised Version

I reviewed your request to send all the sales reps to the training seminar in Cincinnati. Oscar, I agree that this training would help your staff be more productive. However, our budget for . . .

Inappropriate Level

Choose conversational words, but make fitting choices about contractions, personal pronouns, use of names, and forms of politeness. *Don't* use words that are too formal—or too informal.

Original Passage

Hey, Lois, I sure hope that you'll keep helping us get all adults up and reading. You can do that by writing us a check and sending it back ASAP to us in this envelope.

Revised Version

Please continue to support our effort to get every adult reading. If you wish to send a check, make it out to National Campaign for Literacy and return it in the enclosed envelope.

EDITING FOR SENTENCE SMOOTHNESS

Read your draft aloud. When you stumble over phrasing or get confused, it's time to edit. Here are three editing tips, along with three common sentence problems that you may need to address. (See pages 152-155.)

- **Highlight** the first few words of each sentence. Do several sentences start the same way?
- **List word counts** for each sentence. Are many sentences similar in length?
- **Examine** the verbs. Are there strong action verbs, or weak linking verbs (*is, are, was*)?

Choppy Sentences

Do you have a series of short sentences with poor flow, simplistic thoughts, or poor connections?

Solution: **Combine Sentences**
- Combine related ideas.
- Add transitions.

Original Passage

I am responding to your job advertisement. It appeared in the *Seattle Times*. The date was June 12, 2003. I am applying for the Software-Training Specialist position.

Revised Version

In response to your advertisement in the *Seattle Times* on November 12, 2003, I am applying for the position of Software-Training Specialist.

Tired Sentences

Are your sentences sluggish, overly negative, or repetitive?

Solution: **Energize Sentences**
- Use the active voice.
- Change negative statements to positive statements.
- Vary sentence openings.

Original Passage

Your getting back to me in a short time was greatly appreciated. Some people take a lot longer. Some of your other people may also want to meet me next Thursday, and that's fine with me.

Revised Version

Thank you for your quick response to my letter of application for the position of Software-Training Specialist. I look forward to meeting you and the staff at Evergreen Medical Center next Thursday.

Rambling Sentences

Are your sentences strung out, confusing, or packed with too many ideas?

Solution: **Divide Sentences**
- Control ideas with lists.
- Divide sentences, or cut sentence parts.

Original Passage

I enjoyed touring your facilities and meeting your office managers, and I would enjoy contributing to the work that you and other staff members do at Evergreen, and I believe that my hospital training would be an asset.

Revised Version

After touring your facilities and meeting your office managers, I am certain that I would enjoy working at Evergreen Medical Center. I believe that my hospital training would be an asset.

PROOFREADING FOR CORRECTNESS

In addition to spelling errors and typos, the issues listed below commonly plague business documents. When refining your writing, use this list to find and correct the problems. For more information, consult your "Proofreader's Guide," pages 187-266.

- **Pronoun-Antecedent Agreement** (page 263)

  him or her

  To help a new employee learn our day-to-day procedures, please take ~~them~~ through the orientation program.

- **Shift in Person** (page 264)

  they   *their jobs*

  When new employees go through this orientation, ~~you~~ learn ~~your job~~ more quickly.

- **Subject-Verb Agreement** (page 261)

  covers

  The procedure, as well as the attached checklist of steps and items, ~~cover~~ key orientation topics.

- **Dangling Modifier** (page 265)

  you should send the form

  After filling in the review form for the new employee, ~~the form should be sent~~ to Human Resources.

- **Unparallel Construction** (page 264)

  The form describes issues at each stage in the evaluation process: after 1 day,

  after   *after*   *after*

  1 week ~~later, then~~ 2 weeks ~~after starting,~~ and ~~when~~ 30 days.

- **Sentence Fragment** (page 266)

  and shorten the

  The form will streamline orientation for new employees, ~~Much less~~ time it takes them to learn their assignments.

- **Comma Splice** (page 156)

  The new checklist includes more information than the old one; therefore, the new one will take more time to complete.

- **Comma Omission After Introductory Phrases and Clauses** (page 190)

  After the final review, the supervisor and the employee will sign the form.

- **Comma Omission Between Independent Clauses** (page 190)

  Reviewers should use the form for 30 days, and then they should forward the form to Human Resources.

- **Comma Omission Around Nonrestrictive Modifiers** (page 192)

  For each new employee, Human Resources, which is responsible for the initial orientation, will prepare a checklist with the employee's name on it.

CHECKLIST The Writing Process

PREWRITING

- ☐ **Ideas:** Have I analyzed my purpose and audience; developed a measurable goal; and collected information through techniques such as brainstorming, clustering, freewriting, consulting, completing planners, and doing research?
- ☐ **Organization:** Have I organized my thoughts by using graphic organizers and/or outlining?
- ☐ **Voice:** Have I determined what tone fits the audience and situation?
- ☐ **Design:** Have I selected and mapped out a format? Have I consulted models and style guides?

DRAFTING

- ☐ **Ideas:** Have I recorded all my key points and essential information?
- ☐ **Organization:** Have I arranged my ideas and details into an opening, middle, and closing?
- ☐ **Voice:** Have I maintained a person-to-person tone from start to finish?

REVISING

- ☐ **Ideas:** Have I fixed problems with the draft's overall focus, clarity, and content? If appropriate, have I gotten feedback from a colleague?
- ☐ **Organization:** Have I sharpened the opening to pull readers in, reworked the middle paragraphs to improve flow and coherence, and improved the closing to help readers take the next step?
- ☐ **Voice:** Have I fixed any lapses in attitude, level, or energy so that the topic and reader are in the foreground and I am in the background?

REFINING

- ☐ **Word Choice:** Have I eliminated cliches, jargon, and redundancy so that wording is concise, clear, and positive?
- ☐ **Sentence Smoothness:** Have I edited choppy, tired, and rambling sentences by using combining, parallelism, transitions, active voice, and variety?
- ☐ **Correctness:** Have I proofread for sentence, punctuation, mechanics, spelling, and usage errors (using but not relying solely on a grammar check and a spell check)? If appropriate, have I gotten editing help?
- ☐ **Design:** Have I fine-tuned the format, page layout, and typography to make the document professional, inviting, and readable?

Benchmarking Writing with the Seven Traits

What makes business writing work? From a brief e-mail message to a lengthy proposal, business writing works best when it exhibits these seven traits: *strong ideas, logical organization, a conversational voice, clear words, smooth sentences, correct copy,* and *a reader-friendly design.*

How can learning about these seven traits help you succeed as a business writer? The traits can help you do three things:

1. Evaluate your personal writing using the seven traits as benchmarks of quality writing.
2. Improve your writing using guidelines and checklists based on the seven traits.
3. Develop a common vocabulary with your colleagues that will help you improve writing throughout your organization.

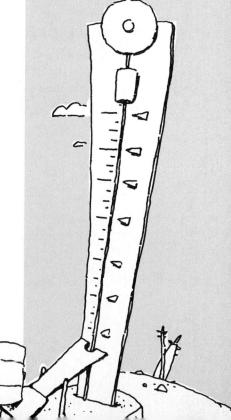

Trait 1: Strong Ideas

(**BENCHMARK:**) Your goal as a business writer is to create a quality document that gets results. You can do this by focusing on a main point; developing that point logically; and providing accurate, current, and complete supporting details. To achieve this benchmark, use the three suggestions below:

STATE IDEAS CLEARLY

If a good idea is stated clearly, the reader can understand it and can use it. You can construct a clear idea statement by following this pattern:

Pattern: *A specific subject*
+ a specific thought, conclusion, opinion
= a good idea statement or claim

Example: *Rankin* **has been recording high carbon monoxide (CO) in Area 3 of the warehouse.**

A clear idea statement will help you shape an argument, develop a paragraph, share information effectively, and state recommendations.

QUALIFY YOUR IDEAS

Statements that use overly positive or negative words (such as *best, worst,* or *never*) may sound unconvincing. To make your statements strong but reasonable, use accurate numbers (*nearly two-thirds*), specific limits (*in Area 3*), or qualifiers (*probably, usually, often, some*).

SUPPORT YOUR IDEAS

If you want readers to accept an idea, support it with details that are concrete, complete, and accurate. To develop this type of support, use provable facts that answer readers' main questions:

- **What do you mean?**
  Clarify, expand, or restate the idea as necessary.
- **Can you prove it?**
  Add supporting details, such as facts and examples to prove your point.
- **Why is it important?**
  Summarize possible outcomes and effects.

Problem: Emissions from Lift Trucks

*The topic sentence clearly **states** the idea.*

From November 2002 through March 2003, Rankin has been recording high levels of carbon monoxide (CO) in Area 3 of the warehouse. General CO levels in the area have exceeded 35 ppm, and many office spaces showed levels of 40-80 ppm (OSHA recommends 25 ppm).

These CO levels are a concern for three reasons:

*Data and the list of reasons **support** the idea.*

1. High CO levels cause sickness and lower productivity.

2. Using summer exhaust fans in winter results in low humidity that shrinks wood used for manufacturing.

3. High CO levels could result in a substantial OSHA fine.

*Phrases "From November 2002" and "in Area 3" **qualify** the idea.*

USE RELIABLE THINKING METHODS

To be clear in your writing, you must first be clear in your thinking. Using a reliable method of thinking can help you develop ideas quickly and effectively. To shape your ideas, start with the basic thinking moves below.

Whenever you need to	Then
INFORM list describe name label share forward summarize reply	**Share what you know:** • Collect and organize information. • Clarify main points. • Supply details.
EXPLAIN define clarify restate illustrate demonstrate show model outline	**Answer questions and apply knowledge:** • Clarify the meaning of terms. • Give examples. • Rephrase ideas and restate information. • Provide steps in a process. • Show how something works.
ANALYZE break down rank conclude classify compare contrast tell why give results examine categorize	**Break down a topic to show how it works:** • Carefully examine a topic. • Partition the topic into parts and subparts. • Create categories of information. • Show connections and cause/effect links. • Discuss similarities and differences. • Prioritize points.
SYNTHESIZE combine connect speculate design compose create predict develop rearrange imagine	**Reshape knowledge into new forms:** • Invent a better way of doing something. • Blend the old with the new. • Predict or hypothesize. • Mix concepts and practices from different fields.
PERSUADE recommend judge criticize argue evaluate rate convince assess	**Convince others to believe and act:** • Evaluate a subject's quality or worth. • Explain what needs to be done and why. • Point out strengths and weaknesses, benefits and costs. • Inspire readers.

Trait 2: Logical Organization

BENCHMARK: Your goal is to organize your writing logically so that readers grasp your message quickly. To reach this benchmark, (1) arrange your points by deciding what readers need first, second, third, and so on; (2) control the flow of information by moving from main points to supporting points to specific details; and (3) break text into paragraphs joined with transitions and sections labeled with headings. In addition, consider using a number of the organizing strategies that follow on this page and the next.

USE THREE-PART STRUCTURE

Most workplace writing involves working with an opening, a middle, and a closing. For each message you write, select the strategies below that make the most sense.

OPENING

Goals:
To establish the purpose of your writing and get the reader's attention.

Opening Strategies:
- State your reason for writing.
- Greet the reader: start with goodwill.
- Get the reader's attention with a question or a dramatic statement.
- State your main point.
- Summarize your conclusions and recommendations.
- Give background details and context.
- Define key terms.
- Preview your document's contents: map out where you're going.

MIDDLE

Goal:
To provide the full details (answers, causes, effects, problems, solutions).

Middle Strategies: Arrange your details by using one of these patterns.
- Questions/answers
- Specific to general
- Categorizing
- Cause/effect
- General to specific
- Alphabetical order
- Problem/solution
- Spatial order
- Order of importance
- Compare/contrast
- Partitioning
- Chronological order

CLOSING

Goal:
To focus on outcomes, action, and the future.

Closing Strategies:
- Explain how to use the information.
- Stress the importance of the information.
- State conclusions and recommendations.
- State what you will do next.
- Request or clarify what the reader needs to do, when, and how.
- Look forward to future contact.
- Offer further help and provide contact information.

BE DIRECT OR INDIRECT

Consider how your reader will probably respond to your message. Then choose either a direct or an indirect approach and follow the guidelines below.

	Direct	Indirect
	Be direct when the reader's response will be neutral or positive.	**Be indirect when the reader's response will be negative or indifferent.**
Opening	• Supply the necessary context. • State the main point (conclusion, request, information, and so on).	• Get the reader's attention. • Indicate the topic. • Offer necessary background.
Middle	• Discuss the main point and supporting points. • Supply necessary information (information the reader needs or wants, arranged logically).	• Supply information, proof, analysis, supporting details, and reasons that build a persuasive argument. • State your main point. • Offer other options (if appropriate).
Closing	• Restate the main point. • Look forward. • End positively and politely.	• Focus on action, next steps, the future. • End politely.

MAKE USE OF LISTS

To use lists effectively, first decide whether to integrate or display the items. With a few short items, build the list into the paragraph, using transition words like *first, second,* and *finally* or numbering/lettering such as (1), (2), (3).

If you have many items, or you want to stress each item—break out the items into a displayed list using the following helpful tips:

- Introduce the list with a complete sentence and a colon.
- Use numbers where ranking or sequence is important; use bullets where it isn't.
- Single-space within items; double-space between items.
- Make all lists parallel in phrasing.

A Numbered, Displayed List

To make this plan work, follow the procedure below for all your travel arrangements:

1. **Book your flight through The Travel Center and charge it to the Rankin account.**

2. **Sign the invoice when you receive it and specify the account to be charged.**

3. **Return the invoice to Accounting via internal mail.**

Trait 3: Conversational Voice

BENCHMARK: Your goal is to write with a conversational yet professional voice. Your writing should be natural, positive, polite, and attentive to the reader's perspective. To reach this benchmark, follow the guidelines below and on the next three pages.

MAKE YOUR WRITING NATURAL

When writing is natural, it's not stiff or stuffy. In other words, the tone or level of formality is right. To find the right tone, consider your role in the message, your relationship with readers, the topic's seriousness, and the writing medium (letter, memo, e-mail, report).

TONE	Characteristics	Example
Formal *Use for* • major documents • messages to superiors • messages to some people outside your company • bad-news messages with legal implications	• no contractions • few personal pronouns • serious, objective tone • specific (sometimes legal or technical) terminology	The goal of Boniface Sanitation is serving the Tallahassee community. As indicated in the attached client list, Boniface has contracts with 300 organizations for waste removal.
Moderate *Use for* • average documents • messages to coworkers, equals, familiar people outside the company	• occasional contractions and personal pronouns • friendly but professional tone • varied sentence structure	Our goal is serving you well. As Tallahassee's leading waste collector, Boniface serves more than 300 companies like yours.
Informal *Use for* • quick documents (lists, questions) • e-mail and memos to coworkers and some outside people	• frequent contractions and personal pronouns • appropriate humor • some jargon, slang	Could you please cover my pick-up route on Tuesday? My dad's having surgery. Thanks. I owe you one!

Keeping Things Natural

Use words that make your writing sound natural and conversational. The following list will help you determine which words and phrases to eliminate from your business writing.

Unnatural	*Natural*
accordingly	so
according to our records	our records show
acquaint	tell
adhere	stick
afford an opportunity	allow/permit
along the lines of	like
applicable to	apply to
apprise	tell
are in receipt of	have received
are of the opinion that	think that
ascertain	learn/find out
as per	according to
as regards	regarding
awaiting your instructions	please let me know
call your attention to	please note
case in point	example
ceased functioning	quit working
cognizant	aware
commence	begin
concur	agree
configuration	shape
disbursements	payments
do not hesitate to	please
due consideration	careful thought
endeavor	try
enumerate	list
evacuate	leave
expedite	speed up
fabricate	make
facilitate	make easier
finalize	settle/finish
fluctuate	vary

Unnatural	*Natural*
herein	in this
heretofore	until now
in accordance with	as
inasmuch as	as/because
increment	amount/step
indispensable	vital
in lieu of	instead of
in the amount of	for
kindly	please
manifest	show
manipulate	operate
modification	change
necessitate	require
on a daily basis	daily
paradigm shift	major change
parameter	limit
per se	as such
personnel reduction	layoffs
per your request	as requested
precipitate	cause
preliminary to	before
prioritize	rank
procure	buy/get
pursuant to	following up
quantify	measure/count
ramification	result
recapitulate	review
remuneration	pay
reproduction	copy
salient	important
strategize	plan/solve
subsequent	later/after
terminate	end
under separate cover	separately
utilize	use
vacillate	waver
visualize	picture
wherewithal	means

MAKE YOUR WRITING POSITIVE

Put the power of positive thinking to work in your writing by stressing solutions and benefits.

Use positive phrasing.

- Stress what *can* be done, not what can't, nor who's to blame.
- Choose words with positive associations: *strong willed* or *firm*, not *pig-headed*.
- Avoid building sentences on negatives: *no, not, never, no one, nobody*.

Be tactful.

Using tact lets you focus on issues, not personalities. Being blunt or finding fault can make your readers defensive and destroy long-term goodwill.

Offer constructive criticism.

- Mention both strengths and weaknesses.
- Focus on solutions and improvements.
- Direct criticism to the topic, not the person.

DEVELOP A "YOU ATTITUDE"

Using a "you attitude" helps you connect with readers and focus on their needs.

Use common courtesy.

Understanding the reader's needs is where it all starts. Ask, *What does this message mean to the reader?* Also, use those few extra words that show concern and courtesy—they're worth the extra effort.

Pay attention to names.

Spell all names correctly, and use the proper courtesy titles. If appropriate, get your reader's name into the message at a key point or in the closing.

Use personal pronouns effectively.

Personal pronouns, especially *you*, place your readers front and center.

- Use *you* and *your* in a positive manner.
- Avoid *you* and *your* if the message is negative.
- Use *I, we, us,* and *our* when they stress unity.

A Natural, Positive Voice with a "You Attitude"

Focus on reader needs.

Dear Ms. Grey:

Thank you for the opportunity to bid on Millwood's waste removal and recycling needs. Based on the needs you outlined for us, we are pleased to offer you the following proposal:

Use positive words.
- One eight-cubic-yard container for regular refuse, serviced twice a week.
- One eight-cubic-yard container for cardboard, serviced once a week.
- One billing a month at $169.00.
- Extra pick-ups at $30.00 per trip.

Use personal pronouns.
As Tallahassee's leading waste collector, Boniface serves more than 300 organizations. We would like to add you to our list of satisfied customers. If you have questions, Ms. Grey, please call me at 303-555-2356.

Positive use of reader's name.

Sincerely,

Jason Reynolds

Jason Reynolds

Keeping Things Positive

In all your correspondence, keep things as positive as possible. Using negative or accusatory language can lead to lost business and potential lawsuits. In sensitive or potentially damaging situations, seek legal counsel about word choice.

Poor: While your past service may have been adequate, this Snorkel Lift fiasco just goes to show that Industrial Aggregate Equipment, and your project supervisor in particular, Nick Luther, are incompetent, unreliable, and, yes, even dishonest.

BETTER: In the past, we have appreciated your service and assistance. From our experience of the past six months, however, we can only conclude that you are experiencing problems that make it difficult for you to provide the service Rankin Technologies needs.

Write Connection: Due to the sensitive nature of the messages below, they require special attention when it comes to keeping things positive. See the models on the pages indicated.

HIT LIST

Avoid these negative, accusatory words.

alcoholic
bankrupt
bribery
corrupt
discrimination
dishonest
drug addict
exorbitant
extortion
fiscally irresponsible
fraud
gullible
highway robbery
incapable
incompetent
inferior
insane
insolvent
irresponsible
kickback
lazy
liar/lies/lying
misappropriate
misconduct
neurotic
pressure tactics
psychotic
senile
suspicious
threaten to
ultimatum
unbelievable
unheard of
unreliable
worthless

Trait 4: Clear Words

BENCHMARK: Your goal when writing for business is to select fresh, precise words; cut unnecessary words; and use fair, respectful words. By choosing the right words, you can write with clarity and energy.

SELECT FRESH, PRECISE WORDS

The best words are the simplest ones you can use and still get your meaning across. Choose words that are precise, clear, and energetic.

1 **Replace or clarify general words.** Balance general words with concrete, precise terms. Choose specific nouns, vivid verbs, and strong modifiers.

> **Vague:** The equipment doesn't do a good job.
>
> **PRECISE:** The fire hose lacks the pressure needed to remove dried material from walls and equipment and uses 600 gallons per cleanup.

2 **Rewrite unprofessional expressions.** Slang terms and cliches weaken your writing's authority, clarity, and energy.

> **Unprofessional:** This note is a heads-up regarding a tax-collection strategy that's coming your way soon.
>
> **PROFESSIONAL:** I'm writing to let you know about a change in the way we will handle your property-tax payments.

3 **Avoid "business English."** Use plain English instead of language that sounds overly technical, vague, or trendy.

> **Business English:** The benchmark has been established to maximize client satisfaction by supplying an abundance of Southern hospitality. To facilitate that, management has upscaled your room while requiring no monetary outlay.
>
> **PLAIN ENGLISH:** We want to provide you with outstanding service and warm, Southern hospitality. So, we have upgraded your room at no expense.

ELIMINATE WORDINESS

Concise writing involves cutting unneeded words, irrelevant information, and obvious statements. To make your writing concise, follow these tips:

Limit modifiers.

Avoid using too many adjectives and adverbs. Limit intensifying adverbs (*very, really, especially*) and delete meaningless modifiers (*kind of, sort of*).

Replace wordy phrases and clauses.

Locate wordy prepositional phrases and relative clauses (*who, which, that* clauses) and replace them with tighter constructions.

Cut redundancy.

Avoid words and phrases that say the same thing. While well-constructed repetition can add power to your writing, redundancy can bog it down.

Wordy Versus Concise Phrasing

Use concise words and phrasing that deliver your message quickly and clearly. The following list should help you write more precisely.

Wordy	*Concise*
advance forward	**advance**
advance planning	**planning**
a majority of	**most**
any and all	**any/all**
are of the opinion that	**believe**
ask the question	**ask**
assembled together	**assembled**
at an early date	**soon**
attach together	**attach**
at the conclusion of	**after/following**
at the present time	**now**
based on the fact that	**because**
basic essentials	**essentials**
both together	**together**
brief in duration	**brief**
close proximity	**close**
combine together	**combine**
completely unanimous	**unanimous**
connect together	**connect**
consensus of opinion	**consensus**
descend down	**descend**
despite the fact that	**although**
disregard altogether	**disregard**
due to the fact that	**because**
during the course of	**during**
end result	**result**
engaged in a study of	**studying**
few in number	**few**
filled to capacity	**filled**
final conclusion	**conclusion**
final outcome	**outcome**
first and foremost	**first/foremost**
foreign imports	**imports**
for the purpose of	**for**

Wordy	*Concise*
for the reasons that	**because**
free gift	**gift**
free of charge	**free**
having the capacity to	**can**
in connection with	**about**
in light of the fact that	**since**
in order to	**to**
in spite of the fact that	**although**
in the amount of	**for**
in the event that	**if**
in the vast majority	**most**
in view of the fact that	**because**
it is often the case that	**often**
it is our opinion that	**we believe that**
it is our recommendation	**we recommend**
it is our understanding	**we understand**
joint cooperation	**cooperation**
join together	**join**
joint partnership	**partnership**
main essentials	**essentials**
make reference to	**refer to**
meet together	**meet**
more preferable	**preferable**
mutual cooperation	**cooperation**
of the opinion that	**think that**
on a daily basis	**daily**
on a weekly basis	**weekly**
on the grounds that	**because**
over again	**again**
personal in nature	**personal**
personal opinion	**opinion**
pertaining to	**about**
plan ahead	**plan**
postponed until later	**postponed**
present status	**status**
prior to	**before**
repeat again	**repeat**
until such time as	**until**
with regard to	**about**

USE FAIR, RESPECTFUL LANGUAGE

People want respect, and it's your job as a writer to select words that address readers respectfully. To choose appropriate words, follow the guidelines below.

Respect age.

When referring to the age of a person or group, use acceptable, neutral terms and avoid words with negative connotations.

Age Group	Acceptable Term
Up to ages 13 or 14	**boys, girls**
Between 13 and 17	**youth, young people**
Late teens and 20's	**young adults**
30's to 60's	**adults**
60 and older	**older adults**

Respect disabilities.

With disabilities, remember to refer to the person first and the disability second—and always use the preferred term.

Not Recommended	Preferred
an AIDS victim	**person with AIDS**
suffering from cancer	**person who has cancer**
handicapped	**disabled**
stutter, stammer, lisp	**speech impairment**

Respect gender.

Take special care when dealing with occupations, courtesy titles, and salutations. (See "Forms of Address," pages 24-27.)

Not Recommended	Preferred
chairman	**chair, presiding officer, moderator**
salesman	**sales representative, salesperson**
mailman	**mail carrier, postal worker**
businessman	**executive, manager, businessperson**
policeman, policewoman	**police officer**

Respect ethnicity.

When depicting individuals or groups according to their ethnicity, use language that implies equal value and respect for all people.

Acceptable General Terms	Acceptable Specific Terms
Native Americans	**Cherokee people, Inuit people**
Asian Americans	**Chinese Americans, Korean Americans**
Hispanic Americans	**Mexican Americans, Cuban Americans**

African Americans
"African American" has wide acceptance, though the term "black" is preferred by some individuals.
"Person of color" is also used to mean "nonwhite."

Anglo Americans (English ancestry), European Americans
Use the terms to avoid the notion that "American," used alone, means "white."

USE PLAIN ENGLISH FOR ESL READERS

If you are writing to someone who reads English as a second language (ESL), it's very important that you use clear, grammatically correct language. Also, remember that different readers have different levels of fluency with English. Some of your readers may be thoroughly trained in English, while others may be struggling at a basic level with grammar and diction. Given this diversity, follow the tips below.

Avoid humor. Normally, humor doesn't translate well from one culture to another.

Avoid cultural references. Be careful with references to people, places, and events specific to your culture. These may confuse or alienate your reader. Specifically, avoid sports, pop culture, religious, and military references.

Avoid jargon, slang, idioms, acronyms, and abbreviations. Such shorthand has a restricted use that will probably confuse ESL readers. Use plain English instead.

Use simple, objective words. Avoid words that have emotional or historical baggage. Use nouns with clear meanings and verbs that express a clear action. However, don't confuse simplicity with a condescending tone: Don't write as if your reader were a child.

Use clear, obvious transitions. At the beginnings of paragraphs and sentences, use obvious transitions like "however," "in addition," "first," "second," and so on, whenever appropriate. Such transitions highlight relationships between statements and help ESL readers follow your thoughts.

Be grammatically correct. Spelling errors, misplaced modifiers, sentence fragments, and faulty comma usage all confuse ESL readers. Be especially careful with spelling. When a name or word includes accents or other diacritical marks, make sure that you use them.

Keep sentences and paragraphs short. Avoid long, complex sentences (more than 15 words) and big, intimidating paragraphs (8 lines or longer). Such sentences and paragraphs are challenging for ESL readers.

FYI Not all English is the same. For example, U.S. English is different from Canadian English, British English, and Australian English. So even when writing to other cultural groups that use English fluently, use standard English, following many of the tips at the left.

Trait 5: Smooth Sentences

BENCHMARK: Your goal is to write smooth sentences that make your writing easy to read and understand. To achieve this benchmark in your writing, express your ideas in energetic, efficient, and well-crafted sentences. Always check your writing for both short, choppy sentences and tired, rambling sentences.

COMBINE CHOPPY SENTENCES

Short, choppy sentences sound abrupt and disconnected. They often give all ideas equal treatment even though key points should be given more emphasis. Fix choppiness by combining and connecting sentences using the suggestions below.

Combine by coordinating.

Using coordination allows you to join words, phrases, and sentences to show equal relationships between ideas and details.

Choppy: The adjustor examined the roof. She checked the valleys closely. She also inspected the carport.

SMOOTH: The adjustor **examined the roof, checked the valleys, and inspected the carport.**

Combine by subordinating.

All ideas are not equal. Using subordination allows you to place key points in main clauses and secondary points in dependent phrases or clauses.

Choppy: I have done a lot of training in the health-care system. That includes more than 200 clients. My training experience spans seven years.

SMOOTH: **During the last seven years,** I have trained more than 200 clients in the health-care system.

Connect with transitions.

Using links or transitions between sentences allows you to write a series of smooth, efficient sentences. (See page 153.)

Choppy: The starting date of August 24 works well for me. I'll begin to search for housing. Thank you for the material you sent about moving costs and real-estate agencies. Could you please send information about area schools?

SMOOTH: **As we discussed earlier,** the starting date of August 24 works well for me. **Before then,** I'll begin to search for housing. **In addition to** the material you've already provided about moving costs and real-estate agencies, could you **also** please send information about area schools?

TRANSITION AND LINKING WORDS

To unify your writing, you need to link individual sentences and paragraphs into a smooth, easy-to-read document. Transition words help by showing how ideas are linked by location, time, or logic.

Words That Show Location

above	away from	between	in front of	on top of	to the right
across	behind	beyond	inside	onto	under
along	below	by	into	outside	
among	beneath	down	near	over	
around	beside	in back of	off	throughout	

Words That Show Time

about	as soon as	first	next	then	tomorrow
after	before	immediately	next week	third	until
afterward	during	later	second	till	when
again	finally	meanwhile	soon	today	yesterday

Words That Compare Things (Show Similarities)

also	likewise	in the same way	similarly	as	like

Words That Contrast Things (Show Differences)

although	still	in contrast	even though	on the other hand
but	yet	nevertheless	however	otherwise

Words That Emphasize a Point

again	in fact	to repeat	most importantly
for this reason	to emphasize	truly	the main point

Words That Conclude, Summarize, Recommend

all in all	because	in conclusion	therefore
as a result	finally	in summary	to sum up

Words That Add Information

additionally	also	as well	finally	in addition
again	and	besides	for example	likewise
along with	another	next	for instance	moreover

Words That Clarify

for example	for instance	in other words	that is	put another way

ENERGIZE TIRED AND RAMBLING SENTENCES

Because tired sentences lack energy, variety, and rhythm, they can hypnotize readers. Similarly, rambling sentences can overwhelm readers with too much information.

Choose strong verbs.

When verbs are turned into nouns and then get replaced with weak verbs (*be, appear, seem, have, give, do, get*), the result is a sluggish sentence.

Sluggish: When I had a **discussion** of the incident with the Undercoating Crew, they **said** that similar **developments** had occurred before.

ENERGETIC: When I **discussed** the incident with the Undercoating Crew, they **confirmed** that similar problems had **developed** before.

Vary sentence patterns.

Vary the openings, lengths, types, and arrangements of your sentences. (See page 155 for more information.)

Unvaried: **I recently moved** to Seattle, and **I have** continued to pursue my career. **I have** learned of a software-training specialist position at Evergreen Medical Center, and **I have** submitted my application.

VARIED: **Since my move to Seattle,** I've been looking for opportunities in computer services. **Recently,** I applied for a position with Evergreen Medical Center as a software-training specialist.

Divide lengthy sentences.

If a long sentence leaves you breathless, break it into manageable parts. Sometimes you can fix a long, complicated sentence by reshaping it into a list.

Rambling: I agree that this arrangement will offer your clients "one-stop shopping," **and** they can meet all their computer needs with little difficulty, for hardware, software, training, and support, **and** it will benefit all parties.

CONCISE: I agree that this arrangement will benefit all parties involved. You will be able to offer your clients "one-stop shopping" for all their needs for computer hardware, software, training, and support.

Use active voice.

When a verb is active, the subject of the sentence is performing the action. When the verb is passive, the subject is being acted upon, and the sentence tends to be sluggish and impersonal.

Passive: If a meeting must **be missed,** Richard must **be notified** a day in advance.

ACTIVE: If you **can't attend** a meeting, **notify** Richard a day in advance.

Sentence Smoothness in Action

The key to developing smooth sentences is learning to identify and fix common problems in sentence structure. For example, look at the three problems in the original passage below, and note how the problems are fixed in the revision that follows.

Original Passage:

choppy

Let me be the first to offer congratulations. We have made a decision to approve your loan. Next we need to receive an appraisal of the property. Then the closing can occur. I have attached, with these various factors in mind, a commitment letter, in which are listed the conditions that are necessary to be met to achieve successful closure of this loan. Please review these conditions, calling me at 555-6900, in the event that questions may arise.

rambling

passive voice

Preapproval for you to receive a Southeast credit card has also occurred. Taking advantage of this opportunity will result in a $20 reduction on closing costs associated with the completion of the enclosed application. Completion must occur five days prior to the date of the loan closing. This is why an application form and postage-free envelop have been enclosed.

Smoother Passage:

sentence variety

Congratulations, your loan has been approved. Once we receive an acceptable appraisal of the property, we can proceed with the closing. With that in mind, I have attached a commitment letter listing the conditions that need to be met to close your loan successfully. Please review them and call me at 555-6900 if you have any questions.

effective coordination and subordination

varied lengths and openings

You have also been preapproved for a Southeast credit card. If you take advantage of this opportunity, you will receive a $20 reduction on the closing costs for your mortgage loan. To enjoy this reduction, simply return your completed credit card application to me five days before the loan closing. I have enclosed both an application and a postage-free envelope for your convenience.

effective active voice

Trait 6: Correct Copy

(**BENCHMARK:**) Your goal when writing is to create a document free of distracting errors in grammar, punctuation, spelling, usage, and mechanics. Some of the most common errors are pointed out below; for a complete listing of rules and guidelines, see the "Proofreader's Guide," pages 189-266.

UNCLEAR WORDING

Unclear pronoun reference results when the word that a pronoun refers to (its antecedent) is missing or ambiguous.

Unclear:	The building includes both a residence and a small coffee shop. Does **it** conform with zoning bylaws? (*It* refers generally to the preceding sentence.)
CORRECT:	The building includes both a residence and a small coffee shop. Does **this use** conform with zoning bylaws? (*This* refers specifically to *use*.)

Misplaced modifiers are adjectives and adverbs that create confusion because they are poorly placed in the sentence.

Misplaced:	Please review the pamphlet describing my services and equipment **enclosed.**
CLEAR:	Please review the **enclosed** pamphlet describing my services and equipment.

Incomplete comparisons happen when words needed to complete a comparison are left out.

Unclear:	The Interconnect sound system is much more flexible and powerful. (*More flexible and powerful* than what?)
CLEAR:	The Interconnect sound system is much more flexible and powerful than our old Belclear system. (The comparison is now complete.)

FAULTY SENTENCES

Subject-verb agreement errors involve mismatches between subjects and verbs, especially in number. (See pages 261-262.)

Incorrect:	Each TLC **affiliate**, as well as TLC's worldwide partners, **depend** on volunteers. (*Affiliate* is singular; *depend* is plural.)
CORRECT:	Each TLC **affiliate**, as well as TLC's worldwide partners, **depends** on volunteers. (Both words are now singular.)

Pronoun-antecedent agreement errors involve a mismatch between a pronoun and its antecedent. (See page 263.)

Incorrect:	To complete **its** projects uniformly, HP **affiliates** follow the same procedures. (*Its* is singular; *affiliates* is plural.)
CORRECT:	To complete **their** projects uniformly, HP **affiliates** follow the same procedures. (The pronoun and its antecedent are now both plural.)

Sentence errors include comma splices, run-ons, and fragments, which can prevent a sentence from expressing a single, clear thought. (See pages 154, 266.)

Comma Splice:	I have enjoyed serving **you, I** will call to discuss your options.
CORRECT:	I have enjoyed serving **you. I** will call to discuss your options.

COMMA ERRORS

Check your writing for common comma errors and use the following rules to fix them. (See pages 190-193 in the "Proofreaders Guide" for additional rules.)

Set off long introductory phrases or clauses. When a sentence begins with a long modifying phrase or clause before the main idea is expressed, set off that material with a comma.

> **For the past nine months,** In-Bloom Florist has been ordering fresh, dried, and silk flowers from Cottonwood Hills.

Separate independent clauses in a compound sentence by placing a comma before the coordinating conjunction. If the clauses are very short, they do not need a comma between them.

> Our orders have always been accurately and quickly processed, **and** we continue to be impressed with the quality of your products.

Set off all nonessential or explanatory elements (words, phrases, clauses) with commas. (See page 192 for additional information.)

> In-Bloom, **Springfield's fastest growing florist shop,** plans to open a second shop in Greenburg, **which is a growing bedroom community outside Birmingham.**

Place commas between two or more adjectives that equally modify the same noun.

> Using a database software package can be a **reliable, efficient** solution to many small-business problems.

MECHANICAL ERRORS

Look over your writing for errors in capitalization, abbreviations, spelling, usage, and so on. (See pages 205-240 for guidelines.)

Capitalize proper names of people, places, and things—including organizations, events, cultural groups, and specific job titles. Do *not* capitalize general job titles, seasons, or geographical directions. In titles and headings, capitalize the first word, the last word, and all words in between except articles (*a, an, the*), short prepositions (*to, by, with*), and conjunctions (*and, but, or, nor, for, so*).

Vice President of Sales	*Write for Business*
Wagner Manufacturing Co.	supervisor
African Americans	The Tokyo Summit
autumn	southeast

Abbreviate the names and addresses of organizations but only those words abbreviated in the official name (*Co., Corp., Ltd., Inc.*). In addresses, abbreviate states only, not places and names.

> Joseph Whittle, CEO
> Rankin Chemical Corp.
> 2311 Industrial Road
> Fargo, ND 58103-0682

Use acronyms or initialisms only for well-known organizations or after a first, full reference; generally, capitalize all letters and avoid periods.

MADD	HUD	NAACP	IBM

Spell and use words correctly. Check key words, proper names, and commonly confused word pairs. Remember that spell checkers will not catch all your mistakes. (See pages 217-222 for a list of commonly misspelled words.)

Trait 7: Reader-Friendly Design

BENCHMARK: Your final writing goal is to create a page design that is attractive, is easy to read, and reflects well on you and your company. To achieve a reader-friendly design, use the tips below.

REFINING DOCUMENT DESIGN

A document design should (1) follow company standards, (2) make information accessible, and (3) look inviting to the reader. Smart choices about format, page layout, and typography will lead to a successful design.

PAGE LAYOUT

Produce pages that are open, balanced, and readable.

- Balance your pages with an effective combination of print, graphics, and white space.
- Introduce headings to separate blocks of text; keep headings consistent in size and presentation (**boldfaced**, centered, or underlined).
- Use visual cues (like numbers, bullets, or indents) to help distinguish between main and secondary points.
- Maintain a ragged right margin unless full justification is required.
- Do not place headings, hyphenated words, or the first lines of paragraphs at the very bottom of a page or column.
- Avoid placing single words or lines at the top of a page.
- Keep all items in a list on the same page.

TYPOGRAPHY

Choose attractive, easy-to-read typefaces and type sizes.

- Select 10-12 point type for regular text, 14-16 for subheadings, and 16-20 for major headings and titles.
- Choose a readable serif typeface such as Times New Roman, Bookman, Schoolbook, or Garamond (**like this type**).
- Use sans serif type such as Arial or Helvetica (**like this type**) for special text, including headings and on-screen documents.
- Try special type styles and treatments for emphasis: underlining, highlighting, *italics*, boxes, UPPERCASE, and **color**.

FORMAT

Use an appropriate design.

- Follow the rules for the type of document you are writing (memo, letter).
- Plan the overall design by considering the number and the width of columns.
- Consider using graphics. (See pages 161-172.)
- Organize each page by using numbers, headers, lists, bullets, and so on.

CREATING STRONG DESIGN

The document below is designed simply, but effectively. Headings, lists, boldface, white space, and margins are used to make each part of the message clear and easy to follow.

Lines are a moderate length, flush left, and ragged right.

Boldface type is used to draw attention to key information.

White space helps break text into readable units.

Headings and lists separate blocks of text.

Main text is serif; headings are sans serif.

Appropriate margins are used on all sides.

Family and Children Coalition Confidentiality Procedures

The Family and Children Coalition Confidentiality Policy states that all clients have the right to confidentiality. Conduct your work in keeping with this policy by following the procedures below.

Client Intakes:
During the client intake, the Coalition counselor should discuss conditions of confidentiality with the client. The counselor should explain the following:
1. Information will never be shared unless the client has given written permission using the Consent to Release Form.
2. Confidentiality may be limited or canceled if Coalition staff have serious concerns about child abuse or neglect.

Outside Requests for Information:
Coalition counselors will handle outside requests for client information.
1. No client information will be shared without the client's written permission.
2. Clients will be notified of any outside requests for information. If the client gives permission, he or she must sign the Consent to Release Form and indicate what information may be released and to whom.

Breaches of Confidentiality:
If a client believes that Coalition staff have not observed the confidentiality policy and procedures, he or she should be directed to follow the Client-Grievance Process.

By carefully following the procedures above, the Coalition staff can help our clients while also respecting their rights to confidentiality.

CHECKLIST The Seven-Traits Benchmarks

Before sending or distributing a document, use this checklist to make sure that the writing contains the required elements and demonstrates the desired traits.

STRONG IDEAS 140

- ☐ The writing focuses on a main point.
- ☐ Supporting points are developed logically and explained well.
- ☐ Information is complete, accurate, and current.

LOGICAL ORGANIZATION 142

- ☐ A strong three-part structure (opening, middle, closing) guides the reader.
- ☐ The organization is direct or indirect, as appropriate.
- ☐ Details are ordered sensibly (categories, problem/solution, order of importance).
- ☐ Transitions link sentences, paragraphs, and sections.

CONVERSATIONAL VOICE 144

- ☐ The tone is positive, polite, knowledgeable, and natural.
- ☐ The voice connects with the readers.

CLEAR WORDS 148

- ☐ Words are fresh, natural, and understandable.
- ☐ Key words and technical terms are precise—and defined, if necessary.
- ☐ Language is sensitive to age, gender, culture, and ethnicity.

SMOOTH SENTENCES 152

- ☐ Sentences are concise and easy to read.
- ☐ Sentence lengths and patterns are varied.
- ☐ Active and passive voice are used effectively.

CORRECT COPY 156

- ☐ Grammar, punctuation, mechanics, usage, and spelling are correct.
- ☐ Correctness creates logic, guides the reader, and makes a positive impression.

READER-FRIENDLY DESIGN 158

- ☐ Format is correct and consistent with company guidelines.
- ☐ Page layout and typography make the document attractive and easy to read.
- ☐ Lists, headings, and graphics make the information accessible.

LESSON

Using Graphics in Business Documents

In many business documents, graphics like tables, graphs, maps, or photographs can communicate your message more clearly—and more quickly—than words alone. To create effective graphics, you may at some point need help from graphic artists, digital scanners, or desktop publishing programs. The best way to start, however, is by gaining an understanding of some basic principles of using graphics in business documents.

Well-designed graphics can . . .

- grab readers' attention and persuade them.
- make information attractive and readable.
- simplify complex ideas and dramatize important points.
- save words by condensing information.
- help transform a document into a presentation.

"You never get a second chance to make a good first impression."
—Dad

Guidelines for Designing Graphics

1 PREWRITE
Consider your purpose and audience.
- Who are your readers, and how will a graphic help them?
- What key information or ideas should your graphic display?

2 **Choose the right graphic and gather necessary details.**
- Tables share precise numbers or words in a grid.
- Line graphs show numerical trends, bar graphs give numerical differences, and pie graphs indicate proportions or percentages.
- Organizational charts show structure, while flowcharts outline a process.
- Line drawings, maps, and photographs provide informative images.

3 DRAFT
Sketch out your graphic.
- On a computer or on paper, experiment with your design.
- Work on the title, captions, and legends.
- Add labels, keys, and notes.
- Use contrasting colors to show differences and shades of a color for similarities.
- Use bright colors for accents and pale colors for backgrounds.
  Note: (1) Shapes, colors, and icons may have different meanings in different cultures. (2) Color graphics may lose sharpness when photocopied.

4 REVISE
Check for clear ideas, correct details, and strong "pictures."
- Are all your data correct? Is the graphic's message accurate?
- Is the picture you created realistic, or is it distorted?

5 REFINE
Check your graphic for
- ☐ precise wording in titles, labels, and legends.
- ☐ design elements that distract or distort.
- ☐ smooth, crisp sentences or phrases in notes and captions.
- ☐ correctness, clarity, and overall effectiveness.

Parts of Graphics

While each type of graphic has its own guidelines, all graphics share some common elements.

HEADING

Each graphic needs a descriptive title that clearly indicates its topic and purpose. If a document contains more than one graphic, each graphic should be numbered as well. Organize tables in a sequence called "tables" (Table 5), and place graphs, charts, and visuals in a second set called "figures" (Figure 3).

Note: Numbers and *titles* may be placed above or below the graphic. Simply be consistent by using one placement style throughout a document.

BODY

Provide what is needed for the type of graphic: columns, rows, bars, lines, arrows, boxes, and so on. For clarity, include labels (written horizontally whenever possible), numbers and units of measurement, and a legend for symbols and colors.

NOTE OR CAPTION

To explain information in the graphic, provide a footnote or caption. If you requested permission to use the information or graphic, be sure to acknowledge your source below the graphic with *Source:, Adapted from:,* or *Used with permission of.*

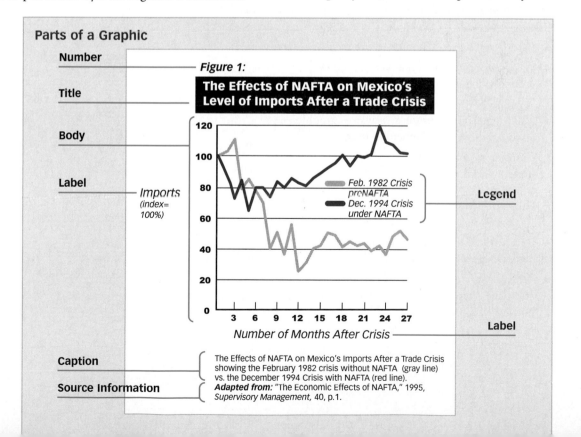

Parts of a Graphic

Number — **Figure 1:**

Title — **The Effects of NAFTA on Mexico's Level of Imports After a Trade Crisis**

Body

Label — *Imports (index= 100%)*

Legend: Feb. 1982 Crisis proNAFTA / Dec. 1994 Crisis under NAFTA

Number of Months After Crisis — Label

Caption — The Effects of NAFTA on Mexico's Imports After a Trade Crisis showing the February 1982 crisis without NAFTA (gray line) vs. the December 1994 Crisis with NAFTA (red line).

Source Information — ***Adapted from:*** "The Economic Effects of NAFTA," 1995, *Supervisory Management,* 40, p.1.

Integrating Graphics into Text

Graphics should enhance your document, whether it's a flyer, a report, or a proposal. Integrate graphics using the tips below and on the next seven pages.

1 **Select an appropriate page design** for the document as a whole. Consider the amount of text and the number of graphics you plan to use, and select a layout to balance the two. Choose from the following designs:

- A single column with a large graphic (**A**).
- Two even columns with a small graphic (**B**).
- Two even columns, one text and one graphics (**C**).
- Two uneven columns, one text and one graphics (**D**).

2 **Position graphics logically.** Insert a graphic close to the first reference to it—preferably *after* the reference.

- Place a *small* graphic on the same page as the reference.
- Place a *large* graphic on a facing page in a double-sided document, or on the page following the reference in a single-sided document.
- Make a *less important* or a *very large* graphic an attachment or an appendix item.
- Comment on the graphics to help readers understand the information.

3 **Follow good page-layout principles,** using white space around and within graphics.

- Position a graphic vertically on the page whenever possible.
- Adjust the size and shape of graphics and place them in boxes at the top or bottom of a page.
- Keep all graphics within the text margins.

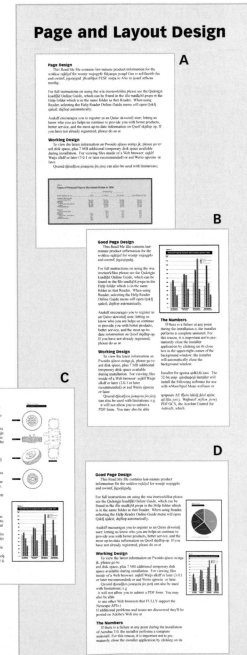

Page and Layout Design

Tables

Tables arrange numbers and words in a grid of rows and columns. Each slot in the grid contains data where two factors intersect (for example, *type of trip* and the *number of days* taken). Use tables when you want to

- categorize data for easy comparison of several factors.
- provide many exact figures in a compact, readable format.
- present raw data that are the foundation of later line, bar, or pie graphs.

DESIGN TIPS

1. **Set up rows and columns in a logical order.** Make tables easy to read by using patterns of organization: *category, time, place, alphabet, ascending,* or *descending order.* Make the columns or rows containing totals clear and prominent.

2. **Label information.** Identify columns at the top and rows at the left. Use short, clear headings and set them off with color, screens (light shades of color), or rules (lines).

3. **Present data correctly.** In a numerical table, round off numbers to the nearest whole (if appropriate) and align them at their right edge. Otherwise, align numbers at the decimal point. Indicate a gap in data with a dash or *n.a.* (not available). In a text table, use parallel wording.

Sample Numerical Table

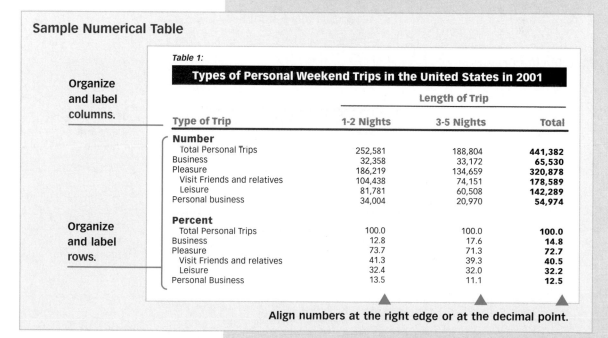

Organize and label columns.

Organize and label rows.

Table 1:

Types of Personal Weekend Trips in the United States in 2001		
	Length of Trip		
Type of Trip	**1-2 Nights**	**3-5 Nights**	**Total**
Number			
Total Personal Trips	252,581	188,804	**441,382**
Business	32,358	33,172	**65,530**
Pleasure	186,219	134,659	**320,878**
Visit Friends and relatives	104,438	74,151	**178,589**
Leisure	81,781	60,508	**142,289**
Personal business	34,004	20,970	**54,974**
Percent			
Total Personal Trips	100.0	100.0	**100.0**
Business	12.8	17.6	**14.8**
Pleasure	73.7	71.3	**72.7**
Visit Friends and relatives	41.3	39.3	**40.5**
Leisure	32.4	32.0	**32.2**
Personal Business	13.5	11.1	**12.5**

Align numbers at the right edge or at the decimal point.

Line Graphs

Graphs show relationships between numbers—differences, proportions, or trends. When properly designed (without distortion), graphs can clearly portray complex ideas.

A line graph reveals trends by showing changes in quantity over time.

- Typically, the horizontal axis measures time (days, months, years), and the vertical axis measures a quantity (costs, products sold).

- The quantity for each time period creates a "data point." When joined, these points create the lines that show the trends.

DESIGN TIPS

1. **Start the vertical axis at zero.** If it's impractical to show all increments, show a break on the axis.

2. **Avoid distortion.** Use all available data points (no skipping). Make sure vertical and horizontal units match well (roughly equal in scale or ratio).

3. **Identify each axis.** Label units measured (years, dollars), and use consistent increments. Print all words horizontally, if possible.

4. **Vary line weights.** Make data lines heavy, axis lines light, and background graph lines even lighter.

5. **Use patterns or colors** to distinguish multiple lines.

6. **Use a legend** if necessary.

Sample Line Graph

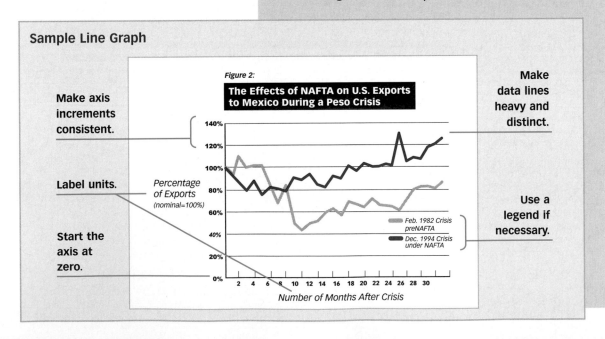

Make axis increments consistent.

Label units.

Start the axis at zero.

Figure 2:

The Effects of NAFTA on U.S. Exports to Mexico During a Peso Crisis

Percentage of Exports (nominal=100%)

Feb. 1982 Crisis preNAFTA

Dec. 1994 Crisis under NAFTA

Number of Months After Crisis

Make data lines heavy and distinct.

Use a legend if necessary.

Bar Graphs

A bar graph compares amounts by using a series of vertical or horizontal bars. The height or length of each bar represents a quantity at a specific time or in a particular place. By comparing bars, readers can quickly see key similarities and differences. Moreover, different designs show different types of information:

- *Single-bar graphs* show quantity differences for one item.
- *Bilateral-bar graphs* show amounts both above and below a zero line.
- *Segmented-bar graphs* divide bars to show what parts make up their wholes.
- *Multiple-bar graphs* present groups of bars so that readers can
  (1) compare bars within each group and
  (2) compare one group to the next.

DESIGN TIPS

1. **Develop bars that are accurate and informative.**
   - Choose a scale that doesn't exaggerate or minimize differences between bars.
   - Maintain a consistent bar width and spacing between bars.
   - Use two-dimensional bars; 3-D bars can blur differences and amounts.

2. **Design bar graphs that are easy to read.**
   - Label bars and axis units clearly.
   - Add a legend if necessary.
   - Use patterns or colors to distinguish between different bars or segments.
   - Present items in a logical order within a group or within single-bar segments (*ascending order, descending order*).

Multiple-Bar Graph

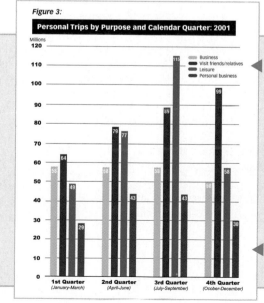

Figure 3:

Personal Trips by Purpose and Calendar Quarter: 2001

Legend

Keep words and numbers horizontal.

◀ Limit to five the number of bars in a group, or the number of segments in a single bar.

Single-Bar Graph

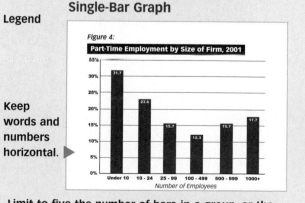

Figure 4:

Part-Time Employment by Size of Firm, 2001

Pie Graphs

Pie or circle graphs divide a whole quantity into parts. They show how individual parts relate to the whole and to each other. Use pie graphs to

- show proportions.
- give the big picture.
- add visual impact.

DESIGN TIPS

1. Keep your graph simple. Divide the circle into six slices or fewer. If necessary, combine smaller slices into a "miscellaneous" category, and explain its contents in a note or in the text.

2. Make your graph clear and realistic. Avoid confusion and distortion.

- Use a moderate-sized circle and avoid 3-D effects.
- Distinguish between slices with shading, patterns, or colors.
- Use a legend if necessary.
- Measure slices (number of degrees) to assure accuracy. Use graphics software or the formula below.

To Calculate Degrees for Each Slice:

Amount of part ÷ whole quantity x 100 = percentage x 3.6 = number of degrees

Slices	$1,936	100%	360 degrees
Part 1	$775	40%	144.1 degrees
Part 2	$484	25%	90.0 degrees
Part 3	$415	21.4%	77.2 degrees
Part 4	$262	13.5%	48.7 degrees

Sample Pie Graph

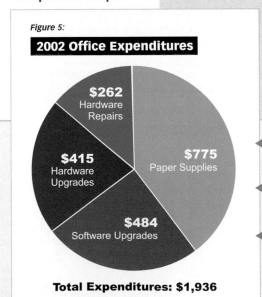

Figure 5:

2002 Office Expenditures

$262 Hardware Repairs

$415 Hardware Upgrades

$775 Paper Supplies

$484 Software Upgrades

Total Expenditures: $1,936

◄ **Start at the 12:00 o'clock position with the largest slice and move clockwise.**

◄ **Follow with the next slices in descending order.**

◄ **Label each slice horizontally and indicate actual percentages and/or amounts.**

Maps

Graphics like maps, drawings, and photographs provide visual images of places, objects, or people. By stressing certain details, these images help readers understand ideas or visualize concepts.

By showing some part of the earth's surface, a map can present a wide range of useful information: communication and transportation data, distances, directions, regions and zones, natural and urban features, market segments, and so on.

FYI To make a map, try an on-line resource such as The National Atlas <http://nationalatlas.gov.>.

DESIGN TIPS

1. Make the geographic area clear. While your map need not be geographically accurate to be highly effective, it should clarify the area in question. Orient the reader by providing a directional arrow (usually north).

2. Provide useful content. Select details carefully, making sure that features, markings, and symbols are distinct and easy to understand. If necessary, use labels and a legend. Add a note or caption to help the reader interpret the map.

3. Indicate differences for regions by
- coloring, shading, cross-hatching, or dotting
- creating bar or pie graphs in each area on the map
- labeling areas with actual numbers

Make the actual geographic area clear.

Indicate differences by using color, shading, or a pattern.

Figure 6:

2001 U.S. Sales by State

2001 Sales by State
Sales above 5 Million
Sales 2.5-5 Million
Sales below 2.5 Million

◀ **Legend**

Line Drawings

Because line drawings screen out unnecessary details, they provide clear, simplified images of objects. Moreover, different types of line drawings focus on different key features.

- *Surface* drawings present objects as they appear externally.
- *Cutaway* drawings or *cross sections* show an object's inside parts.
- *Exploded* drawings "pull apart" an object, showing what individual parts look like and how they fit together.

Sample Exploded Drawing

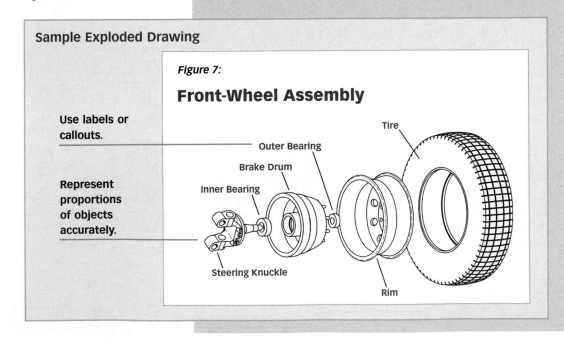

Figure 7:

Front-Wheel Assembly

Use labels or callouts.

Represent proportions of objects accurately.

Outer Bearing

Brake Drum

Inner Bearing

Tire

Steering Knuckle

Rim

Photographs

Unlike line drawings, photographs and other visual images can provide detail. Traditional photographs, back-and-white or color, show surface appearance of reality—from people to things to landscapes.

The very latest photographic technologies can be used to show external and internal images of a different nature: infrared pictures, x-rays, ultrasounds, CAT scans, 2-D and 3-D computer-generated images, and so on.

DESIGN TIPS

1. **Be creative and ethical.** Software such as Adobe Photoshop and Paint Shop Pro allows you to modify images, but make reasonable changes that do not distort or distract.
   - Removing blemishes and cropping images is standard practice.
   - Adding, subtracting, and distorting should be avoided or well documented.

2. **Take, develop, and print quality images.**
   - Use good equipment or seek expert help, if needed.
   - Select distances and angles to clarify size and details.
   - Enlarge and crop images to focus on key objects.
   - Place images on the page or import them digitally into documents.

3. **Obtain permission** to use any recognizable photo of a person or place.

4. **Clarify images.** Use labels, arrows, size references, and so on to help the reader get an accurate picture.

Sample Photographs

Figure 8:

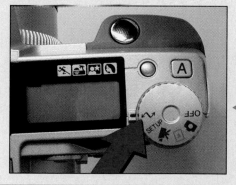

Indicate a specific portion of an image with an arrow.

Figure 9:

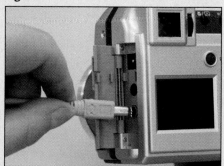

▲ Consider including a hand or a ruler as a size reference.

CHECKLIST The Graphics . . .

STRONG IDEAS   140

- ☐ communicate important ideas clearly, with no distortion or deception.
- ☐ fit the content, audience, purpose, and document type.
- ☐ share accurate information.

LOGICAL ORGANIZATION   142

- ☐ have descriptive titles and appropriate numbers (tables or figures).
- ☐ have complete parts, including labels and legends as needed.
- ☐ have necessary notes or captions.

EFFECTIVE VISUAL "TONE"   144

- ☐ create a tone in words and images that is professional, attractive, informative, and helpful.

CLEAR WORDS   148

- ☐ use precise wording in titles, labels, legends, and notes.
- ☐ use terms that are consistent with terms used in the written text.

SMOOTH SENTENCES   152

- ☐ use phrases or complete sentences as needed.
- ☐ include clear and smooth captions or notes.

CORRECT COPY   156

- ☐ avoid grammar, spelling, and punctuation errors.

READER-FRIENDLY DESIGN   158

- ☐ make information accessible through an attractive, functional design.
- ☐ use colors, shapes, patterns, and white space to clarify information and create strong pictures.
- ☐ avoid fancy but irrelevant material.
- ☐ fit well in the document: they are set off in boxes or framed by white space, located within the margins, and placed close to related text.

Writing and Giving Presentations

In the course of doing business, people get together regularly to make presentations that demonstrate new products, introduce new programs, or give reports. The challenge is being able to share ideas in a clear, concise, effective manner.

This chapter includes information that will help you plan, write, and deliver a presentation, whether it's a one-minute impromptu talk, or an hour-long report with presentation software. There are practical strategies for drafting an attention-grabbing introduction, organizing the body, and developing a focused conclusion. Also, there are tips on how to use visual support and rehearse the delivery.

Giving Presentations

Regardless of the topic, form, or length of your presentation, you can follow the same basic steps to develop and present it.

GETTING STARTED

The first step in preparing an oral presentation is getting an overview of the task. Begin by asking yourself, *What is my purpose? Who is my audience?* and *What is my topic?* Answering these questions will help you write the presentation and shape its delivery.

1 What is my purpose?

- Am I going to explain something?
- Am I trying to persuade or inspire my audience to do something?
- Am I hoping to teach my audience about something?

2 Who is my audience?

- Is it an in-house group or an outside group?
- How many people are in the group, and what are their ages, backgrounds, and interests?
- What will people already know about the topic, and what will they want or need to know?
- What will their attitude be toward the topic and toward me?

3 What is my topic?

- What do I already know about the topic?
- What do I need to learn, and where can I find the information?
- What support materials (displays, computer projections, handouts) would help me present my message?

STATING YOUR MAIN IDEA

After you've made decisions about your purpose, audience, and topic, it's a good idea to write out the main idea you want to communicate.

Begin with the simple statement "My purpose is . . . " and then add a phrase like *to explain, to persuade,* or *to inform.* Finish by inserting your topic, along with the main idea of the presentation.

> *My purpose is* **to explain to the Board of Directors** how our new Confidentiality Procedure will help our staff serve our clients better.

Note: The outline that develops this idea is on pages 180-181.

> "It usually takes me more than three weeks to prepare a good impromptu speech."
> —Mark Twain

Planning Your Presentation

DRAFTING AN OUTLINE

After you've clarified your purpose, audience, and topic—and you've written your purpose statement—think about how to present your message. Begin by brainstorming points that you want to communicate, and then organize the points into a list or working outline. For a brief, informal presentation, this list or outline may be the only script you need.

On the other hand, for a longer, more challenging presentation, you may need to significantly revise and develop the outline as you research and write the script. This outline is your tool for gathering and organizing your thoughts. (See page 125.)

THINKING ABOUT SUPPORT MATERIALS

As you gather information, keep a list of graphics, displays, and handouts that could make your presentation clearer and more interesting. For example, charts, tables, and graphs can help an audience grasp the meaning of complex data. Technical drawings or sketches can help listeners visualize a product or site. Demonstrations or video clips can help listeners better understand a process or connect with the people involved.

Review the list below for items appropriate to your topic, audience, and setting (including available equipment). Then, as you do your research, make a note about an item that you could use and how you could use it (as a display, projection, handout, and so forth).

audio clip (music)	key quotation
bibliography	list of authorities
brochure	overhead
cartoon	photograph
chart	sample product
company document	sketch
demonstration	table
graph	technical drawing
handheld prop	video clip

GATHERING INFORMATION

Using your outline as a guide, gather the information you need. Begin by reviewing key documents, manuals, and company material related to the topic. If necessary, read current articles, review videos, explore the Internet, and talk with other people. What you gather will depend on your purpose, topic, resources, and available time.

For help in finding and organizing information, see pages 123-124.

Organizing Your Presentation

After you've gathered your information, you must organize and develop the message. How? Start by thinking about your presentation as having three distinct parts: (1) introduction, (2) body, and (3) conclusion. The guidelines on this page and the following two pages will help you integrate, organize, and refine all the parts so that they communicate the message and achieve your purpose.

INTRODUCTION

> "What this
> country
> needs is
> more free
> speech
> worth
> listening
> to."
> —Hansell
> B.
> Duckett

For any speaking situation, you should develop an introduction that does the following:

- greets the audience and grabs their attention.
- communicates your interest in them.
- introduces your topic and main idea.
- shows that you have something worthwhile to say.
- establishes an appropriate tone.

You may greet the audience in many ways, including the following: introducing yourself; thanking people for coming; or making appropriate comments about the occasion, the individuals present, or the setting. Following these comments, introduce your topic and main idea as quickly and as clearly as you can. For example, you could open with one of these attention-grabbing strategies:

- a little-known fact or statistic
- a series of questions
- a humorous story or anecdote
- an appropriate quotation
- a description of a serious problem
- a cartoon, picture, or drawing
- a short demonstration
- a statement about the topic's importance
- an eye-catching prop or display
- a video or an audio clip

> "When high words confuse the talk,
> low words will untangle it."
> — Jobo proverb

2 BODY

The body of your presentation should deliver the message—and supporting points—so clearly that the audience understands the presentation after hearing it only once. The key to developing such a clear message is choosing an organizational pattern that fits your purpose statement.

So before you outline the body, take a moment to review what you want your presentation to do: explain a problem? promote an idea? teach a process? Be sure the organizational pattern will help you do that. For example, if you want to teach a process, the outline should list the process steps in chronological order. If your outline is clear, you may begin to write. Organizational patterns for explaining a process and other purposes are listed below.

- **Chronological Order:** Arrange information according to the time order in which events (steps in a process) take place.
- **Order of Importance:** Arrange information according to its importance: greatest to least, or least to greatest.
- **Comparison/Contrast:** Give information about subjects by comparing and contrasting them.
- **Cause and Effect:** Give information about a situation or problem by showing (1) the causes and (2) the effects.
- **Order of Location:** Arrange information about subjects according to where things are located in relation to each other.
- **Problem/Solution:** Describe a problem and then present a solution for it.

After deciding how to organize your message, write it out in either outline or manuscript form. For help, see the tips at the right and the models on pages 180-183.

Body-Building Tips

1. Build your presentation around several key ideas. (Don't try to cover too much ground.)

2. Write with a personal, natural voice.

3. Support your main points with reliable facts and clear examples.

4. Present your information in short, easy-to-follow segments.

5. Use positive, respectful language. (Avoid jargon.)

6. Use graphic aids and handouts.

CONCLUSION ③

A strong introduction and conclusion work like bookends supporting the body of the presentation. The introduction gets the audience's attention, sets the tone, states the main idea, and identifies the key points of the message. Almost in reverse, the conclusion reviews those points, restates the main idea, reinforces the tone, and refocuses the audience on what it should think about or do. Together, those bookends emphasize and clarify the message so that the audience understands and remembers it.

Here are some strategies—which you can use alone or in combination—for concluding a presentation:

- Review your main idea and key points.
- Issue a personal challenge.
- Come "full circle." (State those arguments or details that back up your original point.)
- Recommend a plan of action.
- Suggest additional sources of information.
- Thank the audience and ask for questions.

Q & A

Following your presentation, you may want to invite your audience to ask questions. Very often, a Q & A session is the real payoff for participants. They can ask for clarification of points or ask how your message applies to their personal situations. Audience members may even offer their own insights or solutions to problems mentioned in the presentation. The following suggestions will help you lead a good Q & A session:

- Listen carefully and think about each part of the question.
- Repeat or paraphrase questions for the benefit of the entire group.
- Answer the question concisely and clearly.
- Respond honestly when you don't know the answer, and offer to find an answer.
- Ask for a follow-up question if someone looks confused after your answer.
- Look directly at the group when you answer.
- Be prepared to pose an important question or two if no one asks a question.
- Conclude by thanking the audience for their participation.

"We cannot ignore tone of voice or attitude. These may be just as important as the words used."
—Maurice S. Trotter

Writing Your Presentation

How much of your presentation you actually write out depends on your topic, audience, purpose, and—of course—your personal style. The three most common forms to use to make a presentation are a list, an outline, and a manuscript.

List: Use a list for a short, informal speech such as an after-dinner introduction. Think about your purpose and then list the following:

- your opening sentence (or two)
- a summary phrase for each of your main points
- your closing sentence

1. Opening sentence or two
2. Phrase #1
Phrase #2
Phrase #3
3. Closing sentence

Outline: Use an outline for a more complex or formal topic. You can organize your material in greater detail without tying yourself to a word-for-word presentation. Here's one way you can do it:

- opening (complete sentences)
- all main points (sentences)
- supporting points (phrases)
- quotations (written out)
- all supporting technical details, statistics, and sources (listed)
- closing (complete sentences)
- notes on visual aids (in caps or boldface)

I. Opening statement
   A. Point with support
   B. Point (purpose or goal)
      [VISUAL 1]
II. Body (with 3-5 main points)
   A. Main point
     1. Supporting details
     2. Supporting details
   B. Main point
     1. Supporting details
     2. Supporting details
   C. Main point
     1. Supporting details
     2. Supporting details
III. Closing statement
   A. Point, including
      restatement of purpose
   B. Point, possibly a call
      to action [VISUAL 2]

Manuscript: Use the guidelines below if you plan to write out your presentation word for word as you plan to give it:

- double-space pages (or cards)
- number pages (or cards)
- use complete sentences on a page (do not run sentences from one page to another)
- mark difficult words for pronunciation
- mark script for interpretation (See symbols on page 185.)

PRESENTATION IN OUTLINE FORM

Report on FACC's Confidentiality Procedure

[opening]

The opening is written out word for word and placed in boldface.

I. **Good afternoon, everyone. I appreciate this opportunity to report on our work here at the Family and Children's Coalition. Today I want to focus on one topic that impacts all of our work—the new Confidentiality Procedure that was adopted last week. We believe this procedure will help us serve our clients more effectively. We think it's an effective tool because . . .**

- **it is based on sound policy,**
- **it will help the staff implement the policy in a uniform manner, and**
- **it will enable staff and clients to develop trusting relationships with each other.**

Italics and brackets signal a speaker's prompt.

[Identify the handout and read the policy.]

[middle]

Main points are stated as full sentences (word for word).

II. **First, let's examine four strengths of the policy on which the new procedure is based. Note how the policy . . .**

- enables clients to control most personal information.
- calls for written records of who receives case-related information.
- satisfies legal requirements related to privacy issues.
- helps staff and clients develop trust.

Supporting details are listed as phrases.

[Identify the handout and read the procedure.]

III. **Second, the Confidentiality Procedure will help staff members deal with confidentiality issues in a consistent, uniform manner. Note how the procedure . . .**

- lists issues that counselors must explain to clients at intake.
- sets guidelines for releasing information to outside parties.
- explains a client's recourse to a staff member's breach of confidentiality.
- promotes the uniform application of the Confidentiality Policy— particularly by new staff and student interns.

The speaker uses the phrases as cues and comments on each point.

2

IV. **Third, the Confidentiality Procedure will help staff and clients establish the trusting relationships FACC needs in order to provide its services.**

- Clients, needing a confidential advocate, often come to intake sessions fearful and suspicious.
  - abused wife with child: ***"How do I know he won't find out that we are here? He said if I say anything, . . . he'll kill me."***
  - pregnant teenager: ***"Thanks for listening . . . I just had to tell somebody."***
- Clients become less fearful because they view the policy and procedure as contracts—that the information collected will be kept in confidence.
- Clients become less fearful because they feel information will be kept private from outsiders—staff can say that the Confidentiality Procedure does not allow them to release information.

V. **As you know, the work that we do at the Family and Children's Coalition requires that our staff and clients have trusting, confidential relationships with each other. To build such relationships, and to satisfy legal requirements related to privacy issues, FACC has long had a Confidentiality Policy. However, the staff believes that the new Confidentiality Procedure will help them provide better service to clients because the procedure is (1) based on sound policy, (2) improves uniform application of that policy, and (3) helps staff members and clients develop trusting relationships.**

Are there any questions?

PRESENTATION IN MANUSCRIPT FORM

[opening]

[SLIDE 1]
The title is
projected.

The speaker
delivers the
speech as it
appears on
the page.

[SLIDE 1] **Abix Technologies: Finding the Right Solutions**

Good afternoon, everyone, and welcome to Abix Technologies! This is
Lynn, your tour guide, and I'm Zachary Clark, Director of Public Relations at
Abix. Lynn will soon be taking you on a walk through our Reception Center,
a research lab, and a manufacturing facility. During that tour, she will give
you a lot of information and answer all of your questions. However, before
Lynn takes over, I want to personally welcome each of you to Abix. In
addition, I'd like to introduce you to our company by saying a few things
about who we are, what we produce, and the people we serve.

[middle]

[SLIDE 2]
monument

[SLIDE 3]
inscription

[SLIDES 4-8]
people
mentioned

[SLIDE 9]
company
headquarters

All points and
supporting details
are stated.

First, who are we? [SLIDE 2] The inscription on the monument that
you passed when entering the building answers the question with these
words: [SLIDE 3] "Abix Technologies is an international corporation that
provides technological solutions to environmental wastewater problems."
What does that mean? It means that at Abix Technologies, [SLIDE 4]
we have scientists who research wastewater problems and propose solutions.
[SLIDE 5] We have engineers who develop products to implement those
solutions. [SLIDE 6] We have people who produce the products. [SLIDE 7]
We have sales personnel who market our products around the world.
[SLIDE 8] And finally, we have technicians who service what we sell,
wherever we sell it.

[SLIDE 9] **Second, what do we produce?** While Abix Technologies
makes a wide variety of products for many different applications, it
specializes in technology that disinfects wastewater. These products are
- well researched,
- environmentally safe, and
- cost effective.

2

[middle]

[SLIDE 10]
researchers

[SLIDE 11]
products

[SLIDES 12-19]
markets
mentioned

[SLIDE 20]
statement 1

[SLIDE 21]
statement 2

[SLIDE 22]
monument

[closing]

The main point
is restated and
a polite close
is added.

[SLIDE 10] For example, as you tour the laboratory today, you'll meet researchers who have been working on a particularly challenging problem for more than 3 years. Though they needed only 10 months to find a solution, more than 2 years later, they're still refining it. Why? Because at Abix, products must not only solve problems—they must do so in ways that are environmentally safe and cost effective. [SLIDE 11]

Third, who uses our products? The short answer to this question is "Smart people around the world!" In fact, as you visit the Shipping Department today, you'll see crews packaging products that will be sent to sites on three continents.

However, the longer answer to the question about our customer base is that our markets include [SLIDE 12] the United States, [SLIDE 13] Canada, [SLIDE 14] South America, [SLIDE 15] Europe, [SLIDE 16] Australia, [SLIDE 17] New Zealand, [SLIDE 18] the Middle East, [SLIDE 19] and the Far East. While serving such a broad clientele is not easy, we do it well for two reasons: [SLIDE 20]

1. We carefully assess each customer's needs to make sure that the products we sell meet those needs. [SLIDE 21]
2. We have offices in Sydney, Australia; London, England; Flint, Michigan; and Toronto, Ontario. Each office has highly trained technicians who respond to our customers quickly and effectively. [SLIDE 22]

While I'd like to tell you more, Lynn will show you these things for yourselves. So once again, welcome to Abix Technologies! I'm glad that you're here, and I hope that you enjoy the tour!

Developing Computer Presentations

Business people commonly use computers to make presentations because this multimedia approach can powerfully reinforce and clarify a message. To use presentation software effectively, follow the guidelines below.

1   **Develop a design.** Be sure your graphic design fits your topic and your audience—businesslike for a serious topic, casual for a team meeting, and so on.

2   **Create pages.** If a main idea has several parts, present each one on its own page. Each click of the mouse button (or computer key) should reveal a new detail.

3   **Use transitions.** Dissolves, fades, wipes, and other transitional effects refine a computer presentation and keep the audience's attention (as long as the devices don't detract from the message).

4   **Try animation.** Text can be animated to appear from off screen at just the right moment. Graphics can be made to appear one element at a time, and illustrations can change before the viewer's eyes. Remember to use special effects, especially animation, wisely.

5   **Add sound.** Just as graphics and animation can enhance a presentation, so, too, can sound. Music can serve as an intro or backdrop, and sound effects can add emphasis. Voice recordings can add authority and help drive home key points.

6   **Fine-tune your presentation.** Practice delivering your presentation while clicking through your pages. Try it with an audience of coworkers, if possible, and ask for their input.

7   **Check for word choice and style.** Make sure that the words on the screen are key words. Use these words as talking points—don't try to cover any point word for word. Also, check that transitions, animations, and sounds are smooth and not disruptive.

8   **Edit the final version.** Check spelling, punctuation, usage, and other mechanics. Remember: On-screen errors are glaringly obvious to everyone.

9   **Rehearse.** Practice running the equipment until you can use it with confidence.

10   **Make a backup copy.** Protect all the effort you invested in your presentation.

> "When you say something, make sure you have said it. The chances of having said it are only fair."
> —E. B. White

Practicing Your Delivery

Research shows that less than 40 percent of your message is communicated by your words. More than 60 percent is communicated by your delivery—your voice, body language, and attitude. In other words, rehearsing the delivery of a presentation is at least as important as revising the script.

REHEARSING YOUR PRESENTATION

Keep going over your presentation until you're comfortable with it. Ask a family member or co-worker to listen to you and offer feedback, or use a video recorder so that you can see and hear yourself. Practice these things:

1 **Maintain eye contact with your audience.** It helps people feel that you care about them. It also helps you notice how people are responding to your message.

2 **Speak loudly and clearly.** Also speak at an appropriate speed.

3 **Take your time.** Glance at your notes when necessary.

4 **Use your hands to communicate.** Practice using natural, unforced gestures.

5 **Maintain a comfortable, erect posture.** *Avoid the following:*
- folding your arms across your chest.
- clasping your hands behind you.
- keeping your hands on your hips.
- rocking back and forth.
- fidgeting with objects.
- chewing gum.

6 **Use your voice effectively.** You can mark your copy for vocal variety by using the techniques on the right.

Marking Your Script

Inflection
(arrows) . . . . for a rise in pitch,
for a drop in pitch

Emphasis
(underline or boldface) . . . . for additional
drive or **force**

Color
(curved line or italic) . . . . . . for additional
feeling or *emotion*

Pause
(diagonal) . . . . for a pause/or
break in the flow

Directions
(brackets) . . . . for movement
[walk to chart]
or use of visual aids
[hold up chart]

Pronunciation
(parentheses) . . . . for phonetic *(fō NE tic)*
spelling of words that are
difficult to pronounce

CHECKLIST Overcoming Stage Fright

While it's okay to feel a little nervous before a presentation (the emotion keeps you alert), stage fright can limit your ability to communicate. The remedy for stage fright is confidence—confidence in what to say and how to say it. To develop that confidence, consider doing the following:

PERSONAL PRESENTATION

☐ Know your subject well.
☐ Rehearse the presentation thoroughly, including the use of visuals.
☐ Schedule your time carefully, making sure to arrive early.
☐ Relax before the presentation by stretching or doing a deep-breathing exercise, remembering that your presentation can be successful without being perfect.

THE ROOM AND EQUIPMENT

☐ See that the room is clean, comfortable, and well lit.
☐ Make sure tables and chairs are set up and arranged correctly.
☐ Check that AV equipment is in place and working.
☐ Test microphone volume.
☐ Position the screen and displays for good visibility.

PERSONAL DETAILS

☐ Check clothing and hair.
☐ Arrange for drinking water to be available.
☐ Put your script and handouts in place.

SPEAKING STRATEGIES

☐ Greet individuals as they arrive for the presentation.
☐ Learn some people's names.
☐ Be confident, positive, and energetic.
☐ Provide for audience participation; survey the audience: "How many of you . . . ?"
☐ Speak up and speak clearly—don't rush.
☐ Reword and clarify when necessary.
☐ After the presentation, ask for questions and answer them clearly.
☐ Thank the audience.

Section 4:
Proofreader's Guide

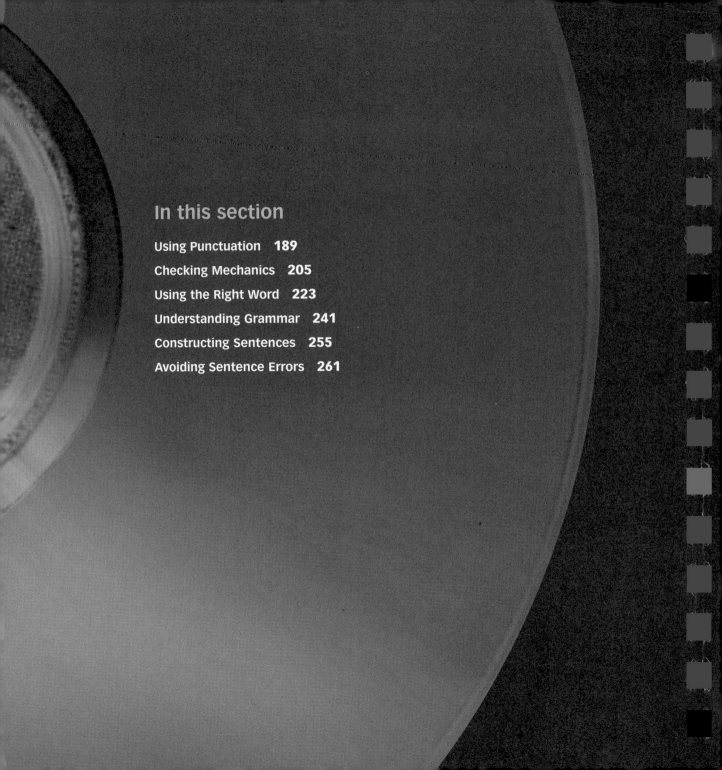

In this section

Using Punctuation

PERIOD

To End a Sentence

- Use a **period** to end a sentence that makes a statement, requests something, or gives a mild command.

    (Statement) **"A gold mine is a hole in the ground with a liar at the top."**
    —Mark Twain

    (Request) **Please arrange an on-site meeting.**

    (Mild Command) **"Concentrate on finding your goal; then concentrate on reaching it."**
    —Michael Friedsam

Note: Omit a period after a statement that has parentheses around it if it is part of another sentence.

These early entrepreneurs (some of them were true visionaries) often met skepticism.

After an Initial or an Abbreviation

- A period should be placed after an initial and after most abbreviations.

Ms.	Inc.	O.D.	M.A.
C.E.	a.m.	U.S.A.	Joan Q.

Note: When an abbreviation is the last word in a sentence, do not add a second period.

Tom recently received his M.B.A.

After an Indirect Question

- Use a period, not a question mark, after an indirect question.

    I wonder how much that will cost us.

ELLIPSIS

To Show Omitted Words

- Use an **ellipsis** (three spaced periods) to indicate that words have been omitted in a quoted passage. Leave one space before and after each period.

    (Original) **All new employees must fill out the standard work forms—social security, insurance, and payroll. The forms, which may be obtained from your immediate supervisor, should be completed before beginning work. If you have any questions, please contact Rosa for assistance.**

    (Quotation) **"All new employees must fill out the standard work forms . . . which may be obtained from your immediate supervisor . . . before beginning work."**

At the End of a Sentence

- If words from a quoted passage are omitted at the end of a sentence, the ellipsis follows the period.

    "All new employees must fill out the standard work forms—social security, insurance, and payroll. . . . If you have any questions, please contact Rosa for assistance."

If the quoted material is a complete sentence (even if it was not in the original), use a period, then an ellipsis.

"All new employees must fill out the standard work forms. . . . Please contact Rosa for assistance."

Note: The first word of a sentence following a period and an ellipsis may be capitalized, even though it was not capitalized in the original.

COMMA

To Join Independent Clauses

- Use a **comma** before a coordinating conjunction (such as *and, but, or, nor, for, so*) when it is used to link two independent clauses.

  Ability may get you to the top, but only character will keep you there.

  "A doctor can bury his mistakes, but an architect can only advise his client to plant vines." —Frank Lloyd Wright

Note: Do not mistake a sentence containing a compound verb for a compound sentence. (No comma is needed with a compound verb.)

  Marva quickly checked the document and corrected a few minor errors.

To Separate Phrases and Clauses

- A comma should follow an introductory adverb clause or a long introductory phrase.

  "If you don't learn from your mistakes, there's no sense making them."
  —Laurence J. Peter

Note: The comma is usually omitted if the phrase or adverb clause follows the independent clause.

  There's no sense making mistakes if you don't learn from them.

After Introductory Words

- Use commas after introductory words that answer the questions *When? How often? Where? Why?*

  Tomorrow, I will circulate the latest draft of our new mission statement.

  Occasionally, we ask for input from outside consultants.

To Set Off Information

- Commas are used to set off explanatory phrases.

  Drive-in banks, according to E. Joseph Cossman, were established so most of the cars could see their real owners.

To Set Off Contrasted Elements

- Commas are used to set off contrasted elements in a sentence.

  This is real life, not fantasy.

To Separate Adjectives

- Commas are used between two or more adjectives that modify the same noun *equally*.

  Using a database software package can be a reliable, efficient solution to many small-business problems.

A Closer Look

Use the tests below for help in deciding whether adjectives modify *equally*.

1. **Switch the order of the adjectives.**
   If the sentence is still clear, the adjectives modify equally. (If *reliable* and *efficient* were shifted in the example above, the sentence would still be clear; therefore, use a comma.)

2. **Place *and* between the adjectives.**
   Does the sentence still sound all right? If so, insert a comma (without *and*). (If *and* were inserted in the sentence above, it would still read well.)

For Items in a Series

- Commas are used to separate three or more items (words, phrases, or clauses) in a series.

   The best workplace chair is one with a **padded seat, an adjustable backrest, and a lumbar support system.**

Note: Do not use commas when all the items in a series are connected with *or, nor,* or *and.*

   Vision problems can be caused by improper lighting or by computer glare or even by letters that are difficult to read.

   The best workplace chair is one with a padded seat and an adjustable backrest and a lumbar support system.

In Addresses and Dates

- Commas are used to set off items in an address and in a date.

   Send for your personal copy of *Write for Business* before December 31, 2003, from UpWrite Press, 35115 West State Street, Burlington, Wisconsin 53105.

Note: No comma is placed between the state and ZIP code. Also, no comma is needed if only the month and year are given: *December 2003.*

To Separate a Vocative

- A comma is used to separate a **vocative** (noun of address) from the rest of the sentence. (A vocative is the noun that names the person or persons spoken to.)

   Jamie, would you like to join me for lunch today?

To Set Off Interruptions

- Commas are used to set off a word, a phrase, or a clause that interrupts the flow of a sentence. The following tests can help identify such expressions. The meaning of the sentence does not change if the expression is (1) omitted or (2) placed nearly anywhere in the sentence.

   The problems, in the final analysis, were due largely to a lack of planning.

   In the final analysis, the problems were due largely to a lack of planning.

For Clarity or Emphasis

- A comma may be used to clarify or to emphasize. Sometimes no specific rule calls for a comma, but one is needed to avoid confusion or to emphasize an important idea.

   What he says, says volumes.

To Set Off Exact Words

- Commas are used to set off the exact words of the speaker from the rest of the sentence.

   "Nothing in fine print is ever good news," quipped Andy Rooney.

Do not use a comma before an indirect quotation. (The comma circled below should not be used.)

   The computer technician said, that he would be here shortly. (misuse of a comma before an indirect quotation)

To Set Off Nonrestrictive Modifiers

- Commas are used to set off nonrestrictive phrases and clauses used as modifiers. Nonrestrictive phrases or clauses are those that are not essential to the basic meaning of the sentence.

    Roy, who is training to be a supervisor, is an asset to our service department. (nonrestrictive)

    Good service at a reasonable rate, which sums up the department's philosophy, is the reason for the dealership's success. (nonrestrictive)

Note: The two clauses shown above in red are merely additional information; they are *nonrestrictive* (not required). If the clauses were left out of the sentences, the meaning of the sentences would remain clear.

- Restrictive phrases or clauses—phrases or clauses that are needed in the sentence because they restrict or limit the meaning of the sentence—are not set off with commas.

    Employees who are praised for new ideas are apt to be creative. (restrictive)

    Companies that offer flexible hours usually have happier, more efficient workers. (restrictive)

Remember: *Restrictive* phrases are required in a sentence; *nonrestrictive* phrases are not required. Compare the following phrases:

    The humorist Will Rogers was born in Oklahoma. (*Will Rogers* is required; do *not* use commas.)

    Will Rogers, the humorist, was born in Oklahoma. (*The humorist* is not required; use commas.)

A Closer Look

Which and That: Use *which* to introduce nonrestrictive (unnecessary) clauses; use *that* to introduce restrictive (necessary) clauses. Doing so will help readers quickly distinguish essential information from nonessential information.

    The system that we implemented in March 2002 was selected after a year-long study.

Note: The clause beginning with *that* is necessary to identify which system.

    The new system, which was implemented in March, has already improved productivity 40%.

Note: The main clause tells the reader important information about the new system; the clause beginning with *which* gives additional—or nonessential information.

To Set Off Appositives

- Commas are used to set off an **appositive**, a noun or phrase that identifies the noun or pronoun it follows. (A *restrictive appositive* is essential to the basic meaning of the sentence; do not set it off with commas. See the second example below.)

    Scott Erickson, a landscape designer, uses his laptop computer in the office and in the field. (nonrestrictive appositive)

    Landscape designer Scott Erickson uses his laptop computer in the office and in the field. (restrictive appositive)

In Large Numbers

- Commas are used to separate numerals or "digits" in large numbers. For numbers of four digits or more, place a comma before every third digit, counting from the right.

    This printer costs $3,045.

Note: It is also acceptable to omit the comma in numbers with only four numerals or "digits."

Exceptions: Commas are not used in address numbers or in identification numbers.

**12345 Karry Place   room 5496
invoice 17823**

Note: Spaces, not commas, are used in metric measurements. (This avoids confusion in those countries where commas are used as decimal points.)

**14 267.9 hectares (U.S.A.) or
14 267,9 hectares (European)**

To Enclose a Title

- Commas are used to enclose initials, a title, or names that follow a surname.

    Mr. Anton Sellek, Sr., and James Matthews, Esq., will arrive at noon.

    Daly, C. U., and Herr, I. M., are not alphabetized correctly on this list.

Note: It is also acceptable to use *Jr.* and *Sr.* without commas.

John Kennedy Jr. had a variety of careers.

Roman numeral suffixes are never set off by commas.

John Williams III is the CEO.

Before Tag Sentences

- A comma is used before a tag sentence, which is a short statement or question at the end of a sentence.

    You took the job, didn't you?

To Separate Interjections

- A comma is used to separate an interjection or a weak exclamation from the rest of the sentence.

    OK, I'll pass the latest sales figures on to the Accounting Department.

A Closer Look

In addition to understanding when and where to use commas correctly, you should also know when *not* to use commas.

Do **not** use a comma between compound predicates.

We started the van, and discovered a problem.

Do **not** use a comma between a subject and a verb.

Recent articles on Internet marketing, are available on-line.

Do **not** use a comma between a verb and its object or complement.

My supervisor said I should read, The Business Journal.

SEMICOLON

To Join Two Independent Clauses

- A **semicolon** is used to join two closely related independent clauses. (**Remember:** Independent clauses can stand alone as separate sentences.)

  When business is good, it pays to advertise; when business is bad, you've got to advertise.

  Note: A comma may be used if the two clauses are short or express a contrast in ideas.

  Acquiring new technology is one thing, using it efficiently is another.

With a Conjunctive Adverb

- A semicolon is used before a conjunctive adverb (*also, besides, however, instead, then, therefore*) that connects two independent clauses; a comma is used after the adverb.

  Too many overtime hours can lead to insanity; however, you'll probably be too busy to notice.

To Separate Items in a Series

- A semicolon is used between items in a series if any of those items already have commas.

  When renting a car, consider your budget restrictions; the model, type, and size of the car required; and any mileage, insurance, or additional charges that may apply.

To Separate Independent Clauses

- A semicolon is used to separate independent clauses joined by a coordinating conjunction if one or both of the clauses are long or contain commas.

  Tomorrow afternoon, please use the Main Street entrance; but if it's after 5:00, use the First Street entrance.

COLON

After a Salutation

- A **colon** should be used in business communications after salutations and memo headings.

  Dear Mr. Buffet: To: Jeani Schultz

To Indicate Time and Ratios

- A colon is used between the parts of a number indicating time and between numbers in a ratio.

  1:00 p.m.   6:30 p.m.   7:50 p.m.
  The ratio of managers to workers is 1:15.

To Introduce Explanatory Material

- A colon may be used to introduce a word or words that explain or summarize the main clause.

  There is no future in any job: The future lies in the person who holds the job.

As a Formal Introduction

- A colon may be used following an independent clause that introduces a formal statement, a question, or a quotation.

  Malcolm Forbes once offered this thought: "Failure is success if we learn from it."

To Introduce a List

- A colon is used to introduce a list.

  A good employee needs two things: a good attitude and a willingness to learn.

  Note: Don't use a colon to introduce a list if no summary words are used. (The summary words *two things* appear in the sentence above; there are no summary words in the sentence below.)

  A good employee needs a positive attitude and a willingness to learn.

✳ ✳ ✳ ✳ ✳ ✳ ✳ ✳ ✳ ✳ ✳ ✳ ✳ ✳ ✳ ✳ ✳ ✳ If it ain't broke, don't fix it—

HYPHEN

To Join Words in Compound Numbers

- A **hyphen** is used to join compound numbers from twenty-one to ninety-nine when they must be written out. A hyphen is also used when the numbers in a ratio are spelled out.

   twenty-one   sixty-six

   "There are some people who, in a fifty-fifty proposition, insist on getting the hyphen, too."
   —Laurence J. Peter

To Make a Compound Noun

- A hyphen can be used to create a compound noun.

   secretary-treasurer   city-state

To Join Letters and Words

- A hyphen is used to join a capital or lowercase letter to a noun or a participle.

   O-ring   G-rated   x-axis
   x-rayed   L-shaped   A-frame

Between Numbers in a Fraction

- A hyphen is used between the numerator and denominator of a fraction, but not when one or both of those elements are already hyphenated.

   one-third   seven-eights
   twenty-one thirty-seconds

When Words Have Common Elements

- A hyphen is used when two or more words have one or more common elements that are omitted in all but the last term.

   The new travel policy applies to lower-, mid-, and upper-level management.

To Make a Compound Adjective

- A hyphen can be used to join two or more words that form a single adjective (a single grammatical unit) before a noun. Do not hyphenate the words forming the adjective when they follow the noun.

   Only double-insulated wire should be used in this situation.

   Only wire that is double insulated should be used in this situation.

Note: Do not use a hyphen when the first of these words is an adverb ending in *ly* or when a letter or number ends the grammatical unit.

   freshly painted conference room
   (adverb ending in *ly*)

   grade A milk
   (the letter *A* is the final element)

Also Note: When such a group of words is used as a noun, it is usually not hyphenated.

   She usually takes a middle-of-the-road position. (adjective)

   He usually takes the middle of the road. (noun)

To Create New Words

- A hyphen is usually used to form new words after the prefixes *self, ex, all,* and *half.* Also, a hyphen is used to connect any prefix to a proper noun, a proper adjective, or the official name of an office. A hyphen is also used with the suffix *elect.*

   self-portrait   all-inclusive
   half-finished   ex-employee

To Divide a Word at the End of a Line

- The hyphen is used to divide a word at the end of a line of print. A word may be divided only between syllables.

Guidelines for Word Division

DIVIDE:

1. Always divide a compound word between its basic units: *attorney-at-law*, not *at-tor-ney-at-law*.

2. When a vowel is a syllable by itself, divide the word after the vowel: *ori-gin*, not *or-igin*.

3. Divide at the prefix or suffix whenever possible: *bi-lateral*, not *bilat-eral*.

DO NOT DIVIDE:

1. Never divide a word so that it is difficult to recognize.

2. Never divide a one-syllable word: *filed*, *trains*, *rough*.

3. Avoid dividing a word of five letters or fewer: *final*, *today*, *radar*.

4. Never leave a single letter at the end of a line: *omit-ted*, not *o-mitted*.

5. Never divide contractions or abbreviations: *couldn't*, not *could-n't*.

6. Avoid dividing a number written as a figure: *42,300,000*, not *42,300-000*.

7. Avoid dividing the last word in a paragraph.

8. Avoid ending two consecutive lines with a hyphen.

DASH

For Emphasis

- **Dashes** are used to set off material (a word, phrase, or clause) for emphasis.

  Before you have an argument with your boss, take a good look at both sides—her side and the outside.

  If they try to rush me, I always say, "I've only got one other speed—and it's slower."
  —Glenn Ford

To Set Off an Introductory Series

- A dash is used to introduce a statement that explains or summarizes a series or list before it.

  Widgets, carburetors, or bologna sandwiches—she could successfully market anything.

To Set Off Explanations and Examples

- A dash may be used to set off examples, explanations, and definitions.

  Three of the applicants—James Johnson, Shiere Melin, and Santana Garcia—have been called back for a second interview.

  The new network—which will be installed tomorrow—will allow us to link directly to our Chicago office.

To Indicate Interrupted Speech

- A dash is used to show interrupted or faltering dialogue in reports of speeches or conversations.

  "The—ah—fourth item on the agenda is not really—is actually no longer a concern."

QUESTION MARK

In a Direct Question

- A **question mark** is used after a direct question.

  Have you had any experience with *Expedite*?

  Note: A question mark is *not* used after an indirect question.

  I asked him if he had any experience with *Expedite*.

When Two Clauses Ask Questions

- When a question ends with a quotation that is also a question, only one question mark is used; it is placed inside the quotation marks.

  On a day off, do you ever wake up in a panic, asking, "Am I late for work?"

To Show Uncertainty

- A question mark is placed within parentheses to show that an item (e.g., a date or number) is uncertain.

  This August will be the 25th (?) anniversary of the fax machine.

In a Series of Questions

- A question mark is used after each question in a series of questions.

  When can we expect the order? Monday? Tuesday? Next week?

For a Parenthetical Question

- A question mark is used for a short question within parentheses or a question set off by dashes.

  You must check your company handbook (do you have a handbook?).

EXCLAMATION POINT

To Express Strong Feeling

- An **exclamation point** is used to convey strong feeling and should be used sparingly.

  Service! Service! Service! These are the three laws of business.

  Note: When an exclamation is mild, a comma or period may be used.

  Yes, we just found out that we got the account with no strings attached.

With Quotation Marks

- When used with quotation marks, the exclamation mark goes outside, unless the quotation itself is an exclamation.

  Remember what she said: "Service!"

  You absolutely must read her latest article, "We Are Here to Serve"!

A Closer Look

Exclamation points show special emphasis. If you overuse them, they lose their effect. Also, avoid combining exclamation points and question marks.

QUOTATION MARKS

To Punctuate Titles

- **Quotation marks** are used to enclose titles of speeches, short stories, songs, poems, episodes of radio or television programs, chapters or sections of books, unpublished works, and articles found in magazines, journals, newspapers, or encyclopedias. (Also see page 200.)

  "Walk This Way" (song)

  "Over the Top" (short story)

  "Tricks of Trade" (magazine article)

  "Managing in the Dark" (chapter in a book)

  "Costo" (television episode)

  "Oh, My Aching Back" (encyclopedia article)

  "Ansett Blues" (poem)

  "Natural Gas Prices March Higher" (journal article)

Placement of Periods and Commas

- Periods and commas at the end of quoted material are always placed inside the quotation marks.

  "Double-check the hotel reservations, Dave," remarked Mr. Schmidt. "Our flight is going to be late."

Placement of Semicolons and Colons

- Semicolons and colons at the end of quoted material are always placed outside the quotation marks.

  I just read "Computers and Creativity"; the chapter talks about the role of computers in the arts.

Placement of Other Punctuation

- An exclamation point or a question mark is placed inside quotation marks when it is part of the quotation; it is placed outside when it is *not* part of the quotation.

  I almost laughed when he asked, "That won't be a problem, will it?"

  Did you hear Molly say, "Oh, no, sir"?

For Special Words

- Quotation marks also may be used (1) to show that a word is being referred to as the word itself; (2) to indicate that a word is jargon, slang, or a coined word; or (3) to indicate that a word is being used in a special sense.

  (1) What does the term "integrity" mean to you?

  (2) Oh man, that group is so "DOA"!

  (3) One person showed up for the "team" meeting.

Note: Italics may be used in place of quotation marks for special words. (See page 200.)

A Closer Look

Do **not** use quotation marks as a way to emphasize key words.

We offer "fast" and "friendly" service.

The quotation marks actually call into question whether the service is either fast or friendly.

MARKING QUOTED MATERIAL

1. Quotation marks are placed before and after the words in a direct quotation—a person's exact words—but are not used with indirect quotations.

> **You may have heard Ms. Clark say that all supervisors should *adopt* the new report form. Actually, she said, "All supervisors should *adapt* the new report form for use in their departments."**

2. Quotation marks are placed before and after a quoted passage. Any word or punctuation mark that is not part of the original quotation must be placed inside brackets.

> (Original) **"All supervisors should adapt the new report form for use in their departments."**

> (Quotation) **"All supervisors should adapt [not adopt] the new report form for use in their departments."**

Note: If only part of the original passage is quoted, make sure that the sentence is accurate and grammatically correct.

> **Ms. Clark has directed all supervisors to "adapt the new report form for use in their departments."**

3. If more than one paragraph is quoted, quotation marks are placed before each paragraph and at the end of the last paragraph (Example A).

Quotations that are more than four lines on a page are usually set off from the text by indenting 10 spaces from the left margin. Quotation marks are not used before or after the quoted material, unless they appear in the original passage (Example B).

Example A   **Example B**

4. Single quotation marks are used to show a quotation within a quotation.

> **Her exact words were "Bring your copy of the article 'Right for Business' to the afternoon workshop."**

ITALICS

To Punctuate Titles

- **Italics** are used to indicate the titles of newspapers, magazines, journals, pamphlets, books, plays, films, radio and television programs, ballets, operas, lengthy musical compositions, cassettes, CD's, software programs, and legal cases, as well as the names of ships, trains, aircraft, and spacecraft. (Also see page 198.)

    Forbes (magazine)

    Our Town (play)

    It's a Wonderful Life (film)

    The First 20 Million Is Always the Hardest (book)

    Nova (television program)

    Washington Post (newspaper)

    Boston Business Journal (journal)

    Small Business Resource Guide (CD)

    Office Array (software program)

For Foreign Words and Phrases

- Italics are used for foreign words and phrases that have not been fully assimilated into the English language.

    All U.S. coins contain the phrase *e pluribus unum*. It means "out of many, one."

For a Word as a Word

- Italics (or quotation marks) are used to indicate that a word is being referred to as a word. (If the word is defined, the definition is placed in quotation marks.)

    In computer language, the term *cookie* means "a unique identifier used to track visitors on a Web site."

For Technical Words

- Italics (or quotation marks) are used to denote technical, scientific, or other specialized terms that may be unclear to most readers.

    Mail sent via the postal service is often referred to as *snail mail*.

Note: A technical term is italicized or set off by quotation marks only once; thereafter, it is set in regular type. For in-house reports or memos, technical terms that are commonly used within your company are not italicized.

SLASH

To Form a Fraction

- A **slash** is used to separate the numerator from the denominator in a fraction.

    Lamar has been in this department only 2 1/2 months.

With Abbreviations

- The slash is sometimes used in abbreviations.

    c/o (in care of)   w/o (without)

To Express Alternatives and Two Functions

- The slash can be used in place of "or" to show alternatives; it can also be used to show two functions.

    his/her   either/or   and/or
    secretary/treasurer
    coach/general manager

PARENTHESES

To Enclose References

- **Parentheses** are often used to enclose references to authors, titles, or pages.

  The latest numbers support our plan (see page 12) and show a need for expansion.

To Enclose Dates and Explanatory Material

- Parentheses are used to enclose dates or explanatory material that interrupts the normal sentence structure.

  The average worker works 128 days each year (from January 1 to May 7) to pay all federal, state, and local taxes.

  The Walk for Life event is set for early spring (Tuesday, March 12) and will be held at the Performing Arts Center.

Placement of Punctuation

- When a parenthetical sentence comes *after* the main sentence, capitalize and punctuate the parenthetical sentence the same way you would any other complete sentence.

  Depending on the meeting's purpose, you may want to use small groups. (Small groups promote discussion.)

  When adding a parenthetical sentence *within* another sentence, do not capitalize it or use a period inside the parentheses.

  The T-shaped setup (this can also accommodate small groups) is good for panel discussions.

Around Numerals in a Numbered List

- Parentheses are used to set off numerals or letters that introduce items in a list within a sentence.

  A good used car will have (1) low mileage, (2) new tires, and (3) a clean interior.

For Parentheses Within Parentheses

- For unavoidable parentheses within parentheses, use brackets: (. . . [. . .] . . .).

BRACKETS

Around Comments Added for Clarity

- **Brackets** are used before and after comments added to explain, clarify, or correct what another person has said or written.

  "They [20th Century Fox] said they had no interest in seeing a picture with the word 'star' in it."

  —Sidney Gains, on *Star Wars*

  "The funny thing is better [TV] shows don't cost that much more than lousy shows."

  —Warren Buffet

Note: The brackets point out that the words *20th Century Fox* and *TV* are not in the original quotations but were added for clarification.

Around the Letters *sic*

- Brackets should be placed around the word *sic* (Latin for "thus" or "so") when it appears within a quoted passage. *Sic* indicates that an error was made by the original speaker or writer.

  "With this sales staff, your *[sic]* bound to succeed."

APOSTROPHE

In Place of Numbers or Letters

● An **apostrophe** is used to show that one or more numerals or letters have been left out of numbers or words that are spelled as they are actually spoken.

>**class of '85** (*19* is left out)
>**good mornin'** (*g* is left out)
>**they'll** (*wi* is left out)
>**I'm** (*a* is left out)

To Form Plurals

● An apostrophe and *s* are used to form the plural of a letter, an abbreviation, a number, a sign, or a word referred to as a word.

>**M's   8's   #'s   MD's   p's and q's**
>**This letter contains five *actually's* and seven *really's*.**

Note: It is now acceptable to omit the apostrophe when forming the plurals of letters, numbers, and the like—as long as no confusion results (*CDs, Bs, and 7s*; but *M's, i's,* and *U's*). Choose the best way to handle these plurals, following any preferences your company may have established—and be consistent.

Also Note: If the same word calls for two apostrophes, omit the second one.

>**Please change the *can'ts* [not *can't's*] to *can's.***

To Form Singular Possessives

● An apostrophe is used with a noun to show ownership. The possessive form of a singular noun is usually made by adding an apostrophe and *s*.

>**Brent's résumé**
>**the office's main entrance**

Note: When a singular noun of more than one syllable ends with an *s* or a *z* sound, the possessive may be formed by adding just an apostrophe. (If, however, the possessive form is pronounced with an extra syllable, it is acceptable to use an apostrophe and *s*. Choose the best way to form these possessives and be consistent.)

>**Kansas' (or Kansas's) cornfields**
>**Dallas' (or Dallas's) skyline**
>**a waitress' (or waitress's) tips**

Also Note: One-syllable nouns ending in an *s* or a *z* sound usually form the possessive by adding an apostrophe and *s*.

>**Jones's work   Banks's portfolio**
>**the dress's length**

To Show Joint Possession

● To indicate ownership shared by more than one noun, use the possessive form for only the last noun in the series.

>**Yolanda, Sara, and Elana's project**
>(All work together on one project.)
>**Yolanda's, Sara's, and Elana's projects**
>(Each works on her own project.)

To Form Plural Possessives

- The possessive form of a plural noun ending in *s* or *es* is usually made by simply adding an apostrophe.

  Sass' family reunion

  bosses' assistants

Note: To punctuate correctly, keep in mind that the word immediately preceding the apostrophe is the "owner."

  coordinator's summary
  (*coordinator* is the owner)
  coordinators' summary
  (*coordinators* are the owners)

  class's instructor (*class* is the owner)
  classes' instructor (*classes* are the owners)

To Express Time or Amount

- An apostrophe and an *s* are used with a singular noun that is part of an expression indicating time or amount.

  today's stock quotes   **two cents' worth**
  a year's experience

With Indefinite Pronouns

- The possessive form of an indefinite pronoun is made by adding an apostrophe and *s* to the pronoun. (See pages 243 and 244.)

  everyone's input   **anyone's guess**
  no one's fault

Note: In expressions using *else*, add the apostrophe and *s* after *else*.

  somebody else's turn

In Compound Nouns

- The possessive of a compound noun is made by placing the possessive ending after the last word.

  attorney-at-law's (singular) **advertisement**
  the attorneys-at-law's (plural) **advertisements**

  manager in training's (singular) **enthusiasm**
  the managers in training's (plural) **enthusiasm**

Note: It is usually a good idea to rephrase an awkward-sounding possessive.

  the advertisements of the attorneys-at-law
  the enthusiasm of the managers in training

With Descriptive Words

- Check a dictionary or your company's stylebook for descriptive words ending in *s*.

  traveler's check   **user's manual**
  writers club

With Names of Companies or Organizations

- The possessive of a company or organization name that contains a preposition is formed by adding an apostrophe and *s*, if the name doesn't end in an *s*. If the name does end in an *s*, only an apostrophe is added.

  The Bank of Madison's new building
  The State Bank of Texas' expansion

APOSTROPHE (continued)

With Stand-Alone Possessives

- Use an apostrophe with a possessive noun that appears without the word it modifies.

  The meeting will be at the Campbells'.

  This quarter's sales are running behind last quarter's.

In Holidays

- Most of the possessive holiday names are formed as if the names were singular nouns.

  Mother's Day   **New Year's Day**
  Valentine's Day

  Note: There are a couple of exceptions to the rule.

  Presidents' Day   **April Fools' Day**

PUNCTUATION MARKS

´ (é) Accent, acute	..... Leaders
` (è) Accent, grave	( ) Parentheses
' Apostrophe	. Period
* Asterisk	? Question mark
{ } Braces	" " Quotation marks (double)
[ ] Brackets	' ' Quotation marks (single)
Ç (ç) Cedilla	
^ (â) Circumflex	§ Section
: Colon	; Semicolon
, Comma	/ Slash/Diagonal
— Dash	~ (ñ) Tilde
¨ (ü) Dieresis	__ Underscore
... Ellipsis	
- Hyphen	

Checking Mechanics

The following information and examples will help you edit your writing with confidence. Use them to check capitalization, form plurals, use abbreviations, and improve your spelling. The chart on page 208 provides an overview of capitalization rules.

CAPITALIZATION

Proper Nouns and Proper Adjectives

- Capitalize all proper nouns and proper adjectives (adjectives formed from proper nouns).

   The owner, Lynn Taylor, would like to thank Rankin Technologies.

   I have a Cartesian philosophy: "I think, therefore I am . . . promoted."

First Words

- Capitalize the first word in a sentence and in a direct quotation.

   Advertising staffers gathered for the usual Monday meeting.

   Ms. Beggs began, "A lie may take care of the present, but it has no future."

Note: Also capitalize the first word of a saying, a slogan, a motto, or dialogue when it appears within a sentence. A question within another sentence may or may not be capitalized.

   Marsha believes the saying All's well that ends well.

   The first rule is, When in doubt, leave it out.

   My question is, How (or how) are we going to pay for this?

First Words in Lists

- Capitalize the first word in each item in a list typed in an outline style.

   Come to the meeting prepared to do the following:
   1. **Share your thoughts on the latest building plan.**
   2. **Explain the changes to the original blueprint.**
   3. **Provide an updated cost analysis and environmental impact statement.**

Note: *Do not* capitalize the first words in such a list if all together the items compose a complete sentence.

   Come to the meeting prepared with the following:
   1. **a presentation of the latest building plan,**
   2. **an explanation of the changes to the original blueprint, and**
   3. **an updated cost analysis and environmental impact statement.**

Salutation and Complimentary Closing

- Capitalize the first and all major words in the salutation of a letter, but only the first word in the complimentary closing.

   Dear Sherry,
   Dear Production Manager:
   Dear Sir or Madam:

   Best wishes,
   Sincerely yours,

First Words Enclosed in Parentheses

- Capitalize the first word in a sentence that is enclosed in parentheses, and that does not appear within another sentence.

    Some writers were unsure of the product's worthiness. (Exaggerating seemed necessary.)

Note: *Do not* capitalize a sentence that is enclosed in parentheses and is located in the middle of another sentence.

    Pat and Meg both volunteered to do the copywriting (we were relieved), and they immediately began tossing ideas back and forth.

After a Colon

- Capitalize the first word in a complete sentence that follows a colon when that sentence is (1) a formal statement, (2) a quotation, or (3) a sentence you want to emphasize.

    It was Sydney Harris who said this about computers: "The real danger is not that computers will begin to think like people, but that people will begin to think like computers."

Organizations

- Capitalize the name of an organization, or a team and its members.

    Toledo Mud Hens

    American Indian Movement

    Republican Party

    Business Products Association

Particular Sections of the Country

- Words that indicate sections of the country are proper nouns and should be capitalized; words that simply indicate direction are common nouns and should be lowercased.

    Many businesses are moving to the sunny South. (section of the country)

    Businesses move south to cut fuel costs and other expenses. (direction)

Abbreviations

- Capitalize abbreviations of titles and organizations. (A number of other abbreviations are also capitalized. See pages 213-215.)

    FTC   **BBB**   **P.A.**   **YWCA**
    SSA   **OSHA**   **LBO**

Numerical Designations

- Capitalize nouns used with reference numbers or letters when they are used in headings, titles, or captions.

    Flight 709   **Order 312**   **Form 411**
    Appendix B

Letters Used to Indicate Form or Shape

- Capitalize the letters used to indicate form or shape.

    B-pillar   **A-frame**   **O-ring**
    T-bar   **L-bracket**   **T-shirt**

Words Used as Names

- Capitalize words like *dad, mother, aunt,* and *judge* when they are part of a title that includes a personal name, or when they are substituted for a proper noun (especially in direct address).

  Hi, Aunt Mae! (*Aunt* is part of the name.)

  My aunt is a doctor.

  The senator said his favorite legislator was Senator Hubert Humphrey.

  Please, Mom, stay for dinner.

A Closer Look

Here is a way to tell if a word is being substituted for a proper noun: read the sentence with a proper noun in place of the word. If the proper noun fits in the sentence, the word being tested should be capitalized. (*Note:* Generally the word is not capitalized if it follows a possessive noun or pronoun, such as *Tonya's, her, my.*)

  Did Dad (Alex) get the promotion? (*Alex* works in this sentence.)

  Did your dad (Alex) get the promotion? (*Alex* does not work here; also, the word *dad* follows the possessive *your.*)

Names for the Supreme Being

- Nouns that refer to the Supreme Being, the title *Bible,* the books of the Bible, and the names of other holy books are all capitalized.

God	**Jehovah**	**the Savior**
Allah	**Genesis**	**The Koran**

Titles

- Capitalize the first and last word of a title and every word in between with the following exceptions: articles (*a, an, the*), short prepositions, and coordinating conjunctions. This applies to titles of books, newspapers, periodicals, poems, plays, films, works of art, articles, and photographs.

  Write for Business

  Journal of Office Professionals

Formal Titles

- Capitalize the fist letter of each major word of an employee's title when it precedes that person's name.

  Marketing Manager Diane Barnhart will give her report at today's meeting.

  The marketing manager will give her report at today's meeting.

Note: Also capitalize the formal names of entities within a company.

  Research and Development

  Human Resources

Titles of Specific Courses

- Words such as *history, business, science,* and *technology* are proper nouns when they are used in the titles of specific courses, but they are common nouns when they name a field of study.

  Professor Sajev teaches Global Business Ethics. (title of a specific course)

  Which professor teaches the biology course? (a field of study)

Note: Language classes and school subjects that are followed by a number should be capitalized.

  Ms. Ott teaches Spanish and Geography 101.

PROPER NOUNS AND PROPER ADJECTIVES

● Capitalize all proper nouns and all proper adjectives (adjectives formed from proper nouns). The chart below provides an overview of capitalization rules.

Capitalization at a Glance

Periods, events in history	Dark Ages, Great Depression
Special events	Vietnam War
Months	February, September, December
Days of the week	Wednesday, Thursday, Saturday
Holidays, holy days	Labor Day, Ash Wednesday, Kwanzaa
Political parties	Libertarian Party, Democratic Party
Government bodies	Congress, the House, the Senate
Official documents	Bill of Rights
Awards, honors	Academy Award, Nobel Prize
Corporations	Microsoft; Jackson Farms, Inc.
Trade names	Honda Civic, Krispy Kreme doughnut
Formal nicknames	Ivan the Terrible, the Big Three
Official titles	Senator Edward Kennedy, Training Director John Thatch
Official state nicknames	the Keystone State, the Wolverine State

Geographical names

Planets and other heavenly bodies	Mars, Earth, Big Dipper
Continents	Africa, North America
Sections of a country or the world	the Northwest, the Mideast
Countries	Peru, Congo, Malasia
States, provinces	Idaho, Iowa, Manitoba
Cities, towns, villages	San Diego, Lyons, East Troy
Localities	the Loop, the Twin Cities
Streets, roads, highways	Sunset Boulevard, Highway 18, Pennsylvania Turnpike
Landforms	the Mojave Desert, the Alps
Bodies of water	the Chang and Huang Rivers, Lake Superior, Hudson Bay
Public areas	Empire State Building, Denali National Park

FORMING PLURALS

Formed by Adding *s*

- The plurals of most nouns are formed by adding *s* to the singular.

  book – books

  pen – pens

Compound Nouns

- The plurals of compound nouns are usually formed by adding *s* or *es* to the important word in the compound.

  sisters-in-law   **attorneys-at-law**

  secretaries of state

Nouns Ending in *ch, s, sh, x*, and *z*

- The plurals of nouns ending in *ch*, *s*, *sh*, *x*, and *z* are made by adding *es* to the singular.

  business – businesses   **wish – wishes**

  fax – faxes

Nouns Ending in *y* Preceded by Consonants

- The plurals of common nouns ending in a *y* that's preceded by a consonant are formed by changing the *y* to *i* and adding *es*.

  phony – phonies

  balcony – balconies

Note: The plurals of proper nouns ending in *y* are formed by adding *s* (*The department has three Marys, two Randys, and four Bobbys*).

Nouns Ending in *y* Preceded by Vowels

- The plurals of nouns ending in a *y* that's preceded by a vowel are formed by adding only an *s*.

  key – keys   **bay – bays**

Nouns Ending in *o* Preceded by Vowels

- The plurals of nouns ending in an *o* that's preceded by a vowel are formed by adding only an *s*.

  cameo – cameos

  zoo – zoos

Nouns Ending in *o* Preceded by Consonants

- The plurals of most nouns ending in an *o* that's preceded by a consonant are formed by adding *es*.

  potato – potatoes

  embargo – embargoes

Exception: All musical terms ending in an *o* form plurals by adding only an *s*.

  soprano – sopranos   **duo – duos**

  piano – pianos

Other exceptions include *memos* and nouns ending in *o* that can form plurals by adding either *s* or *es*, such as *mementos/mementoes* and *cargos/cargoes*.

A Closer Look

A plural generic term used before or after multiple proper names should be capitalized.

Lakes Michigan, Erie, and Huron

the Nile and Euphrates Rivers

the Ural and Rocky Mountains

Symbols, Letters, Numbers, and Words Discussed as Words

- The plurals of symbols, letters, numbers, and words discussed as words are formed by adding an apostrophe and an *s*.

  Using &'s, @'s, and %'s in place of the words *and, at,* and *percent* will save room in this report. Don't forget to cross your *t*'s. And, avoid using too many *and*'s in your writing.

  Note: It is permissible to omit the apostrophe when the omission does not cause confusion, but be consistent. Also, spelled-out numbers do not require an apostrophe.

  DVD's or DVDs   fives and sixes

Nouns Ending in *f* or *fe*

- The plurals of nouns ending in *f* or *fe* are formed in one of two ways: If the final *f* sound is still heard in the plural form of the word, add only an *s*; if the final *f* sound becomes a *v* sound, change the *f* to *ve* and add *s*.

  Plural ends with *f* sound:
  proof – proofs; safe – safes
  Plural ends with *v* sound:
  shelf – shelves; life – lives
  Plural ends with either sound:
  scarf – scarfs, scarves

Nouns Ending in *ful*

- The plurals of nouns ending with *ful* are formed by adding an *s*.

  four cupfuls   six cupfuls

  Note: When referring to separate cups full of something, use *four cups full* or *six cups full.*

Collective Nouns

- When a collective noun refers to a group as a unit, it is singular. (Use the singular pronoun *its*.)

  The Advertising Department meets weekly. Its goal is to meet every day.
  (group as a unit)

  A collective noun that refers to a group's individual members is plural. (Use the plural pronoun *their*.)

  The Advertising Department clapped their hands when their manager was introduced.
  (group as individuals)

Irregular Spelling

- Some English words, including many borrowed from Latin or Greek, form a plural by taking on an irregular spelling; others are now acceptable with the commonly used *s* or *es* ending.

  Foreign Words
  alumnus – alumni
  datum – data (datums)
  phenomenon – phenomena

  English Words
  mouse – mice
  tooth – teeth
  ox – oxen

NUMBERS

Writing Numbers

- Normally use words for numbers from one to nine and use numerals for numbers 10 and over.

  one   four   eight   12   530   2,113

  Note: When comparing numbers, keep them in the same style.

  Four vice presidents and twelve managers will conduct the sixteen meetings.

  The three tool attachments cost $1.85, $1.42, and $.59. (For the sake of consistent style, use $.59, not 59¢.)

Addresses and Time

- Spell out the number *one* in addresses (One Elmbrook Blvd.). You may spell out even, half, and quarter hours in text, but do not use *a.m.* or *p.m.* in this case.

  a quarter to four   nine o'clock tonight
  half past two

Abbreviations and Symbols

- Use numerals with abbreviations and symbols.

  7° C   4 lbs.   3 oz.   2 tsp.
  12'6"   5 ft.   9%

NUMBERS IN DIFFERENT FORMS

- Use numerals to express numbers in the following forms: money used with symbols ($ or ¢), decimals, percentages, chapters, pages, addresses, exact times, identification numbers, statistics, measurements used with abbreviations, and dates.

  Money . . . . **$20.00** (but **twenty dollars**)

  Decimals **26.25**

  Percentages. . . . . **8 percent**

  Chapters . . . . **chapter 7**

  Pages . . . . **pages 287-289**

  Addresses . . . . **7100 Second Avenue**

  Times . . . . **4:30 p.m., 8:00 this morning** (but **eight o'clock**)

  Identification numbers . . . . **Serial number 3126598**

  Statistics. . . . . **a vote of 23-4**

  Measurements . . . . **24 mph, 2 tsp.**

  Dates. . . . . **44 B.C.E.; 79 C.E.; July 10, 1997** (domestic),
  10 July 1997 (international)

To Begin a Sentence

- Use words to express numbers when they begin a sentence.

  Twelve customers have complained so far.

Note: If this rule creates an awkward sentence, reword the sentence.

  Clumsy: **Seven hundred forty-two employees signed up for dental care last year.**

  Better: **Last year, 742 employees signed up for dental care.**

Before a Compound Modifier

- Unless they cannot be expressed in one or two words, use words for numbers that precede a compound modifier that includes another number.

  She sold twenty 35-millimeter cameras in one day.

  The prescription called for 120 25-milligram doses.

Note: You may use a combination of words and numerals for very large numbers.

  6-8 million   2 billion to 2.9 billion

  7 trillion

Hyphenating Numbers

- Hyphens are used to form compound modifiers indicating measurement. They are also used for inclusive numbers and fractions when written out.

  a 500-mile flight

  the fiscal year 2001-2002

  a two-thirds majority

  a three-hour drive

Dates

- In letters and most other business writing, dates are indicated by the month, day, and year with a comma separating the figures.

  June 15, 2002

The military and most European companies use the day-month-year system with no commas.

  5 June 2002

Note: Avoid using slashes with numbers.

  In many countries 6/8/03 would mean August 6, 2003.

ABBREVIATIONS

Acceptable Forms

- An abbreviation is the shortened form of a word or a phrase. In general, use abbreviations only in tables, graphs, charts—places where space must be conserved. The following abbreviations, however, are acceptable in any form of writing:

  Mr.   Ms.   Mrs.   Dr.   Jr.   a.m. (A.M.)

Note: In the body of a letter or a report, spell out the names of states, countries, months, days, or units of measure. Also spell out the words *Avenue, Street, Road, Company,* and similar words when they are part of a proper name. Use words rather than signs or symbols (&, %, #, @).

A Closer Look

Avoid beginning a sentence with an abbreviation. Also, spell out abbreviations the first time they are used; then abbreviate, if appropriate.

Common Abbreviations

aac average annual cost

aae average annual earnings

abr. abridged; abridgment

acct. account; accountant

ACV actual cash value

addn. addition

addnl. additional

adm. administration; administrative

advt. advertisement

aff. affiliate

afft. affidavit

agcy. agency

agt. agent

a.k.a. also known as

A.M., a.m. before noon

amt. amount

ann. annual; annually

AP accounts payable

APR annual percentage rate

AR accounts receivable

ASAP as soon as possible

ASCII American Standard Code for Information Interchange

assn. association

asst. 1. assistant 2. assorted

attn. attention

atty. attorney

aux. auxiliary

avg., av. average

BBB Better Business Bureau

B.C.E. before common era

biog. biographer; biographical; biography

BO back order

c. 1. circa (about) 2. cup(s)

CAD computer-aided design

cc carbon copies; copies

CDT, C.D.T. central daylight time

C.E. common era

CEO chief executive officer

CFO chief financial officer

chap. chapter

c.i.f. cost, insurance, and freight

ck. check

cm centimeter(s)

c/o care of

COD, c.o.d. collect on delivery

C of C Chamber of Commerce

COLA cost of living allowance

contd. continued

COO chief operating officer

co-op cooperative

Corp. Corporation

CPA certified public accountant

CPM cost per thousand

CST, C.S.T. central standard time

cu 1. cubic 2. cumulative

d/b/a, d.b.a. doing business as

dept. department

dev. development

disc. discount

doc. document

DST daylight saving time

dup. duplicate

ea. each

ed. edition; editor

EDT, E.D.T. eastern daylight time

e.g. for example

EIN employer identification number

e.o.m. end of month

encl. enclosure

EST, E.S.T. eastern standard time

et al. and others

etc. and so forth

ex. example

exec. executive

FAQ frequently asked question

fin. finance; financial

F.O.B., f.o.b. free on board

FMV fair market value

ft. foot; feet

fwd. forward

FY fiscal year

FYI for your information

g gram(s)

gal. gallon(s)

gds. goods

GM general manager

GNP gross national product

govt. government

hdqrs. headquarters

hp horsepower

i.e. that is

illus. illustration

Inc. Incorporated

inst. institute

invt. inventory

IRA Individual Retirement Account

IRS Internal Revenue Service

kc kilocycle(s)

kg kilogram(s)

Common Abbreviations

km kilometer(s)
kw kilowatt(s)
l liter(s)
lat. latitude
lb. pound(s)
l.c. lowercase
lg. large
L.L.C. limited liability company
long. longitude
Ltd., ltd. limited
m meter(s)
man. manual
Mc, mc megacycle(s)
mdse. merchandise
MDT, M.D.T. mountain daylight time
mfg. manufacturing
mgr. manager
mgt., mgmt. management
mi. 1. mile(s) 2. mill(s) (monetary unit)
misc. miscellaneous
mkt. market
ml milliliter(s)
mm millimeter(s)
mo. month(s)
mpg, m.p.g. miles per gallon
mph, m.p.h. miles per hour
MST, M.S.T. mountain standard time
mtg. meeting
N/A not available; not applicable
natl. national
neg. negative
N.S.F., n.s.f. not sufficient funds

num. number(s)
org. organization
orig. original
o.t., o/t overtime
oz, oz. ounce(s)
P & I principal and interest
P & L profit and loss
pat. patent
pct. percent
pd. paid
PDT, P.D.T. Pacific daylight time
P/E price/earnings
pg., p. page **pp.** pages
PIN Personal Identification Number
P.M., p.m. after noon
pmt. payment
PO purchase order
P.O. Post Office
POA power of attorney
POP point of purchase
ppd. 1. postpaid 2. prepaid
PR, P.R. public relations
psi, p.s.i. pounds per square inch
PST, P.S.T. Pacific standard time
QA quality assurance
QTD quarter to date
qty. quantity
R&D research and development
recd. received
resp. respectively
retd. returned
ROI return on investment
r.p.m., rpm revolutions per minute
R.S.V.P., r.s.v.p. please reply

S&H shipping and handling
S&L savings and loan
sal. salary
SASE self-addressed stamped envelope
shpt. shipment
sm. small
SOP standard operating procedures
SRO, S.R.O. standing room only
SSN social security number
std. standard
syn. synonymous; synonym
tbs., tbsp. tablespoon(s)
TM trademark
tsp. teaspoon(s)
UHF, uhf ultrahigh frequency
v. 1. *Physics:* velocity
   2. *Electricity:* voltage
   3. volume
VA, V.A. Veterans Administration
VIP very important person
vol. 1. volume 2. volunteer
vp vice president
vs. versus
whse., whs. warehouse
whsle. wholesale
wkly. weekly
w/o without
wt. weight
yd. yard(s) (measurement)
yr. year(s)
YTD year to date

Acronynms

- An acronym is a word formed from the first (or first few) letter of each word in a compound term. Periods are not used within acronyms.

  LAN – Local Area Network

  radar – radio detecting and ranging

  RICO – Racketeer Influenced and Corrupt Organizations (Act)

  scuba – self-contained underwater breathing apparatus

Initialisms

- An initialism is similar to an acronym except that the initials are pronounced as individual letters.

  FDA – Food and Drug Administration

  ICC – Interstate Commerce Commission

  SUV – Sport-Utility Vehicle

Note: Spell out an acronym or initialism the first time you use it, followed by its abbreviation in parentheses. Once the term has been identified in this way, you may use just the abbreviation.

COMMON ACRONYMS AND INITIALISMS

AFL	American Federation of Labor	**MADD**	Mothers Against Drunk Driving
AIDS	acquired immunodeficiency syndrome	**NASA**	National Aeronautics and Space Administration
BBB	Better Business Bureau	**NATO**	North Atlantic Treaty Organization
CIA	Central Intelligence Agency	**NYSE**	New York Stock Exchange
CT	CAT(scan) Computerized Axial Tomography	**OEO**	Office of Economic Opportunity
DOD	Department of Defense	**OEP**	Office of Emergency Preparedness
EPA	Environmental Protection Agency	**OPEC**	Organization of Petroleum Exporting Countries
FAA	Federal Aviation Administration	**OSHA**	Occupational Safety and Health Administration
FBI	Federal Bureau of Investigation		
FCC	Federal Communications Commission	**PAC**	political action committee
FDA	Food and Drug Administration	**PIN**	personal identification number
FDIC	Federal Deposit Insurance Corporation	**PSA**	public service announcement
FHA	Federal Housing Administration	**REA**	Rural Electrification Administration
FICA	Federal Insurance Contributions Act	**ROTC**	Reserve Officers' Training Corps
FmHA	Farmers Home Administration	**SEC**	Securities and Exchange Commission
FTC	Federal Trade Commission	**SSA**	Social Security Administration
GAO	General Accounting Office	**SWAT**	Special Weapons and Tactics
HUD	Housing and Urban Development	**VISTA**	Volunteers in Service to America
IRS	Internal Revenue Service		

SPELLING RULES

i Before *e*

- Use *i* before *e* except after *c*, or when sounded like *a* as in *freight* and *eighty*.

  deceit   ceiling   belief   piece

  Exceptions: This sentence can help you remember eight exceptions:

  Neither sheik dared leisurely seize either weird species of financiers.

Final Consonant

- If a single-syllable word (for example, *sad)* ends with a consonant (*d*) preceded by a single vowel (*a*), double the final consonant before adding a suffix beginning with a vowel (*saddest*).

  tap — tapping   plan — planner

  If a multisyllable word (*admit*) ends in a consonant (*t*) preceded by a single vowel (*i*), the accent is on the last syllable (*ad-mit'*), and the suffix begins with a vowel (*ed*)—the same rule holds true: double the final consonant (*admitted*).

  occur — occurrence
  refer — referring

Silent *e*

- If a word ends with a silent *e*, keep the *e* when adding a suffix beginning with a consonant. Drop the *e* when adding a suffix beginning with a vowel.

  hope — hopeful — hoping
  care — careless— caring
  value — valueless — valuable
  love — lovelorn — lovable

  Exceptions: *courageous, noticeable, judgment*

y as the Last Letter

- If a word ends in a *y* preceded by a consonant, change the *y* to *i* before adding any suffix, unless the suffix is *ing*.

  worry — worrisome — worrying
  study — studious — studying
  lazy — laziness
  try — tried — trying

  If a word ends in a *y* preceded by a vowel, form the plural by simply adding an *s*.

  key — keys   day — days
  play — plays

> **FYI** The list of words on the next six pages can be used to double-check both spelling and hyphenation. Remember, even the best spell checker is not foolproof, nor is the hyphenation software for most word processing programs.

* * * * * * * * * Influence is like a savings account. The less

Commonly Misspelled/Misdivided Words

A

ab-bre-vi-ate
abrupt
ab-scess
ab-sence
ab-so-lute (-ly)
ab-sorb-ent
ab-surd
abun-dance
ac-cede
ac-cel-er-ate
ac-cept (-ance)
ac-cep-table
ac-ces-si-ble
ac-ces-so-ry
ac-ci-den-tal-ly
ac-com-mo-date
ac-com-pa-ny
ac-com-plice
ac-com-plish
ac-cor-dance
ac-cord-ing
ac-count
ac-crued
ac-cu-mu-late
ac-cu-ra-cy
ac-cu-rate
ac-cus-tom (-ed)
achieve (-ment)
ac-knowl-edge
ac-quaint-ance
ac-qui-esce
ac-quire
ac-qui-si-tion
acre-age
ac-tu-al
adapt (-er)
ad-di-tion (-al)
ad-dress
ad-e-quate

ad-ja-cent
ad-journed
ad-just-ment
ad-mi-ra-ble
ad-mis-si-ble
ad-mit-tance
ad-van-ta-geous
ad-ver-tise-ment
ad-ver-tis-ing
ad-vice (n.)
ad-vis-able
ad-vise (v.)
ae-ri-al
af-fect (-ed)
af-fi-da-vit
against
ag-gra-vate
ag-gres-sion
agree-able
agree-ment
al-co-hol
align-ment
al-leged
al-lot-ted
al-low-ance
all right
al-most
al-ready
al-though
al-to-geth-er
alu-mi-num
al-ways
am-a-teur
amend-ment
among
am-or-tize
amount
anal-o-gous
anal-y-sis
an-a-lyze

an-cient
an-ec-dote
an-es-thet-ic
an-gle
an-ni-hi-late
an-ni-ver-sa-ry
an-nounce
an-noy-ance
an-nu-al
anon-y-mous
an-swer
ant-arc-tic
an-tic-i-pate
anx-i-ety
anx-ious
apart-ment
apol-o-gize
ap-pa-ra-tus
ap-par-ent (-ly)
ap-peal
ap-pear-ance
ap-pe-tite
ap-pli-ance
ap-pli-ca-ble
ap-pli-ca-tion
ap-point-ment
ap-prais-al
ap-praise
ap-pre-ci-ate
ap-prise
ap-proach
ap-pro-pri-ate
ap-prov-al
ap-prox-i-mate-ly
ar-bi-trary
ar-chi-tect
ar-gu-ment
arith-me-tic
ar-range-ment
ar-riv-al

ar-ti-cle
ar-ti-fi-cial
as-cend
as-cer-tain
as-i-nine
as-sess (-ment)
as-sign-ment
as-sist-ance
as-so-ci-ate
as-so-ci-a-tion
as-sume
as-sur-ance
as-ter-isk
ath-let-ic
at-tach
at-tack (-ed)
at-tempt
at-tend-ance
at-ten-tion
at-ti-tude
at-tor-ney
at-trac-tive
au-di-ble
au-di-ence
au-then-tic
au-thor-i-ty
au-to-mo-bile
au-tumn
aux-il-ia-ry
avail-a-ble
av-er-age
aw-ful-ly
awk-ward

B

bach-e-lor
bag-gage
bal-ance
bal-loon
bal-lot

ban-dage
bank-rupt-cy
bar-gain
bar-rel
base-ment
ba-sis
bat-tery
beau-ti-ful
beau-ty
be-come
be-com-ing
beg-gar
be-gin-ning
be-hav-ior
be-lief
be-lieve
ben-e-fi-cial
ben-e-fit (-ed)
be-tween
bi-ased
bis-cuit
bliz-zard
book-keep-er
bouil-lon
bound-ary
break-fast
breath (n.)
breathe (v.)
brief
bril-liant
bro-chure
brought
bruise
budg-et
bul-le-tin
buoy-ant
bu-reau
bu-reau-cra-cy
bur-glar
busi-ness

Commonly Misspelled/Misdivided Words

C

caf-e-te-ria
caf-feine
cal-en-dar
cal-i-ber
cam-paign
can-celed
can-cel-la-tion
can-di-date
can-dor
can-is-ter
ca-pac-i-ty
cap-i-tal
cap-i-tol
car-bu-re-tor
ca-reer
car-i-ca-ture
car-riage
cash-ier
cas-se-role
cas-u-al-ty
cat-a-log
ca-tas-tro-phe
cat-e-go-ry
cel-e-bra-tion
cem-e-ter-y
cen-sus
cen-tu-ry
cer-tain
cer-tif-i-cate
ces-sa-tion
chal-lenge
change-a-ble
chan-nel
char-ac-ter (-is-tic)
chauf-feur
chief
chim-ney
choc-o-late
cir-cuit

cir-cu-lar
cir-cum-stance
civ-i-li-za-tion
cli-en-tele
cli-mate
co-er-cion
col-lar
col-lat-er-al
col-lege
col-lo-qui-al
col-o-nel
co-los-sal
col-umn
com-e-dy
com-mence
com-mer-cial
com-mis-sion
com-mit
com-mit-ment
com-mit-ted
com-mit-tee
com-mu-ni-cate
com-mu-ni-ty
com-par-a-tive
com-par-i-son
com-pel
com-pe-tent
com-pe-ti-tion
com-pet-i-tive-ly
com-plain
com-ple-ment
com-plete-ly
com-plex-ion
com-pli-ment
com-pro-mise
con-cede
con-ceit (-ed)
con-ceive
con-cern-ing
con-cert

con-ces-sion
con-clude
con-crete
con-curred
con-cur-rence
con-demn
con-de-scend
con-di-tion
con-fer-ence
con-ferred
con-fi-dant
con-fi-dence
con-fi-dent
con-fi-den-tial
con-grat-u-late
con-nois-seur
con-science
con-sci-en-tious
con-scious
con-sen-sus
con-se-quence
con-ser-va-tive
con-sid-er-ably
con-sign-ment
con-sis-tent
con-sti-tu-tion
con-tempt-ible
con-tin-u-al-ly
con-tin-ue
con-tin-u-ous
con-trol
con-tro-ver-sial
con-tro-ver-sy
con-ven-ience
con-vince
cool-ly
co-op-er-ate
cor-dial
cor-po-ra-tion
cor-re-late

cor-re-spond
cor-re-spon-dence
cor-rob-o-rate
coun-cil
coun-sel
coun-sel-or
coun-ter-feit
coun-try
cour-age
cou-ra-geous
cour-te-ous
cour-te-sy
cov-er-age
cred-i-tor
cri-sis
crit-i-cism
crit-i-cize
cu-ri-os-i-ty
cu-ri-ous
cur-rent
cur-ric-u-lum
cus-tom
cus-tom-ary
cus-tom-er
cyl-in-der

D

dai-ly
debt-or
de-ceased
de-ceit-ful
de-ceive
de-cid-ed
de-ci-sion
dec-la-ra-tion
dec-o-rate
de-duct-i-ble
de-fen-dant
de-fense
de-ferred

def-i-cit
def-i-nite (-ly)
def-i-ni-tion
del-e-gate
de-li-cious
de-pend-ent
de-pos-i-tor
de-pot
de-scend
de-scen-dant
de-scribe
de-scrip-tion
de-sert
de-serve
de-sign
de-sir-able
de-sir-ous
de-spair
des-per-ate
de-spise
des-sert
de-te-ri-o-rate
de-ter-mine
det-ri-men-tal
de-vel-op
de-vel-op-ment
de-vice
de-vise
di-a-mond
di-a-phragm
di-ar-rhe-a
dic-tio-nary
dif-fer-ence
dif-fer-ent
dif-fi-cul-ty
dig-ni-tary
di-lap-i-dat-ed
di-lem-ma
din-ing
di-plo-ma

di-rec-tor
dis-agree-able
dis-ap-pear
dis-ap-point
dis-ap-prove
dis-as-trous
dis-ci-pline
dis-cov-er
dis-crep-an-cy
dis-cuss
dis-cus-sion
dis-ease
dis-sat-is-fied
dis-sim-i-lar
dis-si-pate
dis-tinct-ly
dis-tin-guish
dis-trib-ute
di-vide
di-vine
di-vis-i-ble
di-vi-sion
doc-tor
doesn't
dom-i-nant
dor-mi-to-ry
dos-sier
doubt
drudg-ery
du-pli-cate
dye-ing
dy-ing

E

ea-ger-ly
ear-nest
easily
eco-nom-i-cal
econ-o-my
ec-sta-sy
edi-tion
ef-fer-ves-cent

ef-fi-ca-cy
ef-fi-cien-cy
eighth
ei-ther
elab-o-rate
elec-tric-i-ty
el-e-phant
elic-it
el-i-gi-ble
e-lim-i-nate
el-lipse
em-bar-rass
emer-gen-cy
em-i-nent
em-pha-size
em-ploy-ee
em-ploy-ment
emul-sion
en-close
en-cour-age
en-deav-or
en-dorse-ment
en-gi-neer
enor-mous
enough
en-ter-prise
en-ter-tain
en-thu-si-as-tic
en-tire-ly
en-trance
en-vel-op (v.)
en-ve-lope (n.)
en-vi-ron-ment
equip-ment
equipped
equiv-a-lent
es-crow
es-pe-cial-ly
es-sen-tial
es-tab-lish
es-teemed
et-i-quette

ev-i-dence
ex-ag-ger-ate
ex-ceed
ex-cel-lent
ex-cept
ex-cep-tion-al-ly
ex-ces-sive
ex-cite
ex-ec-u-tive
ex-er-cise
ex-haust (-ed)
ex-hi-bi-tion
ex-hil-a-ra-tion
ex-is-tence
ex-on-er-ate
ex-or-bi-tant
ex-pect
ex-pe-di-tion
ex-pend-i-ture
ex-pen-sive
ex-pe-ri-ence
ex-pla-na-tion
ex-pres-sion
ex-qui-site
ex-ten-sion
ex-tinct
ex-traor-di-nar-y
ex-treme-ly

F

fa-cil-i-ties
fac-sim-i-le
fal-la-cy
fa-mil-iar
fa-mous
fas-ci-nate
fash-ion
fa-tigue (d)
fau-cet
fa-vor-ite
fea-si-ble
fea-ture

Feb-ru-ar-y
fed-er-al
fem-i-nine
fer-tile
fic-ti-tious
fi-ery
fi-nal-ly
fi-nan-cial-ly
fluo-res-cent
fo-li-age
for-ci-ble
for-eign
fore-see
for-feit
for-go
for-mal-ly
for-mer-ly
forth-right
for-tu-nate
for-ward
foun-tain
frag-ile
fran-ti-cal-ly
freight
friend
ful-fill
fun-da-men-tal
fur-ther-more
fu-tile

G

gad-get
gan-grene
ga-rage
gas-o-line
gauge
ge-ne-al-o-gy
gen-er-al-ly
gen-er-ous
ge-nius
gen-u-ine
ge-og-ra-phy

glo-ri-ous
gov-ern-ment
gov-er-nor
gra-cious
grad-u-a-tion
gram-mar
grate-ful
grat-i-tude
griev-ous
grue-some
guar-an-tee
guar-an-teed
guard-i-an
guer-ril-la
guid-ance
gym-na-si-um
gy-ro-scope

H

hab-i-tat
ham-mer
hand-ker-chief
han-dle (d)
hap-haz-ard
hap-pen
hap-pi-ness
ha-rass
har-bor
hast-i-ly
haz-ard-ous
height
hem-or-rhage
hes-i-tate
hin-drance
his-to-ry
hol-i-day
hon-or
hop-ing
hop-ping
hor-ri-ble
hos-pi-tal
hu-mor-ous

Commonly Misspelled/Misdivided Words

hur-ried-ly
hy-drau-lic
hy-giene
hy-poc-ri-sy

I

ide-al-ly
iden-ti-cal
id-io-syn-cra-sy
il-leg-i-ble
il-lic-it
il-lit-er-ate
il-lus-trate
im-ag-i-nary
im-ag-i-na-tive
im-ag-ine
im-i-ta-tion
im-me-di-ate-ly
im-mense
im-mi-grant
im-mor-tal
im-pa-tient
im-per-a-tive
im-por-tance
im-pos-si-ble
im-promp-tu
im-prove-ment
in-ad-ver-tent
in-al-ien-able
in-ci-den-tal-ly
in-con-ve-nience
in-cred-i-ble
in-curred
in-def-i-nite-ly
in-del-i-ble
in-de-pend-ence
in-de-pend-ent
in-dict-ment
in-dis-pens-able
in-di-vid-u-al

in-duce-ment
in-dus-tri-al
in-dus-tri-ous
in-eq-ui-ty
in-ev-i-ta-ble
in-fe-ri-or
in-ferred
in-fi-nite
in-flam-ma-ble
in-flu-en-tial
in-ge-nious
in-gen-u-ous
in-im-i-ta-ble
in-i-tial
ini-ti-a-tion
ini-tia-tive
in-no-cence
in-no-cent
in-noc-u-ous
in-no-va-tive
in-nu-en-do
in-oc-u-la-tion
in-quir-y
in-stal-la-tion
in-stance
in-stead
in-sti-tute
in-sur-ance
in-tel-lec-tu-al
in-tel-li-gence
in-ten-tion
in-ter-cede
in-ter-est-ing
in-ter-fere
in-ter-im
in-ter-mit-tent
in-ter-pret (-ed)
in-ter-rupt
in-ter-view
in-ti-mate

in-va-lid
in-ves-ti-gate
in-ves-tor
in-vi-ta-tion
ir-i-des-cent
ir-rel-e-vant
ir-re-sis-ti-ble
ir-rev-er-ent
ir-ri-gate
is-sue
item-ized
itin-er-ar-y

J

jan-i-tor
jeal-ous
jeop-ard-ize
jew-el-ry
jour-nal
jour-ney
judg-ment
jus-tice
jus-ti-fi-able

K

kitch-en
knowl-edge
knuck-le

L

la-bel
lab-o-ra-to-ry
lan-guage
laun-dry
law-yer
league
lec-ture
le-gal
leg-i-ble
leg-is-la-ture

le-git-i-mate
lei-sure
length
le-nient
let-ter-head
li-a-bil-i-ty
li-a-ble
li-ai-son
li-brar-y
li-cense
lieu-ten-ant
light-ning
lik-able
like-li-hood
like-ly
lin-eage
liq-ue-fy
liq-uid
lit-er-ary
lit-er-a-ture
live-li-hood
liv-ing
log-a-rithm
lo-gis-tics
lone-li-ness
loose (adj.)
lose (v.)
los-ing
love-ly
lun-cheon
lux-u-ry

M

ma-chine
mag-a-zine
mag-nif-i-cent
main-tain
main-te-nance
ma-jor-i-ty
man-age-able

man-age-ment
ma-neu-ver
man-u-al
man-u-fac-ture
man-u-script
mar-riage
mar-shal
ma-te-ri-al
math-e-mat-ics
max-i-mum
may-or
mean-ness
meant
mea-sure
med-i-cine
me-di-eval
me-di-o-cre
me-di-um
mem-o-ran-dum
mer-chan-dise
mer-it
mes-sage
mile-age
mil-len-ni-um
mil-lion-aire
min-i-a-ture
min-i-mum
min-us-cule
min-ute
mi-nu-ti-a
mir-ror
mis-cel-la-neous
mis-chief
mis-chie-vous
mis-er-a-ble
mis-ery
mis-sile
mis-sion-ary
mis-spell
mois-ture

mo-men-tous
mo-not-o-nous
mon-u-ment
mort-gage
mu-nic-i-pal
mus-cle
mu-si-cian
mus-tache
mys-te-ri-ous

N

na-ive
nat-u-ral-ly
nec-es-sary
ne-ces-si-ty
neg-li-gi-ble
ne-go-ti-ate
neigh-bor-hood
nev-er-the-less
nine-teenth
nine-ty
no-tice-able
no-to-ri-ety
nu-cle-ar
nui-sance
nu-mer-ous

O

obe-di-ence
oblige
ob-so-les-cent
ob-sta-cle
oc-ca-sion
oc-ca-sion-al-ly
oc-cu-pant
oc-cur
oc-curred
oc-cur-rence
of-fense
of-fi-cial
of-ten
omis-sion

omit-ted
op-er-ate
opin-ion
op-po-nent
op-por-tu-ni-ty
op-po-site
op-ti-mism
or-di-nance
or-di-nar-i-ly
orig-i-nal (-ly)
out-ra-geous

P

pag-eant
pam-phlet
par-a-graph
par-al-lel
par-a-lyze
pa-ren-the-ses
pa-ren-the-sis
par-lia-ment
par-tial (-ly)
par-tic-i-pant
par-tic-i-pate
par-tic-u-lar-ly
pas-time
pa-tience
pa-tron-age
pe-cu-liar
per-ceive
per-for-mance
per-haps
per-il
per-ma-nent
per-mis-si-ble
per-pen-dic-u-lar
per-se-ver-ance
per-sis-tent
per-son-al (-ly)
per-son-nel
per-spec-tive
per-spi-ra-tion

per-suade
per-tain
phe-nom-e-non
phi-los-o-phy
phy-si-cian
piece
pla-teau
plau-si-ble
pleas-ant
pleas-ure
pneu-mo-nia
pol-i-ti-cian
pos-sess
pos-ses-sion
pos-si-bly
prac-ti-cal-ly
prai-rie
pre-cede
pre-ce-dence
pre-ced-ing
pre-cious
pre-cise-ly
pre-ci-sion
pre-de-ces-sor
pre-dom-i-nant-ly
pref-er-a-ble
pref-er-ence
pre-ferred
prej-u-dice
pre-lim-i-nar-y
pre-mi-um
prep-a-ra-tion
pre-req-ui-site
pre-rog-a-tive
pres-ence
prev-a-lent
pre-ven-tive
pre-vi-ous
prim-i-tive
prin-ci-pal
prin-ci-ple
pri-or-i-ty

pris-on-er
priv-i-lege
prob-a-bly
pro-ce-dure
pro-ceed
pro-cess (-es)
pro-fes-sor
pro-grammed
prom-i-nent
prom-is-so-ry
pro-nounce
pro-nun-ci-a-tion
pro-pa-gan-da
pros-e-cute
pro-spec-tive
pro-tein
psy-chol-o-gy
pub-lic-ly
pur-chase
pur-sue
pur-su-ing
pur-suit

Q

qual-i-fied
qual-i-ty
quan-da-ry
quan-ti-ty
quar-ter
ques-tion-naire
qui-et
quite
quo-tient

R

rap-port
rar-i-ty
re-al-ize
re-al-ly
re-cede
re-ceipt
re-ceive (d)

re-ces-sion
rec-i-pe
re-cip-i-ent
rec-og-ni-tion
rec-og-nize
rec-om-mend
re-cruit
re-cur-rence
re-cy-cla-ble
ref-er-ence
re-ferred
re-gret-ta-ble
re-hearse
reign
re-im-burse
rel-e-vant
re-lieve
re-li-gious
re-mem-ber
re-mem-brance
rem-i-nisce
ren-dez-vous
re-new-al
rep-e-ti-tion
rep-re-sen-ta-tive
req-ui-si-tion
re-scind
re-sem-blance
res-er-voir
re-sis-tance
re-spect-a-bly
re-spect-ful-ly
re-spec-tive-ly
re-spon-si-bil-i-ty
res-tau-rant
ret-ro-ac-tive
rheu-ma-tism
ri-dic-u-lous
route

Commonly Misspelled/Misdivided Words

S

sac-ri-le-gious
safe-ty
sal-a-ry
sal-vage
sand-wich
sat-el-lite
sat-is-fac-to-ry
Sat-ur-day
scarce-ly
scar-ci-ty
scen-er-y
sched-ule
sci-ence
scis-sors
sec-re-tary
seize
sen-si-ble
sen-tence
sen-ti-nel
sep-a-rate
ser-geant
sev-er-al
se-vere-ly
sher-iff
shin-ing
siege
sig-nif-i-cance
sim-i-lar
si-mul-ta-ne-ous
sin-cere-ly
siz-able
skep-tic
ski-ing
sol-emn
so-phis-ti-cat-ed
soph-o-more
so-ror-i-ty
sou-ve-nir
spa-ghet-ti

spe-cif-ic
spec-i-men
sphere
spon-sor
spon-ta-ne-ous
sta-tion-ary
sta-tion-ery
sta-tis-tic
stat-ue
stat-ure
stat-ute
stom-ach
straight
strat-e-gy
sub-si-dize
sub-stan-tial
sub-sti-tute
sub-tle
suc-ceed
suc-cess
suf-fi-cient
sum-ma-rize
su-per-fi-cial
su-per-in-tend-ent
su-pe-ri-or-i-ty
su-per-sede
sup-ple-ment
sup-pose
sure-ly
sur-prise
sur-veil-lance
sur-vey
sus-cep-ti-ble
sus-pi-cious
sus-te-nance
syl-la-ble
sym-met-ri-cal
sym-pa-thy
sym-pho-ny
symp-tom

syn-chro-nous
syn-on-y-mous

T

tar-iff
tech-ni-cal
tech-nique
tele-gram
tem-per-a-ment
tem-per-a-ture
tem-po-rary
ten-den-cy
ten-ta-tive
ter-res-tri-al
ter-ri-ble
ter-ri-to-ry
the-ater
there-fore
thor-ough (-ly)
though
thresh-old
through-out
to-bac-co
to-geth-er
to-mor-row
tongue
to-tal-ing
touch
tour-na-ment
tour-ni-quet
to-ward
trag-e-dy
trai-tor
tran-quil-iz-er
trans-fer-able
trans-ferred
trav-eled
trea-sur-er
tru-ly
Tues-day

tu-i-tion
typ-i-cal
typ-ing

U

unan-i-mous
un-con-scious
un-doubt-ed-ly
un-for-tu-nate-ly
unique
uni-son
uni-ver-si-ty
un-man-age-able
un-nec-es-sary
un-prec-e-dent-ed
un-til
un-wieldy
up-per
ur-gent
us-able
use-ful
usu-al-ly
uten-sil
util-ize

V

va-can-cies
va-ca-tion
vac-u-um
vague
valu-able
va-ri-ety
var-i-ous
veg-e-ta-ble
ve-hi-cle
ve-loc-i-ty
ven-geance
vi-able
vi-cin-i-ty
vig-i-lance

vil-lain
vi-o-lence
vis-i-bil-i-ty
vis-i-ble
vis-i-tor
vol-ume
vol-un-tary
vol-un-teer

W

wan-der
ware-house
war-rant
weath-er
Wednes-day
wel-come
wel-fare
wheth-er
whol-ly
with-hold
wom-en
worth-while
wor-thy
wreck-age
writ-ing
writ-ten

Y

yel-low
yes-ter-day
yield

Z

ze-nith
zig-zag
zo-olo-gy

Using the Right Word

This list contains words that are easily confused and thus misused. The definitions and examples will help clarify how these challenging words ought to be used in your writing.

a, an

- *A* is used before words beginning with a consonant sound; *an* is used before words beginning with a vowel sound.

    a hotel   **an understanding**
    a unified team   **an honest mistake**

accept, except

- The verb *accept* means "to receive" or "to believe"; the preposition *except* means other than; the conjunction means "unless" and the verb means "leave out."

    The supervisor accepted Lu's reason for being late for work.

    Everyone—except Lu and the supervisor— had remembered to switch to daylight savings time.

    Only in rare cases are employees excepted from the policy on punctuality.

adapt, adept, adopt

- *Adapt* means "to modify to make suitable"; *adopt* means "to take and treat as one's own" (as with a concept or a child). *Adept* is an adjective meaning "proficient or well trained."

    We adopted Business Plus accounting software. Now we need an adept accountant to adapt our bookkeeping system to the new software.

adverse, averse

- *Adverse* means "hostile, unfavorable, or harmful." *Averse* means "to have a definite feeling of distaste; disinclined."

    Adverse weather conditions grounded all airplanes.

    The tired staff was averse to the idea of working till midnight.

advice, advise

- *Advice* is a noun that means "recommendation or information"; *advise* is a verb meaning "to counsel or recommend."

    He advised me to value good advice.

affect, effect

- *Affect* is a verb that means "to influence." As a noun, *effect* means "the result"; as a verb it means "to bring about."

    Your performance in the coming year will directly affect the amount of your bonus.

    The effect of the economy is hard to predict.

    The new procedure will effect significant savings in time and cost.

aid, aide

- As a verb, *aid* means "to help"; as a noun, *aid* means "the help given." *Aide* is a person who acts as an assistant.

    This book will aid anyone who wants to improve his or her writing.

    Mr. Young is an aide to the vice president.

allot, alot, a lot

- *Allot* means "to assign a portion or piece." *Alot* is not a word; *a lot* (two words) is correct, but should be used sparingly—especially in formal writing.

allude, elude, refer

- *Allude* means "to indirectly refer to something," *elude* "to escape attention or understanding altogether," and *refer* "to directly call attention to something."

   Don't just allude to proper conduct; instead, refer specifically to required behavior. That way your expectations will not elude your staff.

allusion, illusion

- *Allusion* is an indirect reference; *illusion* is a false impression or image.

   Are you under the illusion that most people understand your allusions to the works of Aristotle?

already, all ready

- *Already* is an adverb meaning "before or by the specified time." *All ready* is an adjective form meaning "completely prepared." (Use *all ready* if you can substitute *ready* alone in the sentence.)

   The shipment already arrived this morning.
   The sales staff is all ready to take orders.

alright, all right

- *Alright* is an incorrect form of *all right*. (Please note that the following words are spelled correctly: *always, altogether, already, almost.*)

alter, altar

- *Alter* means "to change something"; *altar* is "a table or raised area used in worship."

   The secretary altered the form of the company letterhead.
   The couple stood in front of the altar.

alternate, alternative

- *Alternate* is a noun meaning "something or someone that can be used or put in place of another"; it is also a verb meaning "to change back and forth between two things." An *alternative* is a choice derived from two or more possibilities.

   If I'm still sick, Mary can go to the meeting as my alternate.
   Earl and I alternate shifts.
   One alternative to a meeting is a conference call.

altogether, all together

- *Altogether* means "wholly, completely." *All together* means "in a group" or "all at once." (Use *all together* if you can substitute *together* alone in a sentence.)

   All together there are 5,000 jobs listed.
   That's altogether too many to consider.

among, between

- *Among* refers to groups of more than two persons or things; *between* refers to only two.

   Personal leave days are listed among the benefits offered by this company.
   Communication between workers and management is candid.

amount, number

- *Amount* refers to things in bulk or mass. *Number* refers to separate units that can be counted. (See also **fewer, less**.)

  The number of new workers hired next year will depend upon the amount of revenue raised by sales.

and, etc.

- Don't use *and* before *etc.* (See also **etc.**)

  Did you confirm prices, costs, profits, etc.?

annual, biannual, semiannual, biennial, perennial

- *Annual* means "occurring once every year." *Biannual* and *semiannual* mean "twice a year." *Biennial* means "every two years." *Perennial* means "throughout the year, every year."

anxious (about), eager (to)

- *Anxious* indicates that one is worrying; *eager*, that one is gladly anticipating something.

  Margarete is anxious about speaking in public, but she is eager to share her new findings with the research department.

any one (of), anyone

- *Any one* means "a singular thing or person from a group"; *anyone* is a pronoun meaning "any person."

  Choose any one of the proposed weekend schedules. Anyone wishing to work on Saturday instead of Sunday may do so.

any way, anyway, anyways

- *Any way* means "any route, method, or course of action"; *anyway* is an adverb meaning "in any case." (*Anyways* is an incorrect form of *anyway*.)

  Matt couldn't think of any way to change his schedule. I didn't really need a ride from him anyway.

appraise, apprise

- *Appraise* means "to estimate the worth of something." *Apprise* means "to inform."

  The man appraised the house at $150,000 and apprised the owners of its worth.

as, as if, like (See like.)

ascent, assent (to)

- *Ascent* refers to rising or advancement; *assent* refers to agreement.

  The ascent of Mt. Everest is treacherous.

  Because of your inexperience, I cannot assent to your going on the expedition.

assure, ensure, insure (See insure.)

augment, supplement

- Although both words mean "to add something," *augment* indicates a simple increase in size or degree, and *supplement* indicates making something that was deficient, complete.

  Flood warnings augmented the importance of the levee reports.

  This manual supplements the program we purchased last month.

average, median

- The *average* and *median* of a series of numbers can be explained by this example: Seven workers used 0, 2, 3, 3, 5, 7, and 8 sick days respectively. The *average* number of sick days used is the total (28) divided by the number of workers (7): 4. The *median*, or middle number in the series, is 3: 0, 2, 3, 3, 5, 7, 8.

bad, badly

- *Bad* is an adjective and can be used after linking verbs.

   The bad day would not end.

   I feel bad, look bad, and smell bad.

   Badly is an adverb.

   He was driving badly, so I called the 800 number on the truck's bumper sticker.

base, bass

- *Base* is the lowest part or the foundation. *Bass* (when pronounced like *case*) is a low-pitched sound. *Bass* (when pronounced like *pass*) is a fish.

beside, besides

- *Beside* is a preposition that means "next to." *Besides* is an adverb that means "in addition to."

   Put the file cabinet beside the desk.

   Besides the new cabinet, we need better lighting.

between, among (See among.)

biannual, biennial (See annual.)

bring, take

- *Bring* refers to movement toward the writer or speaker; *take* refers to movement away from the writer or speaker.

   Please bring the new product data to the meeting, and remember to take the disks to Personnel beforehand.

by, bye, buy

- *By* is a preposition or an adverb. *Bye*, an inter-jection, is short for "good-bye." *Buy* is a verb meaning "to purchase."

   I cannot walk by a candy store without having an urge to buy some chocolate.

can, may

- *Can* implies ability; *may* indicates permission.

   "I can take your order" literally means "I am physically or mentally able to take the order." "May I take your order?" asks permission to take the order.

capital, capitol

- As a noun, *capital* refers to wealth (money or goods) or to a chief city. The adjective *capital* means "important, excellent, or serious." *Capitol* refers to a government building.

   Capitol buildings are generally in the center of the capital city.

   She grew used to making decisions of capital importance.

   Thought, not money, is the real business capital.   —Harvey Firestone

   New investments contributed capital for the building fund.

* * * * * * * * * * * The by-product is sometimes more valuable

censor, censure

● *Censor* means "to examine in order to delete anything objectionable." *Censure* means "to condemn or criticize."

After the letter was censored, there was little left to read.

The problematic open-campus policy was censured by the school board.

cent, sent, scent

● *Cent* is the value of a penny; *sent* is the past tense of the verb *send*; *scent* is a fragrance or a smell.

The perfume company sent out 75-cent postcards to announce their new scent.

chair, chairperson

● The terms *chair* and *chairperson* refer to the presiding officer of a meeting or board. Use either term, but do not use *chairman* or *chairwoman;* the latter terms are sexually biased.

choose, chose

● *Choose* (chüz) means "to select"; *chose* (chōz) is the past tense.

After being warned to choose her words carefully, Fiona chose to remain silent.

chord, cord

● *Chord* means "the combination of three or more tones sounded at the same time," as with a guitar *chord.* It can also mean "an emotion or a feeling." A *cord* is a string, a rope, or a small electrical cable.

The guitar player strummed the opening chord to the group's hit song, which struck a responsive chord with the audience.

The worn electrical cord for my space heater should be replaced.

cite, sight, site (See sight.)

climactic, climatic

● *Climactic* refers to the climax, or high point, of an event; *climatic* refers to the climate, or weather conditions.

Because we are using the open-air amphitheater, climatic conditions in these foothills will just about guarantee the wind gusts we need for the climactic third act.

clothes, cloths, close

● The word *clothes* means "a covering or garments meant to be worn." *Cloths* are fabrics. As an adjective, *close* means "very near." As a verb, it means "to shut" or "bring to an end."

coarse, course

● *Coarse* is an adjective meaning "common, rough, or crude." *Course* as a noun means "movement, a direction, or a route taken" or "a curriculum or class." *Course* as a verb means "to move swiftly."

Burlap is a very coarse fabric.

The ship's captain mapped out a new course to avoid the hurricane.

I'm taking an Internet course.

compare with, compare to

● Things of the same class are *compared with* each other; things of different classes are *compared to* each other.

Compare your responses with mine.

Ben compared his computer to a sloth.

Note: *Compared to* can also mean "in relation to."

Roberta is Internet savvy compared to me.

complement, compliment

- *Complement* means "to complete or go well with." *Compliment* means "to give praise." Both words can also be used as nouns. The adjective *complementary* means "serving to fill out or complete." *Complimentary* means "given free as a favor."

  "Some folks pay a compliment like they expect a receipt."
  —Frank McKinney Hubbard

  A fine grape jelly is a complement to any peanut butter.

comprehensible, comprehensive

- *Comprehensible* means "capable of being understood"; *comprehensive* means "covering a broad range, or inclusive."

  If the report is comprehensible to the laypeople, it's a great report.

  Comprehensive training sessions ensured the program's success.

comprise, compose

- *Comprise* means "to contain or consist of"; *compose* means "to create or form by bringing parts together."

  The research team comprises three Ph.D.'s and one high school student.

  The research team is composed of [not comprised of] three Ph.D.'s and one high school student.

concave, convex

- *Concave* refers to an object curved inward like the inner surface of a ball; *convex* refers to an object curved outward like the outer surface of a ball.

confidant, confident

- A *confidant* is someone you trust. *Confident* means "self-assured."

  Mr. Barker had no confidant with whom he could share his ideas.

  Confident of her talent, Sharon leapt at any chance to speak.

conscience, conscious

- A *conscience* gives one the capacity to know right from wrong. *Conscious* means "awake or alert, not sleeping or comatose."

  Your conscience will guide you.

  Mr. Kreutz needs two cups of coffee to be fully conscious at this hour.

consequently, subsequently

- *Consequently* means "as a result of"; *subsequently* means "following closely in time or order."

  We were late for the meeting; consequently, we missed the reading of the minutes.

  The general had retired to his study but was subsequently interrupted by a knock at the door.

consul (See counsel.)

continual, continuous

- *Continual* refers to something that happens at intervals over a long period; *continuous* refers to something that happens without stopping.

  The continual interruptions impaired her concentration.

  The company suffered a continuous slump that lasted for five months.

controller, comptroller

- *Controller* refers to someone who either controls air traffic or is the chief accountant in a business or an institution. *Comptroller* refers only to the latter position.

counsel, council, consul

- As a noun, *counsel* means "advice" or "legal or professional adviser"; as a verb, *counsel* means "to advise." *Council* refers to a group that governs, administers, or advises. A *consul* is a government official appointed to a position in a foreign country.

  The consul appointed to Brazil counseled the trade minister there about our new tariff laws.

  The corporate counsel knew the pollution laws by heart.

  The building council offers counsel to dissatisfied tenants.

credible, creditable

- *Credible* refers to someone or something you "can believe." *Creditable* means "deserving of commercial credit" or "limited praise."

  The auditor examined two credible reports.

  The bank believes Joy's Shoe Mart is a creditable business.

criteria, criterion

- *Criteria* is the plural form of *criterion,* a standard on which a judgment is made.

  The most important criterion in the pie judge's mind was taste.

  The exclusive club has a long list of membership criteria.

data, datum

- Informally, the term *data* often defines a single collection of facts.

  The data given in this report *is* interesting and very convincing. (Informal)

  In formal writing, if your emphasis is on the individual facts, *data* is used as the plural form of the singular *datum.*

  These data *were* collected during months of research. (Formal, scientific)

decent, descent, dissent

- *Decent* means "good." *Descent* is the process of going or stepping downward. *Dissent* means "disagreement."

  The plane's descent into the airport was quick and smooth.

  There is clear-cut dissent over which airline offers decent business service.

defective, deficient

- *Defective* means "faulty or imperfect"; *deficient* indicates a shortage or "lacking something necessary."

  The defective part caused the sudden engine failure.

  Our winter food stores were deficient.

device, devise

- *Device* is an "invention for a particular purpose" or a "means to do something." *Devise* means to "form, plan, or arrange."

  That paint-mixing device no longer works.

  He was asked to devise a sales plan for the fourth quarter.

different from, different than

- Use *different from* in most cases; use *different than* when it is followed by a clause and results in a simpler construction.

  His car is different from mine.

  The elevator smells different than it smelled yesterday.

disburse, disperse

- *Disburse* means "to pay out funds"; *disperse* means "to spread out or break up."

  The trustee is the only person who can disburse the inheritance.

  The riot police dispersed the crowd.

discreet, discrete

- *Discreet* means "showing good judgment, modest, unobtrusive"; *discrete* means "distinct, separate."

  The new office dress code mandated businesslike, discreet attire.

  Her advice to me was to keep my home life discrete from my career.

disinterested (See uninterested.)

- Both words mean "not interested." However, *disinterested* is also used to mean "unbiased."

effect, affect (See affect.)

elicit, illicit

- *Elicit* is a verb meaning "to bring out"; *illicit* is an adjective meaning "unlawful."

  The manager's confidence in the team seems to elicit strong morale.

  Illicit home use of shop equipment has been uncovered.

eminent, imminent, emanate

- *Eminent* means "prominent, conspicuous, or famous"; *imminent* means "ready or threatening to happen"; *emanate* is a verb meaning "something coming from a particular source."

  Several eminent CEO's will be flying in for the meeting. A merger of the companies is imminent.

envelop, envelope

- *Envelop* means "to cover or surround"; an *envelope* is a flat paper folder or case (usually for a letter).

  Fog envelopes our seaside cottage each morning in summer.

  The letter arrived in a hot-pink envelope.

etc.

- *Etc.* is an abbreviation for *et cetera,* which means "and others" or "and so forth." Never use *and* before *etc.* (See also **and, etc.**)

example, sample

- The noun *example* means "prototype," or "something that serves as a pattern"; the noun *sample* means a "representative item from a larger whole." As a verb, *sample* means "to take a sample of or from."

  Mr. Dorrit will compose a collection letter to be used as an example for the rest of the clerks.

  Before you purchase the pepper sausage, taste a sample.

except, accept (See accept.)

explicit, implicit

- *Explicit* means "expressed directly, or clearly defined"; *implicit* means "implied, or unstated."

  The directions were explicit and easy for us to follow.

  The implicit message in the boss's glance was understood by all.

fair, fare

- *Fair,* as an adjective, refers to a pleasing appearance; as a noun, it refers to a gathering for buying and selling goods. *Fare* is the charge levied for transportation.

farther, further

- *Farther* refers to physical distance; *further* means "to a greater extent": to additional time, quantity, or degree.

  When we investigated further, we discovered that they had traveled farther than initially thought.

female, woman

- Use *female* in scientific or legal materials; in most other contexts, *woman* is the more personal, acceptable term.

  The female subject received the placebo.

  Women of varying economic backgrounds have been polled.

fewer, less

- *Fewer* refers to a number of countable units; *less* refers to value, degree, or bulk quantity. (See also **amount, number.**)

  Despite fewer benefits and less pay, department morale rose.

first, firstly

- Both words are adverbs meaning "before another in time" or "in the first place." However, do not use *firstly*, which is stiff and unnatural sounding.

  Incorrect: **Firstly, I want to see the manager.**

  Correct: **First, I want to see the manager.**

  When enumerating, use the forms *first, second, third, next, last*—without the "ly."

fiscal, physical

- *Fiscal* means "related to financial matters"; *physical* means "related to material things."

  Physical health requires regular exercise; fiscal health requires careful budgeting.

for, fore, four

- *For* is a preposition meaning "because of," "directed to," or "in favor of." As an adjective, *fore* means "earlier" or "forward"; as a noun, it means "the front." *Four* is the number 4.

  For pity's sake, move to the fore of the boat before this thing capsizes and the four of us take a cold dip!

former, latter

- When speaking of two things, *former* refers to the first thing and *latter* to the second. (See also **later.**)

  Of the two speeches, the former was more polished, but the latter was more entertaining.

Former means "from an earlier time"; *latter* means "closer to the end" or "recent."

  This latter decision was never even hinted at in their former correspondence.

good, well

- *Good* is an adjective, never an adverb. *Well* is nearly always an adverb; when used to indicate state of health, *well* is an adjective.

    Good work should be well rewarded.

    Please go home if you're not feeling well.

guarantee, guaranty

- A *guarantee* is an agreement or assurance that a product or a service will maintain a certain standard. A *guaranty* is an agreement that one will pay another's debt if that person fails to pay.

    The guarantee says I must be completely satisfied with this stove or I'll get my money back.

    My parents signed a guaranty when I got my first car loan.

healthful, healthy

- *Healthful* means "promoting good health"; *healthy* means "possessing good health."

    She has a healthy heart because of her healthful diet.

hear, here

- *Hear* is a verb meaning "to perceive by the ear." *Here* is an adverb meaning "of or in this place."

heard, herd

- *Heard* is the past tense of the verb "hear." As a noun, *herd* means a "group of animals"; as a verb, it means "to keep or move (animals) in a herd."

    When we heard the thundering herd of cattle, we knew it was time to get out of the way.

hole, whole

- *Hole* is a noun meaning "an opening or a gap." As an adjective, *whole* means "complete or entire"; as a noun, it means "an entire or complete entity."

illicit, elicit (See elicit.)

illusion, allusion (See allusion.)

immigrate (to), emigrate (from)

- *Immigrate* means "to come into a new country to reside here." *Emigrate* means "to leave one country to live in another."

    Her family emigrated from Nigeria in 1987.

    Knowing English made it easy for her to immigrate to the United States.

imminent, eminent (See eminent.)

imply, infer

- *Imply* means "to suggest, hint, or communicate indirectly"; *infer* means "to deduce or conclude from." (Writers and speakers *imply*; readers and listeners *infer*.)

    I thought she was implying that I would receive a raise; apparently I inferred incorrectly.

insight, incite

- *Insight* is the ability to see the truth in a situation. *Incite* refers to provoking or encouraging.

    The new employee's insight proved extremely helpful.

    Poor communication can incite distrust in a company.

* * * * * * * * * A pessimist is a person who looks both ways

insure, ensure, assure

- *Insure* means "to secure from harm or loss"; *ensure* means "to make certain of something"; and *assure* means "to put someone's mind at rest."

  We assured Mr. Finn that the drilling would be painless; and to ensure that promise, the dentist used her strongest anesthetic.

  One more gold crown, and I'm going to insure this mouth.

interstate, intrastate

- *Interstate* means "connecting or existing between two or more states"; *intrastate* means "occurring or existing within a state."

irregardless, regardless

- *Irregardless* is the substandard form of *regardless*.

  Incorrect: **Irregardless of the weather, we will go.**

  Correct: **Regardless of the weather, we will go.**

it's, its

- *It's* is the contraction of "it is" or "it has." *Its* is the possessive form of "it."

  It's not simply what you know; it's also whom you know.

  The medical clinic finally remodeled its outdated waiting room.

kind of, sort of

- These phrases are used informally to mean "somewhat" or "rather"; avoid using them in formal business communications.

  Unacceptable: **Sales have been kind of slow this quarter.**

  Acceptable: **Sales have been somewhat slow this quarter.**

knew, new

- *Knew* is the past tense of the verb "know." *New* means "recent, original, or fresh."

  We are wondering if he knew about the new logo before we did.

later, latter

- As an adverb, *later* means "after a period of time"; as an adjective, it is the comparative form of "late." *Latter* is a noun referring to the second of two things mentioned. (See also **former, latter.**)

  We can write the agenda later.

  This report was submitted later than that one.

  Of the two proposals just presented, the latter offers a more workable solution.

lay, lie

- *Lay* means "to put or place something." It is a transitive verb, which means it must be followed by a direct object. (See page 249.) Its principal parts are *lay, laid, laid.*

  Please do not lay that report there.

  Harley's assistant laid down the new carpeting yesterday.

  She had laid down the law about photocopies.

Lie means "to rest or recline." It is an intransitive verb, which means it does not take a direct object. (See page 249.) Its principal parts are *lie, lay, lain.*

  George likes to lie down for a nap after lunch. He lay down Monday at 12:30, but often he has lain down by 12:15.

lead, led

- *Lead* (lēd) is the present tense of the verb meaning "to guide or direct." The past tense of the verb is *led* (lĕd). The adjective *lead* (lēd) means "first." The noun *lead* (lĕd) refers to a heavy metal or graphite.

lean, lien

- As a verb, *lean* means "to incline or bend." As an adjective, *lean* means "having little or no fat." A *lien* is a legal charge or hold on property.

learn, teach

- *Learn* means "to acquire knowledge"; *teach* means "to impart knowledge."

  Someone who learns from experience is often in a better position to teach than someone who learns from a book.

leave, let

- *Leave* means "to depart from" or "to let something remain behind." *Let* means "to permit or allow."

  Leave your work at the office. Don't let it ruin your weekend.

lend, borrow

- *Lend* means "to give or allow the use of temporarily"; *borrow* means "to obtain or receive for temporary use."

  At Thursday's meeting, Rob asked to borrow a copy of the new manual. Laura was happy to lend it.

less, fewer (See fewer.)

liable, libel, likely

- *Liable* means "responsible according to the law" or "exposed to an adverse action"; *libel* is a false or unfavorable written statement about someone; *likely* means "very probable" or "reliable."

  If you take the expressway, you will likely be late.

  Being entirely at fault, Graham was liable for the damages.

  Claiming the charges were untrue, Maria sued for libel.

like, as, as if

- In formal writing, use *as* or *as if* (conjunctions) to introduce clauses.

  Prepare the report as [not like] you were instructed.

  It looks as if [not like] we will need two more tickets.

  Use *like* (a preposition) to introduce a phrase.

  Your office looks like an oversized closet!

loose, loosen, lose, loss

- The adjective *loose* (lüs) means "unfastened or free." The verbs *loosen* and *loose* mean "to release." *Lose* (lüz) is a verb meaning "to misplace" or "to fail to keep control of." *Loss* (lòs) means "deprivation" or "the act of losing possession."

man, mankind

- Do not use the words *man* or *mankind* to mean "the human race" because the terms exclude women. Instead, use *humankind, humans,* or *humanity.* (Also see page 150.)

medal, metal

- *Medal* is a small metal award. *Metal* is a hard substance like silver or aluminum.

media, medium

- *Media* is the plural form of *medium*.

  The media are relentlessly exposing fraud.

  Radio has been an important news medium throughout the world.

miner, minor

- A *miner* is a person who digs for ore. As a noun, *minor* means "someone who is not yet legally an adult." As an adjective, *minor* means "of lesser importance or size."

  The miners were rescued from a shaft 300 feet underground.

  Try to solve minor problems before they become serious.

  A responsible minor has an excellent chance of becoming a responsible adult.

moral, morale

- *Moral* refers to what is right or wrong, or to the lesson a story or situation teaches. *Morale* is a person's attitude or mental condition.

  Human cloning raises a moral question.

  Office morale seems to peak on payday.

number, amount (See amount.)

OK, okay

- This expression (*OK* or *okay*) is used informally; however, avoid using it in formal correspondence of any kind.

oral, verbal

- *Oral* means "uttered with the mouth"; *verbal* means "relating to or consisting of words and the comprehension of words"; it can refer to something oral or written.

  Writing a clear, interesting report requires strong verbal skills.

  Delivering the report from the podium takes oral skill.

partly, partially

- *Partially* is an adverb meaning "to some extent, but not totally"; *partly* is an adverb meaning "in some, but not all parts."

passed, past

- *Passed* (the past tense of the verb "to pass") means "went by" or "gone by." *Past* can be used as a noun ("time gone by"), an adjective ("preceding"), or a preposition ("after" or "beyond").

  The company passed last year's sales in early December. (verb)

  Clinging to policies of the past can be a detriment to the future. (noun)

  For the past two weeks I've entered data into our new computer system. (adjective)

  It takes steel determination to walk past that pastry cart. (preposition)

percent, percentage

- *Percent* means a "part of a hundred" and is used with a specific number. *Percentage* refers to a portion of the whole and is not used with a specific number.

  Maria saves 20 percent of her paycheck each week. That percentage was recommended by her accountant.

personal, personnel

- *Personal* means "private" or "individual." *Personnel* are workers in a particular business or other organization.

     The Human Relations Department keeps a list of all the company's personnel. Some personal information, such as address, phone number, and social security number, is included in the list.

perspective, prospective

- *Perspective* is a person's mental vision or outlook on things; *prospective* is an adjective meaning "expected in or related to the future."

     From my perspective as a recent dorm dweller, your apartment is pure luxury.

     We interviewed five prospective copywriters today.

plain, plane

- As a noun, *plain* means "a large area of level land." As an adjective, it means "easily understood or seen" or "ordinary."

     "The rain in Spain stays mainly on the plain."
     —Alan Jay Lerner

     "There are no plain women on television."
     —Anna Ford

   As an adjective, *plane* means "flat, level, and even." As a noun, it means a "flat surface" or a "tool used to smooth the surface of wood"; it also can mean "airplane."

     The surface of the new desk was a plane; not even a marble would roll off.

     A plane must be sharpened frequently when used on hardwood.

pore, pour, poor

- As a noun, *pore* means "a minute opening"; as a verb, it means "to read intently." *Pour* is a verb meaning "to cause to flow in a stream." *Poor* means "lacking wealth" or "inferior."

     This new fabric is full of pores that let moisture escape.

     Pour yourself some more coffee.

     The poor morale was causing problems.

precede, proceed

- To *precede* means "to go or come before," while *proceed* means "to move on or go ahead."

     A memo that preceded today's meeting told us to proceed with stage two.

preventive, preventative

- These words are synonyms, but *preventive* is the preferred form, meaning "something that prevents or hinders a certain action or disease."

     Preventive measures were taken to avoid the takeover.

principal, principle

- As an adjective, *principal* means "primary or main." As a noun, it can mean "highest-ranking person" or "a sum of invested money." *Principle* is a noun meaning "a guiding doctrine" or "a scientific law."

     His principal gripe is boredom. (adjective)

     Most high school principals are concerned about much more than academics. (noun)

     The buyers made extra payments to more quickly lower the principal. (noun)

     The principle of *caveat emptor* is "let the buyer beware."

quiet, quit, quite

- As an adjective, *quiet* means "free from noise"; it can also be a noun or a verb. *Quit* is a verb meaning "to stop" or "to leave." *Quite* is an adjective meaning "completely" or "to a considerable extent; rather."

   My office is quiet and quite comfortable. I'll miss it when I quit.

quote, quotation

- In formal writing, *quote* should be used as a verb; *quotation* is always a noun.

   The quotation used in your report was very effective, but in your next report, you should also quote what your foreman said to you.

real, very, really

- *Real* is usually used as an adjective meaning "authentic." Do not use it in place of the adverbs *very* or *really*.

   "Real life seems to have no plot."
   —Dame Ivy Compton-Burnett

   Raul's forecasts turned out to be very [not real] accurate.

   The controller was not really in control of that situation.

reason . . . is because, reason why

- Don't use either of these phrases, because they are redundant. The words *because* and *why* both repeat the idea of cause unnecessarily. Instead, use *reason . . . that* or simply *because*.

   The reason I'm late is that I missed the train.

   I'm late because I missed the train.

respectfully, respectively

- *Respectfully* means "showing a high regard for"; *respectively* means "each in the order mentioned."

   The young man respectfully shared his views with his father.

   Awards were given to Mira, John, and Roland respectively.

right, write, wright, rite

- As an adjective, *right* means "righteous, correct, or appropriate"; as a noun, it means "that which is just or legal." *Write* means "to inscribe or compose." A *wright* is someone who builds or repairs something. *Rite* is a ceremonial act.

   Write the memo again, but this time use the right form.

   Get the wheelwright to repair the spokes.

   The initiation rites need to be reviewed.

scene, seen

- *Scene* is a noun that means "a view" or "a place where something happens," or "a spectacle." *Seen* is a form of the verb "see."

   Have you seen Hannah's office?   It looks like the scene of a disaster.

seam, seem

- *Seam* (noun) is a line formed by joining two pieces. *Seem* (verb) means "to give the impression of being."

   The stuffing was coming out of the seams on her chair.

   You seem to be capable of handling this yourself.

set, sit

● The verb *sit* means "to assume a seated position." The verb *set* means "to place or put down." *Set* is transitive (it must take a direct object); *sit* is intransitive (it does not take a direct object).

> **Jay set the package on the scale.**

> **Please sit over there while I do this.**

sight, cite, site

● As a noun, *sight* means "the ability to see" or "something seen"; as a verb, it means "to see something." *Cite* means "to quote," "to officially commend," or "to summon before a court." *Site* means "a place."

> **Before they reached the construction site, they were cited for speeding.**

> **Carolyn had a tendency to cite Dickens when observing the sights of London.**

sole, soul

● As an adjective, *sole* means "single, one and only"; as a noun, *sole* refers to the bottom surface of the foot or a shoe. *Soul* refers to the spiritual part of a person.

> **The sole reason for the success of this paper is that it prints the truth.**

> **Certain experiences nourish the soul.**

some, sum

● *Some* (adjective) refers to unspecified things or numbers. *Sum* means "the whole amount, the total."

> **Some reporters are at the door.**

> **The sum is too high for our budget.**

stationary, stationery

● *Stationary* is an adjective meaning "immobile"; *stationery* is a noun referring to writing materials used in letters.

subsequently (See consequently.)

tenant, tenet

● A *tenant* is one who rents or leases property from a landlord; a *tenet* is a principle, belief, or doctrine.

than, then

● *Than* (conjunction) indicates a comparison; *then* (usually an adverb) refers to time.

> **Michael did not know any more about this than I did.**

> **First write your résumé; then look for a job.**

their, there, they're

● *Their* is a possessive pronoun. As a pronoun, *there* is used to introduce a clause; as an adverb, it is used to indicate place. *They're* is the contraction for "they are."

> **They're planning to leave immediately after their presentation.**

> **"If there isn't a law, there will be."**
> > —Harold Farber

threw, through

● *Threw* (verb) is the past tense of "throw." *Through* (preposition) means "in one side and out the other"; *through* (adjective) means "extending from one place to another."

> **After Marcus threw the ball, he heard it crash through a window.**

to, too, two

- *To* (preposition) indicates direction; it is also used to form an infinitive. *Too* (adverb) means "also," "very," or "excessively." *Two* is the number 2.

  The two friends headed to the cafeteria to eat lunch, which smelled too good to pass up.

toward, towards

- These words are synonyms, but *toward* is the preferred form, meaning "in the direction of" or "in relation to."

  Please point me toward the fitness center.

uninterested, disinterested

- Both words mean "not interested"; *disinterested*, however, is also used to mean "unbiased or impartial."

  A judge is never uninterested in the facts of the case but must hand down a disinterested decision.

vain, vane, vein

- *Vain* (adjective) can mean "valueless" or "fruitless" or "conceited." *In vain* means "to no avail." *Vane* (noun) is an instrument that shows which way the wind blows. *Vein* (noun) refers to a blood vessel or an ore deposit.

  The weather vane twirled about during the spring storm.

  A rich silver vein was discovered beneath the town.

  We searched in vain for the disks.

vary, very

- *Vary* is a verb meaning "to change"; *very* is an adverb meaning "to a high degree."

  When you vary the speed like that, you take a very great risk.

waist, waste

- *Waist* is the part of the body between the rib cage and the hips. As a verb, *waste* means "to use carelessly" or "to cause to lose energy." As a noun, *waste* refers to either a worthless by-product or an act of wasting.

  "Waste neither time nor money, but make the best use of both."

  —Benjamin Franklin

  One's waist size is largely a function of diet and exercise.

wait, weight

- *Wait* (verb) means "to remain somewhere expecting something or someone." As a noun, *wait* refers to the act of waiting. *Weight* is a noun referring to a measure of heaviness.

ware, wear, where

- *Ware* is a noun that refers to manufactured goods. As a verb, *wear* means "to have on one's person"; as a noun, it means "clothing." *Where* refers to location; it can be an adverb, a conjunction, or a noun.

  Where do you plan to sell your wares?

  I never know what I should wear on casual Fridays.

waver, waiver

- *Waver* refers to faltering due to a lack of decision making; *waiver* is a conscious surrender of rights or privileges.

 When Ms. Stewart was asked to make a final decision, she wavered.

 Many ski resorts require skiers to sign a liability waiver.

way, weigh

- *Way* is a noun meaning "path or route"; avoid using it as an adverb meaning "to a great degree." *Weigh* means "to measure weight" or "to evaluate."

 After weighing the possibilities, Kenton decided to take the easy way out.

weather, whether

- *Weather* refers to the condition of the atmosphere. *Whether* refers to a possibility.

 "Everybody talks about the weather, but nobody does anything about it."
 —Mark Twain

 Tell me whether you agree or not.

who, which, that

- *Who* always refers to people. *Which* refers to non-living objects or animals, never to people. *That* may refer to people, animals, or nonliving objects. In formal writing, use *that* to introduce restrictive (necessary) clauses and *which* to introduce nonrestrictive (unnecessary) clauses. (See page 192.)

 The Altina Fitness Center, which was built last year, is filled to capacity after work.

 The exercise and yoga classes that are offered there are especially popular.

who, whom

- *Who* is used as the subject of a clause; *whom* is used as the object of a verb (direct object) or of a preposition.

 To whom should I give this Internet proposal? Give it to Ms. Brown, who is in charge of information technology services.

who's, whose

- *Who's* is the contraction of "who is" or "who has." *Whose* is a possessive pronoun.

 Who's in charge of cleanup?

 "Whose life is it anyway?"
 —Brian Clark

wood, would

- *Wood* is a noun or an adjective referring to the material trees are made of; *would* is a form of the verb "will."

 I would not buy that wood to make the filing cabinets.

your, you're

- *Your* is a possessive pronoun showing ownership. *You're* is the contraction of "you are."

 "Your job is only as big as you are."
 —George C. Hubbs

 "You're never wrong to do the right thing."
 —Malcom Forbes

Understanding Grammar

To understand and use grammar correctly, you need to understand the eight parts of speech and the role each plays in a sentence. Knowing this can help you boost your writing skills.

NOUN

A **noun** is a word that names something.

People: Tony Blair, politician

Places: South Africa, nation

Things: *Working Woman*, magazine

Ideas: business ethics, value system

Classes of Nouns

Nouns are divided into five classes: *proper, common, concrete, abstract,* and *collective.*

Proper Noun

● A **proper noun** names a specific person, place, thing, or idea and is always capitalized.

Bill Gates	Ivory Coast
Sears Tower	World Federalism

Common Noun

● A **common noun** is a general name for a person, a place, a thing, or an idea and is lowercased.

entrepreneur	stock exchange
skyscraper	ideology

Concrete Noun

● A **concrete noun** names something tangible. It can be seen, touched, heard, smelled, or tasted.

odor	desk	piano
Yosemite	Lake Erie	Alabama

Abstract Noun

● An **abstract noun** names something that cannot be seen, touched, heard, smelled, or tasted. It is usually an idea, a condition, or a feeling.

War on Poverty	democracy	Buddhism
freedom	success	happiness

Collective Noun

● A **collective noun** names a group or a unit. Collective nouns can be used in either the singular or the plural form. (See page 242.)

herd	Green Bay Packers	committee
staff	Human Resources Department	

Forms of Nouns

Nouns are grouped according to their *gender, case,* and *number.*

Gender of Noun

Gender of a noun indicates whether a noun is masculine, feminine, neuter, or indefinite. (Also see page 150.)

Masculine: father, nephew, buck, drake

Feminine: sister, niece, doe, hen

Neuter (without sex): rock, keyboard, lake

Indefinite (masculine or feminine): mayor, firefighter, deer

A Closer Look

The eight parts of speech are *noun, pronoun, verb, adjective, adverb, preposition, conjunction,* and *interjection.* See page 254.

Case of a Noun

Case tells how a noun functions in a sentence. Three cases of nouns are *nominative, possessive,* and *objective.*

- **Nominative case** describes a noun used as the subject of a clause.

  Bill Gates heads a multibillion-dollar software company that he founded.

  Nominative case also describes a noun when it is used as a *predicate noun* (or predicate nominative). A predicate noun follows a form of the *be* verb (for example, *is, are, was, were, been*) and repeats or renames the subject.

  Business handbooks are useful tools for every office.

- **Possessive case** describes a noun that shows possession or ownership.

  An employee's desk is a construction site.

  Note: Be sure to follow the rules of punctuation when it comes to possessives, especially the placement of apostrophes in plural words or words expressing joint ownership. (See pages 202-203.)

- **Objective case** describes a noun used as a direct object, an indirect object, or an object of a preposition.

  The delete key can give writers nightmares. (*Nightmares* is the direct object of *can give*; *writers* is the indirect object.)

  But writing without a delete key is also scary. (*Delete key* is the object of the preposition, *without.*)

Number of a Noun

Number indicates whether a noun is singular or plural. (See pages 261 and 263.)

- A **singular noun** refers to one person, place, thing, or idea.

  supervisor   warehouse   monitor

- A **plural noun** refers to more than one person, place, thing, or idea.

  secretaries   closets   calculators

A Closer Look

When it comes to their number, some nouns are not what they appear to be. For example, *earnings* refers to a single thing, but it is actually a plural noun.

Our third-quarter earnings were better than expected.

Singular nouns that appear to be plural:
economics, news, mathematics, mumps, measles, lens, summons

Plural nouns that refer to a single thing:
assets, earnings, media, premises, proceeds, quarters, scissors, trousers, goods, grounds, thanks, dues

Nouns that can be **singular or plural** (depending upon how they are used):
corps, headquarters, gross, means, ethics, data, species, series, class, group, staff, company, committee, board, public

PRONOUN

A **pronoun** is a word used to emphasize or replace a noun.

I	you	she	it
that	myself	someone	who

Almost all pronouns have **antecedents**. An antecedent is the noun that the pronoun refers to or replaces.

> **The workers acted as though they had forgotten the proper procedure.**
> (*Workers* is the antecedent of *they*.)

Note: Each pronoun must agree with its antecedent in number (singular or plural), in person (first, second, or third), and in gender (masculine, feminine, or neuter). (See page 245.)

Classes of Pronouns

All pronouns fall into one of seven classes: *personal, relative, interrogative, demonstrative, indefinite, reflexive,* and *intensive*.

Personal Pronoun

- A **personal pronoun** (*I, you, he, she, it*) takes the place of a noun.

> **Rita Worth is a CEO; she likes to go fishing on her days off.**

Relative Pronoun

- A **relative pronoun** (*who, whose, whom, which, that*) introduces a clause related to another word in the sentence.

> **The person who leaves last should lock the office door.** (The clause beginning with *who* describes *person*.)

Interrogative Pronoun

- An **interrogative pronoun** (*who, whose, whom, which, what*) introduces a question.

> **Who will write the report?**

Demonstrative Pronoun

- A **demonstrative pronoun** (*this, that, these, those*) points out something.

> **This is great! These are our best year-end numbers ever.**

Indefinite Pronoun

- An **indefinite pronoun** (*all, another, any, anyone, anything, both, each, either, everyone, few, many, most, neither, none, no one, one, several, some*) refers to an unspecified person, thing, or group.

> **All are invited to the seminar.**

Reflexive Pronoun

- A **reflexive pronoun** (*myself, yourself, himself*) refers to the subject or the doer of the action.

> **Letta drives herself too hard.**

Intensive Pronoun

- An **intensive pronoun** is a reflexive pronoun (*myself, yourself, himself*) that is used only to emphasize the noun or pronoun it refers to.

> **The club members themselves voted yes on this proposition.**

A Closer Look

See the chart on page 244 for a list of pronouns categorized to help you make better use of them in your writing.

CLASSES OF PRONOUNS

Personal

I, me, my, mine, we, us, our, ours, you, your, yours, they, them, their, theirs
he, him, his, she, her, hers, it, its

Relative

who, whose, whom, which, what, that, whoever, whatever, whomever

Interrogative

who, whose, whom, which, what, whoever, whatever, whomever

Demonstrative

this, that, these, those

Indefinite

all	anyone	each one	everything	much	no one	several	something
another	anything	either	few	neither	nothing	some	such
any	both	everybody	many	nobody	one	somebody	
anybody	each	everyone	most	none	other	someone	

Reflexive and Intensive

myself, himself, herself, itself, yourself, themselves, ourselves, yourselves

FORMS OF PRONOUNS

	Forms of Singular Pronouns			Forms of Plural Pronouns		
	Subjective Pronouns	Possessive Pronouns	Objective Pronouns	Subjective Pronouns	Possessive Pronouns	Objective Pronouns
First Person	I	my, mine	me	we	our, ours	us
Second Person	you	your, yours	you	you	your, yours	you
Third Person	he	his	him	they	their, theirs	them
	she	her, hers	her			
	it	its	it			

Forms of Personal Pronouns

The form of a personal pronoun indicates its *number* (singular or plural), its *person* (first, second, or third), its *case* (nominative, possessive, or objective), and its *gender* (masculine, feminine, or neuter).

Number of a Pronoun

- The **number** of a pronoun can be either singular or plural. Singular personal pronouns include *I, you, he, she, it.* Plural personal pronouns include *we, you, they.* Notice that the pronoun *you* can be singular or plural.

    Have you (singular) **completed the tax forms?**

    Looking at the applicants, he said, "I will contact each of you (plural) **within a week."**

Person of a Pronoun

- The **person** of a pronoun indicates whether that pronoun is speaking, is spoken to, or is spoken about. (See page 244.)

	Singular	Plural
First Person	**I** (am)	**we** (are)
Second Person	**you** (are)	**you** (are)
Third Person	**he / she / it** (is)	**they** (are)

A Closer Look

A pronoun must agree with its antecedent in both *number* and *person*. (See page 263.)

> **Nicole greeted the committee with her** (not *their* or *its*) **distinctive smile.** (*Their* does not agree in number; *its* does not agree in person.

Case of a Pronoun

The **case** of a pronoun indicates how it is used in a sentence. There are three cases of personal pronouns: *nominative* (or *subjective*), *objective*, and *possessive.*

- **Nominative case** pronouns are used in two ways—as subjects and as subject complements (following the linking verbs *am, is, are, was, were, be, being, been*).

    I appreciate a pat on the back when I deserve it. (subjects)

    It was Adam's idea, so the real hero is he. (subject complement)

- **Objective case** pronouns are used in three ways—as direct objects, indirect objects, and objects of prepositions.

    Alex saw it. (direct object)

    Max handed her two cups. (indirect object)

    The manager talked with him. (object of a preposition)

Note: Do not use objective pronouns as subjects.

> *Incorrect:* **Maria and me arrived early.**
>
> *Correct:* **Maria and I arrived early.**

- **Possessive case** pronouns are used in one way—to show possession or ownership.

    Their parents have been business partners for years.

Gender of a Pronoun

- The gender of a pronoun can be masculine, feminine, or neuter.

    He told her about it.

VERB

A **verb** expresses either action (*run, flipped, twisted*) or state of being (*is, are, seemed*).

The different forms of a verb indicate its *number* (singular or plural); *person* (first, second, or third); *voice* (active or passive); and *tense* (present, past, future, present perfect, past perfect, or future perfect).

Number and Person of a Verb

Number indicates whether a verb is singular or plural. **Person** indicates whether the verb is correctly used with a first-, second-, or third-person subject.

	Singular	**Plural**
First Person	(I) **am**.	(We) **are**.
Second Person	(You) **are**.	(You) **are**.
Third Person	(She) **is**.	(They) **are**.

Voice of a Verb

Voice of a verb indicates whether the subject acts or is acted upon.

Active Voice

● **Active voice** means that the subject acts or does something.

The partners talked all afternoon.

Passive Voice

● **Passive voice** means that the subject is acted upon. (Passive verbs always begin with a form of "be"— *am, are, is, was, were, be, being, been,* etc.)

Many topics were discussed.

Tense of a Verb

The **tense** of a verb indicates when the action is taking place or when the condition exists.

Present Tense

● **Present tense** indicates action that is happening at the present time or that happens continually.

More people work in the service industry than in any other industry.

Past Tense

● **Past tense** indicates action that was completed in the past.

In the early twentieth century, heavy industry employed most of the workforce.

Note: Usually the past tense of a verb is formed by adding *ed*; however, many irregular verbs do not follow this pattern. (See page 248.)

Future Tense

● **Future tense** indicates action that will take place in the future.

Many workers wonder how social security will handle baby-boomer retirees.

> **FYI** In most cases, using active voice instead of passive voice will make your writing more direct, lively, and engaging. Reserve passive voice for special types of writing. (See pages 58 and 154.)

Present Perfect Tense

- **Present perfect tense** indicates action that began in the past but continues in the present or is completed in the present.

  Lately, airlines have struggled with rising costs and fewer customers.

Past Perfect Tense

- **Past perfect tense** indicates a past action that began and was completed in the past.

  The investors had expected to see returns.

Future Perfect Tense

- **Future perfect tense** indicates action that will begin in and be completed by a specific time in the future.

  By the end of December, the company will have been sold.

Classes of Verbs

Verbs can be divided into these classes: *auxiliary* (or helping), *linking*, *transitive*, and *intransitive*.

Auxiliary Verbs

- **Auxiliary verbs** *(am, is, are, was, were)* help to form some of the tenses and the voice of the main verb.

Forming tense:

  I enjoy skiing. (present tense verb)

  I will enjoy skiing. (future tense verb formed by adding the auxiliary verb *will*)

Forming voice:

  The gang devoured your salad! (active voice verb)

  Your salad was devoured in no time! (passive voice verb formed by adding the auxiliary verb *was*)

Tense	ACTIVE VOICE		PASSIVE VOICE	
	Singular	**Plural**	**Singular**	**Plural**
Present	I see you see he/she/it sees	we see you see they see	I am seen you are seen he/she/it is seen	we are seen you are seen they are seen
Past	I saw you saw he saw	we saw you saw they saw	I was seen you were seen it was seen	we were seen you were seen they were seen
Future	I will see you will see he will see	we will see you will see they will see	I will be seen you will be seen it will be seen	we will be seen you will be seen they will be seen
Present Perfect	I have seen you have seen he has seen	we have seen you have seen they have seen	I have been seen you have been seen it has been seen	we have been seen you have been seen they have been seen
Past Perfect	I had seen you had seen he had seen	we had seen you had seen they had seen	I had been seen you had been seen it had been seen	we had been seen you had been seen they had been seen
Future Perfect	I will have seen you will have seen he will have seen	we will have seen you will have seen they will have seen	I will have been seen you will have been seen it will have been seen	we will have been seen you will have been seen they will have been seen

that it cannot be done wrong. * * * * * * * * * * * * * * * * *

COMMON IRREGULAR VERBS

Present Tense	Past Tense	Past Participle	Present Tense	Past Tense	Past Participle
am, be	was, were	been	know	knew	known
arise	arose	arisen	lay (put)	laid	laid
bear	bore	borne	lead	led	led
begin	began	begun	lend	lent	lent
bind	bound	bound	lie (deceive)	lied	lied
bite	bit	bitten, bit	lie (recline)	lay	lain
blow	blew	blown	light	lit, lighted	lit, lighted
break	broke	broken	mistake	mistook	mistaken
bring	brought	brought	prove	proved	proved, proven
build	built	built	ride	rode	ridden
burst	burst	burst	ring	rang	rung
catch	caught	caught	rise (get up)	rose	risen
choose	chose	chosen	run	ran	run
cling	clung	clung	see	saw	seen
come	came	come	seek	sought	sought
deal	dealt	dealt	set (place)	set	set
dive	dived, dove	dived	shake	shook	shaken
do	did	done	shine (emit light)	shone	shone
draw	drew	drawn	show	showed	shown
dream	dreamed	dreamed	shrink	shrank	shrunk
	dreamt	dreamt	sing	sang	sung
drink	drank	drunk	sink	sank	sunk
drive	drove	driven	sit	sat	sat
eat	ate	eaten	slay	slew	slain
fall	fell	fallen	speak	spoke	spoken
feed	fed	fed	spring	sprang	sprung
fight	fought	fought	steal	stole	stolen
find	found	found	strike	struck	struck, stricken
flee	fled	fled	swear	swore	sworn
fly	flew	flown	swim	swam	swum
forbid	forbade	forbidden	swing	swung	swung
forgive	forgave	forgiven	take	took	taken
freeze	froze	frozen	tear	tore	torn
give	gave	given	throw	threw	thrown
go	went	gone	wake	woke, waked	woken, waked
grow	grew	grown	wear	wore	worn
hang (execute)	hanged	hanged	weave	wove	woven
hang (suspend)	hung	hung	wring	wrung	wrung
hide	hid	hidden	write	wrote	written

Linking Verbs

- A **linking verb** is a special type of intransitive verb that links a subject to its complement—a noun, a pronoun, or an adjective in the predicate of a sentence.

  Poorly organized reports are not very helpful. (The subject *reports* is linked to the predicate adjective *helpful*.)

  Incorrect: **This is her.** (A linking verb cannot connect the objective pronoun *her* to the subjective pronoun *this*.)

  Correct: **This is she.** (A linking verb can connect the subjective pronoun *she* to the subjective pronoun *this*.)

  COMMON LINKING VERBS: am, is, are, was, were, be, being, been, smell, look, seem, grow, become, appear, sound, taste, feel, remain

Transitive Verbs

- A **transitive verb** indicates action transferred to an object(or, in the passive voice, the subject). In the active voice, a transitive verb transfers its action to a direct object.

  Many people enjoy their jobs. (*Jobs* is the direct object of the verb *enjoy*.)

  A transitive verb may also have an indirect object, which receives the action indirectly.

  Samantha gave Matthew a reassuring glance. (*Glance* is the direct object of the verb *gave*, and *Matthew* is the indirect object.)

  In the passive voice, a transitive verb transfers the action to the subject of the sentence.

  An attempt to fix the copier was made by the receptionist. (The subject *attempt* receives the action of the verb *was made*.)

Intransitive Verbs

- An **intransitive verb** indicates action that is not transferred to anyone or anything. This verb does not need a direct object.

  The worst public speakers mumble and dawdle.

Special Verb Forms

A **verbal** is derived from a verb but functions as a noun, an adjective, or an adverb. There are three types of verbals: *gerunds, infinitives,* and *participles*. (See page 257 for information on verbal phrases.)

Gerunds

- A **gerund** ends in *ing* and is used as a noun.

  Arriving at work on time is important. (subject)

  Another key to success is accomplishing your tasks. (predicate noun)

Infinitives

- An **infinitive** is usually introduced by the word "to" and can be used as a noun, an adjective, or an adverb.

  To write well is not always easy. (noun)

  This is an important point to remember. (adjective)

  Writers are wise to practice their writing often. (adverb)

Participles

- A **participle** ends in *ing* or *ed* and is used as an adjective.

  That employee making clay models is very creative. The completed models will be on display in the coming weeks. (*making* modifies *employee*; *completed* modifies *models*.)

ADJECTIVE

An **adjective** is a word that describes, limits, or in any other way modifies a noun or a pronoun. (The articles *a, an,* and *the* are adjectives.)

Adjectives can appear in different positions. They often come before the words they modify; but as predicate adjectives, they come after the words they modify.

> **The beautiful day ended with Marcia in tears. She was overjoyed.** (*The* and *beautiful* modify the noun *day; overjoyed* is a predicate adjective and modifies the pronoun *she.*)

Common and Proper Adjectives

- Like nouns, adjectives can be **common** (lower-cased) or **proper** (capitalized).

> **The professors at Oxford University agreed that Americanized English was unusual.**

Note: Since *Americanized* is derived from the proper noun *America,* it is considered a proper adjective and is always capitalized. *The* and *unusual* are common adjectives; *the* is capitalized only because it is the first word of the sentence.

A Closer Look

Don't add adjectives to nouns that don't need them. The adjectives listed below are unnecessary and only repeat what the noun already says.

> **basic necessities, end result, exact replica, final outcome, foreign imports, free gift, joint cooperation, mutual cooperations, past history, sum total**

Forms of Adjectives

Adjectives have three forms: *positive, comparative,* and *superlative.*

Positive

- The **positive form** describes without making any comparisons.

> **Good employees are important assets.**

Comparative

- The **comparative form** (*-er, more,* or *less*) compares two persons, places, things, or ideas.

> **Good employees are a more important asset than good buildings.**

Superlative

- The **superlative form** (*-est, most,* or *least*) compares three or more persons, places, things, or ideas.

> **Good employees are the most important asset a business can possess.**

Note: Most one-syllable and some two-syllable adjectives take the *er* and *est* endings. Most two-syllable and most three-syllable adjectives use *more* and *most* (and *less* and *least*).

Positive	Comparative	Superlative
good	better	best
bad	worse	worst
cold	colder	coldest
crabby	crabbier	crabbiest
impressive	more impressive	most impressive

ADVERB

An **adverb** is a word that modifies a verb (or verbal), an adjective, or another adverb. Adverbs tell *how, when, where, why, how often,* or *how much.* (*Not* and *never* are adverbs.)

> **The business was sold quickly.** (*Quickly* modifies the verb *was sold.*)
>
> **The staff was extremely concerned.** (*Extremely* modifies the adjective *concerned.*)
>
> **Management moved very quickly to reassign employees.** (*Very* modifies the adverb *quickly,* which modifies the verb *moved.*)

Note: Most adverbs have an *ly* ending. Some adverbs can be written either with an *ly* or without; when in doubt, use the *ly* form.

> **deep, deeply; tight, tightly; loud, loudly**

A Closer Look

Adverbs can be placed in different positions in a sentence. Usually, they appear in front of the words they modify, but they can correctly follow the words as well. *Caution:* Adverbs should not be placed between a verb and its direct object.

> **The secretary carefully prepared the report.** (adverb before the verb)
>
> **The secretary prepared the report carefully.** (adverb after the verb and its direct object)
>
> **If the problem isn't addressed, these customers will definitely leave.** (adverb between verbs)

Forms of Adverbs

Adverbs have three forms: *positive, comparative,* and *superlative.*

Positive

- The **positive form** describes an action without making any comparisons.

> **This copier operates efficiently.**

Comparative

- The **comparative form** (*-er, more,* or *less*) compares the actions of two persons, places, things, or ideas.

> **This copier operates more efficiently than the one downstairs.**

Superlative

- The **superlative form** (*-est, most,* or *least*) compares the actions of three or more persons, places, things, or ideas.

> **This copier operates most efficiently of all the copiers in the building.**

Special Adverb Form

Conjunctive Adverbs

- A **conjunctive adverb** can both modify and connect words, phrases, and clauses. It can be used at the beginning, in the middle, or at the end of a sentence.

> **Consequently, we believe the profit/earnings ratio will not meet our expectations. We do wish, however, to evaluate your stock again in six months. We will buy another stock instead.**

PREPOSITION

A **preposition** is a word (or word group) used in front of a noun or a pronoun to form a phrase that modifies some other word in the sentence.

The paperwork has been piled onto the file cabinet. (The preposition *onto* begins a phrase that acts as an adverb modifying the verb *has been piled*.)

Prepositional Phrase

● A **prepositional phrase** consists of a preposition, the object of that preposition, and the modifiers of the object.

The flowers on the luncheon table are wilted. (preposition *on*, object *table*, and modifiers *the* and *luncheon*)

COMMON PREPOSITIONS

aboard	back of	excepting	notwithstanding	since
about	because of	for	of	subsequent to
above	before	from	off	together with
according to	behind	from among	on	through
across	below	from between	on account of	throughout
across from	beneath	from under	on behalf of	till
after	beside	in	onto	to
against	besides	in addition to	on top of	toward
ahead of	between	in back of	opposite	under
along	beyond	in behalf of	out	underneath
alongside	by	in case of	out of	unlike
alongside of	by means of	in front of	outside	until
along with	concerning	in place of	outside of	unto
amid	considering	in regard to	over	up
among	contrary to	inside	over to	upon
apart from	despite	inside of	owing to	up to
around	down	in spite of	past	via
as	down from	instead of	prior to	with
as for	due to	into	regarding	within
aside from	during	like	round	without
at	except	near	round about	
away from	except for	near to	save	

CONJUNCTION

A **conjunction** is the part of speech used to connect words, phrases, clauses, or sentences. Used properly, conjunctions can add continuity to your writing.

Kinds of Conjunctions

Subordinating Conjunctions

- **Subordinating conjunctions** connect a dependent clause to an independent clause, completing the meaning of the dependent clause.

  If the trailer is still here tomorrow, it will be impounded. (The dependent clause *If the trailer is still here tomorrow* depends on the rest of the sentence to complete its meaning.)

Correlative Conjunctions

- **Correlative conjunctions** are always used in pairs, linking items of equal weight.

  She decided to neither buy nor lease a new car.

Coordinating Conjunctions

- **Coordinating conjunctions** connect grammatically equivalent elements, that is, a word to a word, a phrase to a phrase, or a clause to a clause.

  "It's not the most intellectual job in the world, but I do have to know the letters."
  —Vanna White

INTERJECTION

- An **interjection** is a word or phrase that expresses strong emotion or surprise. Punctuation (usually a comma or an exclamation point) sets off an interjection from the rest of the sentence.

  Help! The elevator is stuck!
  Oh my, that happens often.

Caution: Use strong interjections sparingly. Like shouting, they can diminish the dignity of your writing.

KINDS OF CONJUNCTIONS

Coordinating

and, but, or, nor, for, yet, so

Correlative

either, or; neither, nor; not only, but (also); both, and; whether, or; though, yet

Subordinating

after	as long as	before	provided that	that	unless	where
although	as though	if	since	though	until	whereas
as	because	in order that	so that	till	when	while

Parts of Speech

1. A **noun** is a word that names something: a person, a place, a thing, or an idea.

Tony Blair/prime minister	South Africa/country
Working Woman/magazine	World Federalism/ideology

2. A **pronoun** is a word used in place of a noun.

I	you	she	it	which	themselves
me	that	he	they	whoever	whatever
my	mine	ours			

3. A **verb** is a word that expresses action or state of being.

fight	walk	drive	rip	dive	jump
play	write	lift	type	call	work
is	are	was	were		

4. An **adjective** describes or modifies a noun or pronoun. (The articles *a*, *an*, and *the* are adjectives.)

good	bad	tall	wide	clear	fast

5. An **adverb** modifies a verb, an adjective, or another adverb. An adverb tells how, when, where, why, how often, or how much. (*Not* and *never* are adverbs.)

tomorrow	near	far	perfectly	well	completely
surely	regularly	greatly	partly	slowly	quickly

6. A **preposition** is a word (or group of words) used in front of a noun or a pronoun to form a phrase that modifies some other word in the sentence.

above	across	after	with	by	for
from	in	of	off	on	out
over	through	to	until	up	away from

7. A **conjunction** connects individual words or groups of words.

and	but	or	nor	for	yet
so	because	when	though	whereas	while

8. An **interjection** expresses strong emotion or surprise.

Help!	Yikes!	Wow!

Constructing Sentences

THE SENTENCE

A **sentence** is one or more words that express a complete thought.

> **"Chop your wood, and it will warm you twice."**
>
> —Henry Ford, Sr.

Subject and Predicate

- A sentence must have a subject and a predicate. The **subject** tells who or what the sentence is about. The **predicate**, which contains the verb, tells or asks something about the subject.

> **"The Edsel is here to stay."**
>
> —Henry Ford II

Note: In the sentence above, *Edsel* is the subject— the sentence talks about the Edsel. *Is here to stay* is the predicate—it says something about the subject.

Understood Subject and Predicate

- Either the subject or the predicate or both may be "absent" from a sentence; however, both must be clearly understood.

> **"What seems to be wrong?"**
> (*What* is the subject; *seems to be wrong* is the predicate.)
>
> **"Everything."**
> (*Everything* is the subject; the predicate *is wrong* is understood.)
>
> **"Be more specific."**
> (The subject *you* is understood; *be more specific* is the predicate.)

THE SUBJECT

The **subject** is a word, phrase, or clause that tells *who* or *what* the sentence is about. It can be a noun, a pronoun, an infinitive, an infinitive phrase, a gerund, a gerund phrase, or a noun clause.

> **Technology has changed the way business is done.** (noun)
>
> **I can get that for you wholesale.** (pronoun)
>
> **To cut costs has been her primary goal.** (infinitive phrase)
>
> **Finding that document will be difficult.** (gerund phrase)
>
> **When your samples arrive is when you should begin your calls.** (noun clause)

Simple Subject

- A **simple subject** is the subject without the words that modify it.

> **"The greatest test of courage on earth is to bear defeat without losing courage."**
> —Robert G. Intersoll

Complete Subject

- A **complete subject** is the simple subject and all the words that modify it.

> **"The greatest test of courage on earth is to bear defeat without losing courage."**
> —Robert G. Intersoll

Compound Subject

- A **compound subject** has two or more subjects.

> **Decisiveness and determination are key ingredients to any successful venture.**

THE PREDICATE

A **predicate** is the sentence part that tells or asks something about the subject; it always contains a verb.

> **"Good management consists in showing average people how to do the work of superior people."**
> —John D. Rockefeller, Sr.

Simple Predicate

- A **simple predicate** is the verb without the words that modify it.

> **"Those who give too much attention to trifling things become generally incapable of great ones."**
> —Francois, Duke of Rochefoucauld

Complete Predicate

- A **complete predicate** is the simple predicate (the verb) and all the words that modify it.

> **"Those who give too much attention to trifling things become generally incapable of great ones."**
> —Francois, Duke of Rochefoucauld

Compound Predicate

- A **compound predicate** consists of two or more simple predicates.

> **Jackie added the figures in both columns and came up with an astonishing total.**

Direct Object

- A **direct object** receives the action of the verb. It's a noun or a noun substitute that answers *what?* or *whom?* after a verb. (See page 242.)

> **Please prepare the income statements.**

USING PHRASES

A **phrase** is a group of related words that lacks a subject, a predicate, or both. It functions as a single part of speech but does not express a complete thought.

> **will be running** (verb phrase; no subject)
> **in the race** (prepositional phrase; no subject or predicate)
> **Marie will be running in the race.** (These two phrases plus a subject make a sentence.)

Types of Phrases

There are six types of phrases: *noun, appositive, verb, prepositional, absolute,* and *verbal.*

Noun Phrase

- A **noun phrase** includes a noun or pronoun plus all related modifiers. It can function as a subject, an object, a complement, or an appositive.

Appositive Phrase

- An **appositive phrase** follows a noun or a pronoun and identifies or explains it; it includes a noun and its modifiers.

> **Denzel, the director of our art department, has been with the company for ten years.**

Verb Phrase

- A **verb phrase** includes a main verb and the preceding helping verb or verbs.

> **Money orders are being issued at the bank and the post office.**

Prepositional Phrase

- A **prepositional phrase** includes a preposition, its object, and any modifiers of the object. It functions as an adjective or an adverb.

    Worthwhile projects are only accomplished with hard work.
    (The prepositional phrase is used as an adverb modifying the verb *are accomplished*.)

    Luck is not a main ingredient in the recipe for success.
    (The prepositional phrase *in the recipe* is used as an adjective modifying the noun *ingredient;* the phrase *for success* is used as an adjective modifying the noun *recipe*.)

Absolute Phrase

- An **absolute phrase** includes a noun or a pronoun and a participle, as well as any modifiers (including any object of the participle).

    His voice rising above the noise, the manager encouraged his team.

    (*Voice* is the noun; *rising* is a present participle modifying voice. The entire absolute phrase modifies *manager*.)

Verbal Phrases: Gerund, Infinitive, Participial

- A **gerund phrase** is a verbal phrase that includes a gerund and its modifiers. It functions as a noun.

    Making rubber tires was once a hot, exhausting job. (The gerund phrase acts as the subject.)

    Workers grew weary of sweating through their shifts. (The gerund phrase is the object of the preposition *of*.)

- An **infinitive phrase** includes an infinitive and its modifiers. It functions as a noun, an adjective, or an adverb.

    To walk outside was a welcomed break.
    (Acting as a noun, this infinitive phrase is the subject of the sentence.)

    After the holiday rush, we wanted some time to relax. (Acting as an adjective, this phrase modifies the noun *time*.)

    He rubbed a rough hand through his bristly white hair to jog his memory. (Acting as an adverb, this phrase modifies *rubbed*.)

- A **participial phrase** includes a past or a present participle and its modifiers. It functions as an adjective.

    Recalling the name of his favorite mystery writer, the man smiled. (The participial phrase modifies *man*.)

    This laborer, retired recently, takes refuge in books. (The phrase modifies *laborer*.)

A Closer Look

Be careful to place participial phrases next to the nouns or pronouns they modify so that you don't create a dangling or misplaced modifier. (See page 265.)

Panicked by the turbulence, I reminded my seatmate to breathe deeply. (This misplaced modifier is confusing: Am *I* panicked, or is *my seatmate*?)

Panicked by the turbulence, my seatmate needed to be reminded to breathe deeply. (Clear)

USING CLAUSES

Independent Clause

- An **independent clause** has both a subject and a predicate and expresses a complete thought; it can stand alone as a sentence.

  An answering machine can record messages, but voice mail can do so much more.

  Note: The above sentence has two clauses; each independent clause can stand alone as a sentence.

Dependent Clause

- A **dependent clause** cannot stand alone. It can, however, add important detail to a sentence.

  When there's no one available to take calls, your voice-mail system can take a message.

Adverb Clause

- An **adverb clause** answers *how? where? when? why? how much?* or *under what condition?* Adverb clauses begin with a subordinating conjunction. (See 253.)

  When your sales staff is on the road, voice mail enables you to leave timely messages.

Adjective Clause

- An **adjective clause** is used to modify a noun or a pronoun by answering the questions *what kind?* or *which one?*

  The person who invented the telephone would marvel at communications today.

Noun Clause

- A **noun clause** functions as a noun and can be used as a subject, an object, or a complement.

  What made voice mail work was combining the telephone and the computer.

USING SENTENCE VARIETY

Kinds of Sentences

As a writer, it makes sense to use sentences of varying kinds, including *declarative, interrogative, imperative, exclamatory,* and *conditional* sentences.

Declarative

- **Declarative sentences** simply state information about a person, a place, a thing, or an idea.

  "Consumers are the most merciless, meanest, toughest market disciplinarians I know."
  —Edwin S. Bingham

Interrogative

- **Interrogative sentences** ask questions.

  Why do some people flit from one job to another, while others stay for decades?

Imperative

- **Imperative sentences** give commands or make requests. Often the subject (*you*) is understood.

  Never rely on your memory—or a computer's.

Exclamatory

- **Exclamatory sentences** express strong emotion.

  Always have a backup plan! Always!

Conditional

- **Conditional sentences** state wishes ("if . . . then" statements) or conditions contrary to fact.

  "If Patrick Henry thought that taxation without representation was bad, he should see how bad it is with representation."
  —*Old Farmer's Almanac*

* * * * * * * * * * Don't talk about yourself; it will be done

TYPES OF SENTENCES

The structure of a sentence is *simple, compound, complex,* or *compound-complex.* This depends on the relationship between the independent and dependent clauses in it.

Simple

● A **simple sentence** has only one clause, which is independent; thus, it has only one subject and one predicate. The subject and/or predicate may be single or compound.

> **My dogs bark.**
> (single subject; single predicate)
> **My dogs and my cat fraternize.**
> (compound subject; single predicate)
> **Their barking and yowling can startle and annoy.**
> (compound subject; compound predicate)

Compound

● A **compound sentence** has two or more independent clauses without any dependent clauses. The clauses are most often joined by a coordinating conjunction (*and, or, so, but*), by punctuation, or by both.

> **The dogs get weekly baths, so what is that smell?**
> **It can't be the cat; Missy is a fastidious self-groomer.**

Note: Correlative conjunctions are also used to join the clauses in a compound sentence. (See page 253).

> **Either the dogs got into the garbage or Missy's been mouse hunting.**

In addition, semicolons and conjunctive adverbs can be used in compound sentences.

> **Cats and dogs can be "friends"; still, there are certain limitations.**

Complex

● A **complex sentence** has only one independent clause (in red) and one or more dependent clauses (in italics). Dependent clauses usually begin with relative pronouns or subordinating conjunctions. (See pages 243 and 253.)

> **When the weather is nice, I walk the dogs for several miles.**
> (one dependent clause; one independent clause)
> **When we get to the parkway, and if there are only a few people around, Felix and Hairy can run free.**
> (two dependent clauses; one independent clause)

Compound-Complex

● A **compound-complex sentence** has two or more independent clauses (in red) and one or more dependent clauses (in italics).

> **If I'm feeling spunky, I run , too, but I can never keep up with the dogs.**
> (one dependent clause; two independent clauses)

A Closer Look

In general, varying sentence structure will enhance your writing style, making it more interesting and engaging. Remember, though, that clarity is still the single most important quality of good writing.

ARRANGEMENT OF A SENTENCE

By arranging words in a particular way, the writer creates a point of emphasis. These arrangements may be classified as *loose, cumulative, periodic,* or *balanced.*

Loose

● In a **loose sentence**, the point of emphasis comes at the beginning. Explanatory material is added as needed.

The press release is a vital tool often used to increase public visibility, to create a positive image, and to market services or products.

Cumulative

● A **cumulative sentence** places the point to be made in the main clause and gives it emphasis with modifying words, phrases, or clauses placed before it, after it, or in the middle of it.

While double-checking the facts for accuracy, press-release writers look for the critical information, the newsworthy data, the new answers to old questions.

Periodic

● A **periodic sentence** moves from specific examples to the main idea.

Putting the critical information in the first paragraph is easier when you visualize a newspaper editor cutting off the end of the release to make it fit in the available space.

Balanced

● A **balanced sentence** features a parallel structure that emphasizes a similarity or a contrast between two or more grammatically equal parts (words, phrases, or clauses).

When writing a press release, start with the most important information and end with the least important data.

Note: Parallelism means "putting elements of equal value into similar constructions." Parallelism can make your sentences especially clear and add emphasis to your ideas.

His first full-time job meant the end of impossible budgeting, with an easier life ahead. (Unparallel)

His first full-time job meant the end of impossible budgeting, and the beginning of an easier life. (Parallel)

FYI Be careful when working with sentences. It's very easy to fall into the trap of writing run-on or rambling sentences. A short, clear sentence beats a long, wordy one every time. (See pages 136 and 154.)

Avoiding Sentence Errors

AGREEMENT OF SUBJECT AND VERB

The subject and verb of any clause must agree in both person and number. Checking sentences for agreement requires a close look at everything you write. The following guidelines should help.

- A verb must agree with its subject in number (singular or plural).

    The members were proud of their sales record. (Both the subject *members* and the verb *were* are plural; they agree in number.)

    Note: Do not be confused by words between the subject and verb.

    Our director, along with most of the associate directors, finds the new procedure awkward at best. (*Director*, not *associate directors*, is the subject.)

Delayed Subjects

- **Delayed subjects** result when the verb precedes the subject (an inverted sentence). In such sentences, the true (delayed) subject must agree with the verb.

    There are many interesting stops along the way. There can be no smoking on the bus. (*Stops* and *smoking* are the subjects of these sentences, not *there*.)

Compound Subjects

- Compound subjects connected with *and* almost always take a plural verb.

    Hard work and attention to detail are her greatest strengths.

Subjects with *or/nor*

- Singular subjects joined by *or* or *nor* require a singular verb.

    Either Spencer or Laura is expected to attend the meeting.

Note: Sometimes one of the subjects joined by *or* or *nor* is singular and one is plural; the verb should agree with the subject closer to the verb.

    Neither his complaints nor his attitude was the reason I changed my mind. (The singular subject *attitude* is closer to the verb; therefore, the singular verb *was* is used to agree with *attitude*.)

Indefinite Pronouns

- The indefinite pronouns *each, either, neither, one, everybody, another, anybody, anyone, anything, everyone, everything, nobody, somebody,* and *someone* are singular; they require a singular verb.

    Everybody is required to leave early today.

Note: Do not be confused by words or phrases that come between the indefinite pronoun and the verb.

    Each of the attendants is [not are] required to bring a notepad and pens to the briefing.

- The indefinite pronouns *both, few, several,* and *many* are plural; they require a plural verb.

    Many are being called, but few are answering their phones.

Indefinite Pronouns with Singular or Plural Verbs

● The indefinite pronouns *all, any, most, none,* and *some* may be either singular or plural. These pronouns are singular if the number of the noun in the prepositional phrase that follows is singular; they are plural if the noun is plural.

Most of the manuals were missing.
(*Manuals*, the noun in the prepositional phrase, is plural; therefore, the pronoun *most* is considered plural, and the plural verb *were* is used to agree with it.)

Much of the meeting was over by the time we arrived. (Because *meeting* is singular, *much* is also singular, requiring the singular verb *was*.)

All are expected to attend.

Collective Nouns

● **Collective nouns** (*class, faculty, family, committee, navy, team, species, band, crowd, pair, squad*) can be singular or plural in meaning. They require a singular verb when they refer to a group as a unit; they require a plural verb when they refer to the group members as individuals.

The team is [not are] required to submit an expense report for the road trip.
(*Team* refers to a group as a unit; it requires the singular verb *is*.)

The faculty are [not is] highly experienced.
(In this example, *faculty* refers to the individuals within the group. If the word *individuals* were substituted for *faculty*, it would become clear that the plural verb *are* is needed.)

Nouns That Are Plural in Form

● Some nouns that are plural in form but singular in meaning require a singular verb: *economics, news, mathematics, summons, mumps,* and so on.

Economics is a social science, not a pure science.

Exceptions: assets, earnings, premises, proceeds, quarters (These plural-form nouns, though singular in meaning, use a plural verb.)

Last year's earnings were up from 2001!

Our greatest assets are our employees.

Relative Pronouns

● When a relative pronoun (*which, who, that*) is used to introduce a dependent clause, the number of the verb must agree with the pronoun's antecedent. (See pages 261 and 263.)

This is one of the reports that are required for this project. (The relative pronoun *that* takes the plural verb [*are*] because its antecedent [*reports*] is plural. To test this type of sentence, read the *of* phrase first: *Of the reports that are . . .*)

"Be" Verbs

● If a form of the *be* verb is used and there is a noun both before and after that verb, the verb must agree with the subject. This holds true even if the predicate noun (the noun coming after the verb) is different in number.

The cause of his health problem was his bad eating habits.

His bad eating habits were the cause of his health problem.

AGREEMENT OF PRONOUN AND ANTECEDENT

A pronoun must agree with its *antecedent* in number, person, and gender. (The antecedent is the word or words to which the pronoun refers.)

Susan paid cash for her lunch.

Note: The antecedent in this sentence is *Susan*; it is to *Susan* that the pronoun *her* refers. Both the pronoun and its antecedent are singular, third person, and feminine; therefore, the pronoun is said to agree with its antecedent.

Singular Pronouns

- Use a singular pronoun to refer to antecedents such as *either, neither each, one, anyone, everyone, everybody, somebody, nobody, another, none,* and *a person.*

  One of the reports is missing its [not their] cover.

Note: When *a person* or *everyone* is used to refer to both sexes or either sex, you will have to choose whether to offer optional pronouns or to rewrite the sentence.

  Everyone will turn in his or her time card. (optional pronouns)

  All employees will turn in their time cards. (rewritten in plural form)

Plural Pronouns

- When a plural pronoun is mistakenly used with a singular indefinite antecedent, you need to change one or the other.

  Everyone must turn in their reports.

  Everyone must turn in his or her report.

Singular and Plural Antecedents

- If one of the antecedents joined by *or* or *nor* is singular and one is plural, the pronoun is made to agree with the closer antecedent.

  Neither the employer nor his employees were ready for their [not his] trip.

Two or More Antecedents

- Two or more antecedents joined by *and* are considered plural; two or more singular antecedents joined by *or* or *nor* are referred to by a singular pronoun.

  Jane and Florence opened their briefcases.

  Either Fred or Stan forgot his laptop in the conference room.

Masculine and Feminine Antecedents

- If one of the antecedents is masculine and one is feminine, the pronouns should also be masculine and feminine.

  Will either Sandra or Rob return her or his extra laptop battery?

FYI For more information on pronouns and antecedents, turn to pages 243-245. Also see "Shifts in Sentence Construction" on page 264.

SHIFTS IN SENTENCE CONSTRUCTION

A shift is an improper change in structure midway through a sentence. The following examples will help you identify and avoid several different kinds of shifts in your writing.

Shift in Number

● **Shift in number** is using both a singular and plural pronoun to refer to the same person or group.

When people get special training, he or she should share what they have learned with their coworkers.
(The sentence shifts from the single pronouns *he or she* to the plural pronoun *they*.)

When people get special training, they should share what they have learned with their coworkers.
(The sentence now contains the plural pronouns *people* and *they*.)

Shift in Person

● **Shift in person** is improperly mixing first, second, or third person within a sentence.

Customers can pay for the items when ordering or when you receive them.
(The sentence shifts from third person, *customers*, to second person, *you*.)

You can pay for the items when ordering or when you receive them.
(Both subjects remain in second person.)

Customers can pay when ordering or when they receive the items. (*Customers*, a third person plural noun, requires a third person plural pronoun, *they*.)

Shift in Tense

● **Shift in tense** is using more than one tense in a sentence when only one tense is needed.

We are currently replacing the regulators in the serial link boxes, even though these units operated satisfactorily. (*Are replacing* is present tense, but *operated* is past tense.)

We are currently replacing the regulators in the serial link boxes, even though these units are operating satisfactorily. (*Are replacing* and *are operating* are both present tense.)

Shift in Voice

● **Shift in voice** is mixing active with passive voice.

As we searched the warehouse for damage, a broken window was discovered. (*Searched* is in the active voice, while *was discovered* is in the passive voice.)

As we searched the warehouse for damage, we discovered a broken window.
(Both verbs are in the active voice.)

Unparallel Construction

● **Unparallel construction** occurs when the kind of words or phrases being used shifts or changes in the middle of a sentence.

All products must be tested, receive approval, and have labeling before shipment.
(The sentence shifts verb forms from *be tested* to *receive approval* to *have labeling*.)

All products must be tested, approved, and labeled before shipment.
(All three verbs end with *ed*—they are consistent or parallel.)

* * * * * * * An honest executive is one who shares the credit

AMBIGUOUS WORDING

Ambiguous wording occurs when the words used in a piece of writing are unclear to the reader because they can have two or more possible meanings. Learn to recognize and avoid ambiguous writing by studying the examples that follow.

Misplaced Modifiers

- **Misplaced modifiers** are words or phrases that are so separated from what they are describing that the reader may be confused.

   The copier has nearly been running three hours straight. (Does the sentence mean the copier has *nearly been running?*)

   The copier has been running nearly three hours straight. (This sentence says the copier has been running for *nearly* three hours.)

Dangling Modifiers

- **Dangling modifiers** are descriptive words or phrases that appear to modify the wrong noun. Dangling modifiers often occur as phrases or clauses containing *ing* words.

   After analyzing all the data, our supervisor asked us for our report. (It sounds as if the supervisor has been *analyzing all the data.*)

   After we analyzed all the data, our supervisor asked us for our report. (This sentence clarifies who *analyzed all the data.*)

Indefinite Pronoun Reference

- An **indefinite reference** is a problem caused by careless use of pronouns. There must always be a word or phrase nearby that a pronoun clearly replaces.

   When the forklift operator placed the pallet on the scale, it broke. (The pronoun *it* could refer to the *scale* or the *pallet.*)

   The pallet broke when the forklift operator placed it on the scale. (Now it is clear which item *broke.*)

Incomplete Comparisons

- **Incomplete comparisons**—leaving out words that show exactly what is being compared to what—can confuse readers.

   The office manager said the U150 is faster. (The *U150* is faster than what?)

   The office manager said the U150 is faster than the R33. (*Than the R33* completes the comparison.)

Unclear Wording

- One type of ambiguous writing is wording that has two or more possible meanings due to an unclear reference to something. (See page 156.)

   Daniel wanted to complete his report after reading the latest research, but he didn't. (It is unclear what Daniel didn't do— *complete his report* or *read the latest research.*)

   Daniel wanted to read the latest research before completing his report, but he didn't have time to do the reading. (This sentence makes it clear that Daniel completed his *report* but not his *reading.*)

NONSTANDARD LANGUAGE

Nonstandard language is language that does not conform to the standards set by schools, businesses, media, and public institutions. It is often acceptable in everyday conversation and in fictional writing, but seldom in formal speech or in formal writing.

Colloquial Language

- **Colloquial language** is wording used in informal conversation that is unacceptable in formal writing.

  How's it goin'? (Colloquial)

  How are you today? (Standard)

Slang

- Avoid the use of slang or any "in" words in formal writing.

  During the staff meeting, I really got ticked off. (Slang)

  During the staff meeting, I got very angry. (Standard)

Double Preposition

- The use of certain double prepositions—*off of, off to, from off*—is unacceptable.

  Place the file up on the shelf. (Double preposition)

  Place the file on the shelf. (Standard)

Substitution

- Avoid substituting *and* for *to*.

  Try and save all the data related to the Swanson project. (Substitution)

  Try to save all the data related to the Swanson project. (Standard)

Double Negative

- A **double negative** is an expression that contains two negative words used to convey a single negative idea. Double negatives are unacceptable in all writing.

  After examining the labels, I don't think none of them are good. (A double negative is created by using *don't* and *none* together.)

  After examining the labels, I don't think any of them are good. (Standard)

  She didn't barely have time to finish her presentation. (A double negative is created by using *didn't* and *barely* together.)

  She barely had time to finish her presentation. (Standard)

Sentence Fragment

- A **sentence fragment** is a group of words that lacks a subject, a predicate, or both.

  Raised the expectation of investors. (lacks a subject)

  All the reports since last year. (lacks a predicate)

  Quite an encouragement. (lacks a subject and predicate)

Note: Repair a sentence fragment by supplying what it lacks.

  The first-quarter earnings raised the expectations of investors.

  All the reports since last year indicate higher profits.

  The sales figures are quite an encouragement.

Section 5:
The Almanac

In this section

World Maps

The maps on the following pages will prove useful if you are planning a business conference with people in a different part of the country—or the world. Keep in mind the change in time you will experience when you travel to that meeting.

Be aware that time zones are designed with not only geography in mind, but also political boundaries. For example, all China is one time zone, while parts of Russia north of China are in earlier and later time zones.

Some states in the United States have two different time zones. Also, remember to check for daylight savings time from April through October, because some parts of the United States stay on standard time throughout the year.

World Time Zones

The world's time zones start at the prime meridian and divide the world into 24 time zones. When going west, travelers must set their watches back one hour for each time zone they cross. Going east, they must set their watches forward one hour for each zone.

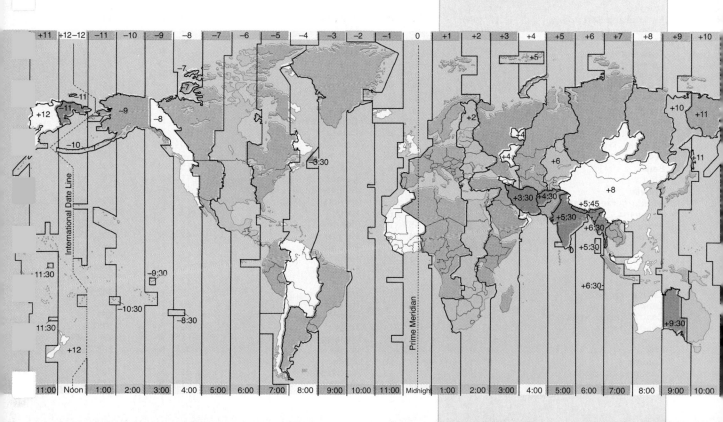

Index to World Maps

Using the latitude and longitude lines listed below allows you to locate any country on any of the maps included on pages 272-282. For example, Brazil has the coordinates 10° S and 55° W (latitude is always listed first). Find the equator (0° latitude) and locate the 10° S latitude line. Then start with the prime meridian (0° longitude) and move to longitude 55° W. Where those two lines intersect, you'll find Brazil.

Country	Latitude		Longitude	
Afghanistan	33°	N	65°	E
Albania	41°	N	20°	E
Algeria	28°	N	3°	E
Andorra	42°	N	1°	E
Angola	12°	S	18°	E
Antigua and Barbuda	17°	N	61°	W
Argentina	34°	S	64°	W
Armenia	41°	N	45°	E
Australia	25°	S	135°	E
Austria	47°	N	13°	E
Azerbaijan	41°	N	47°	E
Bahamas	24°	N	76°	W
Bahrain	26°	N	50°	E
Bangladesh	24°	N	90°	E
Barbados	13°	N	59°	W
Belarus	54°	N	25°	E
Belgium	50°	N	4°	E
Belize	17°	N	88°	W
Benin	9°	N	2°	E
Bhutan	27°	N	90°	E
Bolivia	17°	S	65°	W
Bosnia-Herzegovina	44°	N	18°	E
Botswana	22°	S	24°	E
Brazil	10°	S	55°	W
Brunei	4°	N	114°	E
Bulgaria	43°	N	25°	E
Burkina Faso	13°	N	2°	W
Burundi	3°	S	30°	E
Cambodia	13°	N	105°	E
Cameroon	6°	N	12°	E
Canada	60°	N	95°	W
Central African Republic	7°	N	21°	E
Chad	15°	N	19°	E
Chile	30°	S	71°	W
China	35°	N	105°	E
Colombia	4°	N	72°	W
Congo, Democratic Republic of the	0°	SN	25°	E

Country	Latitude		Longitude	
Congo, Republic of the	1°	S	15°	E
Costa Rica	10°	N	84°	W
Côte d'Ivoire	8°	N	5°	W
Croatia	45°	N	16°	E
Cuba	21°	N	80°	W
Cyprus	35°	N	33°	E
Czech Republic	50°	N	15°	E
Denmark	56°	N	10°	E
Djibouti	11°	N	43°	E
Dominica	15°	N	61°	W
Dominican Republic	19°	N	70°	W
East Timor	8°	S	125°	E
Ecuador	2°	S	77°	W
Egypt	27°	N	30°	E
El Salvador	14°	N	89°	W
England	53°	N	2°	W
Equatorial Guinea	2°	N	10°	E
Eritrea	15°	N	38°	E
Estonia	59°	N	26°	E
Ethiopia	8°	N	38°	E
Fiji	19°	S	174°	E
Finland	64°	N	26°	E
France	46°	N	2°	E
Gabon	1°	S	11°	E
The Gambia	13°	N	16°	W
Georgia	43°	N	45°	E
Germany	51°	N	10°	E
Ghana	8°	N	2°	W
Great Britain	54°	N	2°	W
Greece	39°	N	22°	E
Greenland	70°	N	40°	W
Grenada	12°	N	61°	W
Guatemala	15°	N	90°	W
Guinea	11°	N	10°	W
Guinea-Bissau	12°	N	15°	W
Guyana	5°	N	59°	W
Haiti	19°	N	72°	W
Honduras	15°	N	86°	W
Hungary	47°	N	20°	E
Iceland	65°	N	18°	W
India	20°	N	77°	E
Indonesia	5°	S	120°	E
Iran	32°	N	53°	E
Iraq	33°	N	44°	E
Ireland	53°	N	8°	W
Israel	31°	N	35°	E
Italy	42°	N	12°	E
Jamaica	18°	N	77°	W
Japan	36°	N	138°	E
Jordan	31°	N	36°	E
Kazakhstan	45°	N	70°	E
Kenya	1°	N	38°	E

Country	Latitude		Longitude		Country	Latitude		Longitude	
North Korea	40°	N	127°	E	Saint Vincent				
South Korea	36°	N	128°	E	and the Grenadines	13°	N	61°	W
Kuwait	29°	N	47°	E	Samoa	13°	S	172°	W
Kyrgyzstan	42°	N	75°	E	San Marino	44°	N	12°	E
Laos	18°	N	105°	E	São Tomé and Príncipe	1°	N	7°	E
Latvia	57°	N	25°	E	Saudi Arabia	25°	N	45°	E
Lebanon	34°	N	36°	E	Scotland	57°	N	5°	W
Lesotho	29°	S	28°	E	Senegal	14°	N	14°	W
Liberia	6°	N	10°	W	Serbia and Montenegro	45°	N	21°	E
Libya	27°	N	17°	E	Sierra Leone	8°	N	11°	W
Liechtenstein	47°	N	9°	E	Singapore	1°	N	103°	E
Lithuania	56°	N	24°	E	Slovakia	49°	N	19°	E
Luxembourg	49°	N	6°	E	Slovenia	46°	N	15°	E
Macedonia	43°	N	22°	E	Solomon Islands	8°	S	159°	E
Madagascar	19°	S	46°	E	Somalia	10°	N	49°	E
Malawi	13°	S	34°	E	South Africa	30°	S	26°	E
Malaysia	2°	N	112°	E	Spain	40°	N	4°	W
Maldives	3°	N	73°	E	Sri Lanka	7°	N	81°	E
Mali	17°	N	4°	W	Sudan	15°	N	30°	E
Marshall Islands	9°	N	168°	E	Suriname	4°	N	56°	W
Mauritania	20°	N	12°	W	Swaziland	26°	S	31°	E
Mexico	23°	N	102°	W	Sweden	62°	N	15°	E
Micronesia	5°	N	150°	E	Switzerland	47°	N	8°	E
Moldova	47°	N	28°	E	Syria	35°	N	38°	E
Monaco	43°	N	7°	E	Taiwan	23°	N	121°	E
Mongolia	46°	N	105°	E	Tajikistan	39°	N	71°	E
Morocco	32°	N	5°	W	Tanzania	6°	S	35°	E
Mozambique	18°	S	35°	E	Thailand	15°	N	100°	E
Myanmar	23°	N	95°	E	Togo	8°	N	1°	E
Namibia	22°	S	17°	E	Tonga	20°	S	173°	W
Nauru	1°	S	166°	E	Trinidad and Tobago	11°	N	61°	W
Nepal	28°	N	84°	E	Tunisia	34°	N	9°	E
The Netherlands	52°	N	5°	E	Turkey	39°	N	35°	E
New Zealand	41°	S	174°	E	Turkmenistan	40°	N	55°	E
Nicaragua	13°	N	85°	W	Tuvalu	8°	S	179°	E
Niger	16°	N	8°	E	Uganda	1°	N	32°	E
Nigeria	10°	N	8°	E	Ukraine	50°	N	30°	E
Northern Ireland	55°	N	7°	W	United Arab Emirates	24°	N	54°	E
Norway	62°	N	10°	E	United Kingdom	54°	N	2°	W
Oman	22°	N	58°	E	United States	38°	N	97°	W
Pakistan	30°	N	70°	E	Uruguay	33°	S	56°	W
Palau	8°	N	138°	E	Uzbekistan	40°	N	68°	E
Panama	9°	N	80°	W	Vanuatu	17°	S	170°	E
Papua New Guinea	6°	S	147°	E	Vatican City	41°	N	12°	E
Paraguay	23°	S	58°	W	Venezuela	8°	N	66°	W
Peru	10°	S	76°	W	Vietnam	17°	N	106°	E
The Philippines	13°	N	122°	E	Wales	53°	N	3°	W
Poland	52°	N	19°	E	Western Sahara	24°	N	13°	W
Portugal	39°	N	8°	W	Western Samoa	10°	S	173°	W
Qatar	25°	N	51°	E	Yemen	15°	N	48°	E
Romania	46°	N	25°	E	Zambia	15°	S	30°	E
Russia	60°	N	80°	E	Zimbabwe	20°	S	30°	E
Rwanda	2°	S	30°	E					
St. Kitts and Nevis	17°	N	62°	W					
Saint Lucia	14°	N	61°	W					

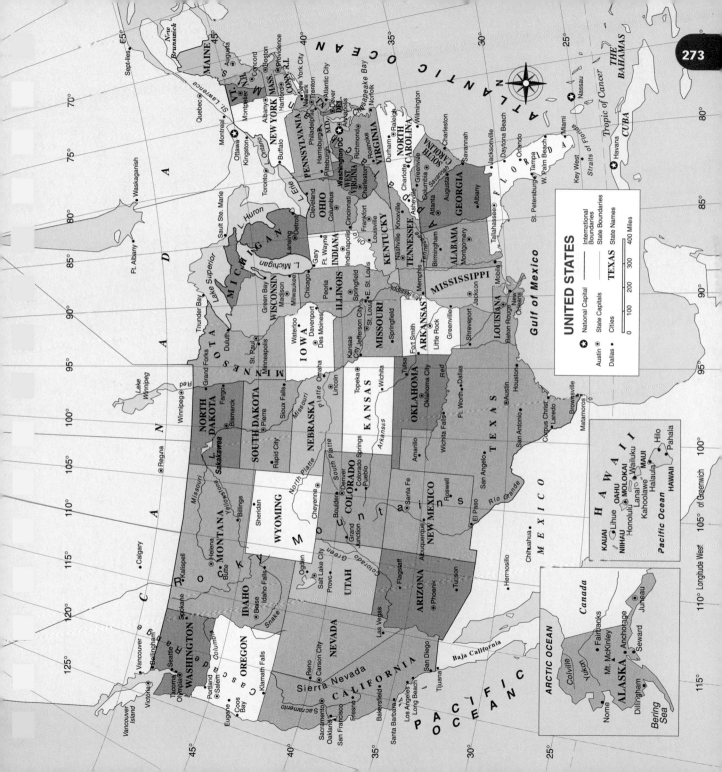

UNITED STATES

★ National Capital
● State Capitals
● Cities

| | International Boundaries |
| | State Boundaries |

Austin   **TEXAS** State Names
Dallas

0   100   200   300   400 Miles

CANADA

Legend:
- ⊛ National Capital
- ⊙ Provincial/Territorial Capital
- • Cities

- International Boundaries
- Provincial/Territorial Boundaries
- **QUEBEC** Provincial/Territorial Names

Scale: 0 — 250 — 500 Miles

Oceans and Seas
- ARCTIC OCEAN
- ATLANTIC OCEAN
- PACIFIC OCEAN
- Norwegian Sea
- Greenland Sea
- Denmark Strait
- Davis Strait
- Baffin Bay
- Labrador Sea
- Hudson Strait
- Hudson Bay
- Ungava Bay
- Gulf of St. Lawrence
- Beaufort Sea
- Chukchi Sea
- Bering Strait
- Gulf of Alaska

Regions and Countries
- ICELAND
- GREENLAND
- ASIA
- ALASKA
- UNITED STATES

Provinces and Territories
- YUKON TERRITORY
- NORTHWEST TERRITORIES
- NUNAVUT
- BRITISH COLUMBIA
- ALBERTA
- SASKATCHEWAN
- MANITOBA
- ONTARIO
- QUEBEC
- LABRADOR
- NEWFOUNDLAND
- PRINCE EDWARD ISLAND
- NOVA SCOTIA
- NEW BRUNSWICK

Cities
- Whitehorse
- Tuktoyaktuk
- Yellowknife
- Port Radium
- Iqaluit
- Inukjuak
- Baker Lake
- Rankin Inlet
- Churchill
- Bear Lake
- Dawson Creek
- Prince Rupert
- Prince George
- Kamloops
- Vancouver
- Victoria
- Kelowna
- Trail
- Grande Prairie
- Fort Chipewyan
- Fort McMurray
- Edmonton
- Red Deer
- Calgary
- Lethbridge
- North Battleford
- Prince Albert
- Saskatoon
- Swift Current
- Regina
- Flin Flon
- Thompson
- Brandon
- Winnipeg
- Moosonee
- Timmins
- Thunder Bay
- Sudbury
- North Bay
- Sault
- Toronto
- Kingston
- Ottawa
- Amos
- Trois-rivières
- Montreal
- Quebec
- Labrador City
- Corner Brook
- St. John's
- Charlottetown
- Sydney
- Halifax
- Moncton
- Fredericton

Rivers and Lakes
- Mackenzie R.
- Yukon R.
- Peace R.
- Athabasca
- Columbia R.
- Churchill R.
- Nelson R.
- Saskatchewan R.
- Great Bear Lake
- L. Superior
- L. Huron
- L. Michigan
- L. Erie
- L. Ontario
- Smallwood Res.
- St. Lawrence

Islands
- Queen Elizabeth Islands
- Ellesmere Island
- Axel Heiberg Island
- Sverdrup Islands
- Devon Island
- Patrick Island
- Melville Island
- Banks Island
- Victoria Island
- Prince of Wales Island
- Baffin Island
- Queen Charlotte Islands

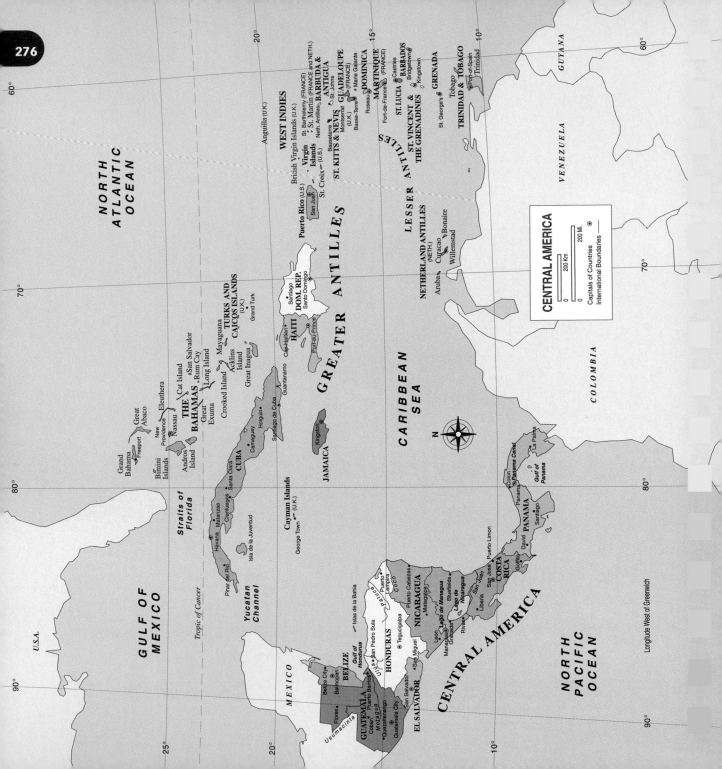

276

NORTH ATLANTIC OCEAN

U.S.A.

GULF OF MEXICO

Tropic of Cancer

MEXICO

Straits of Florida

Yucatan Channel

Grand Bahama
Bimini Islands
Freeport
New Providence
Nassau
Andros Island
Eleuthera
Great Abaco
Cat Island
San Salvador
Rum Cay
Long Island
THE BAHAMAS
Great Exuma
Crooked Island
Acklins Island
Mayaguana
Great Inagua

TURKS AND CAICOS ISLANDS (U.K.)
Grand Turk

Pinar del Río
Havana
Matanzas
Cienfuegos
Santa Clara
Camaguey
Holguín
CUBA
Isla de la Juventud
Santiago de Cuba
Guantanamo

Cayman Islands (U.K.)
George Town

JAMAICA
Kingston

GREATER ANTILLES

Cap-Haïtien
Santiago
HAITI
Port-au-Prince
DOM. REP.
Santo Domingo

CARIBBEAN SEA

WEST INDIES

Anguilla (U.K.)

British Virgin Islands (U.K.)
Puerto Rico (U.S.)
San Juan
Virgin Islands (U.S.)
St. Croix

St. Barthelemy (FRANCE)
St. Martin (FRANCE and NETH.)
Neth. Antilles
Basseterre
ST. KITTS & NEVIS
Montserrat (U.K.)
BARBUDA & ANTIGUA
St. Johns
GUADELOUPE (FRANCE)
Basse-Terre
Marie Galante
Roseau
DOMINICA
Fort-de-France
MARTINIQUE (FRANCE)
Castries
ST. LUCIA
BARBADOS
Bridgetown
ST. VINCENT & THE GRENADINES
St. George's
GRENADA
Kingstown
Tobago
TRINIDAD & TOBAGO
Port-of-Spain
Trinidad

LESSER ANTILLES

NETHERLAND ANTILLES (NETH.)
Aruba
Curaçao
Bonaire
Willemstad

VENEZUELA

GUYANA

COLOMBIA

N

CENTRAL AMERICA
200 Km
200 Mi.
Capitals of Countries
International Boundaries

Colón
Panama Canal
Gulf of Panama
La Palma
Panama
PANAMA
Santiago
David
Golfito
San José
Puerto Limon
COSTA RICA
Liberia
Puerto Cabezas
San Juan
Bluefields
Rivas
Granada
NICARAGUA
Lago de Nicaragua
Matagalpa
Managua
Lago de Managua
León
Islas de la Bahía
Puerto Lempira
PATUCA
La Ceiba
San Pedro Sula
HONDURAS
Tegucigalpa
Belize City
Belmopan
BELIZE
Gulf of Honduras
Puerto Barrios
Cobán
Flores
GUATEMALA
Quezaltenango
Guatemala City
San Salvador
San Miguel
EL SALVADOR
Usumacinta

CENTRAL AMERICA

NORTH PACIFIC OCEAN

Longitude West of Greenwich

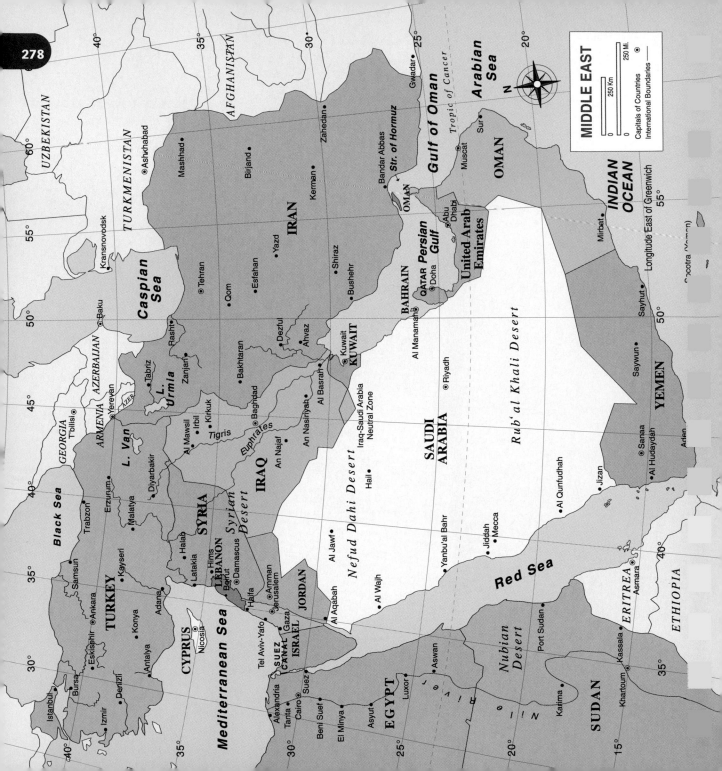

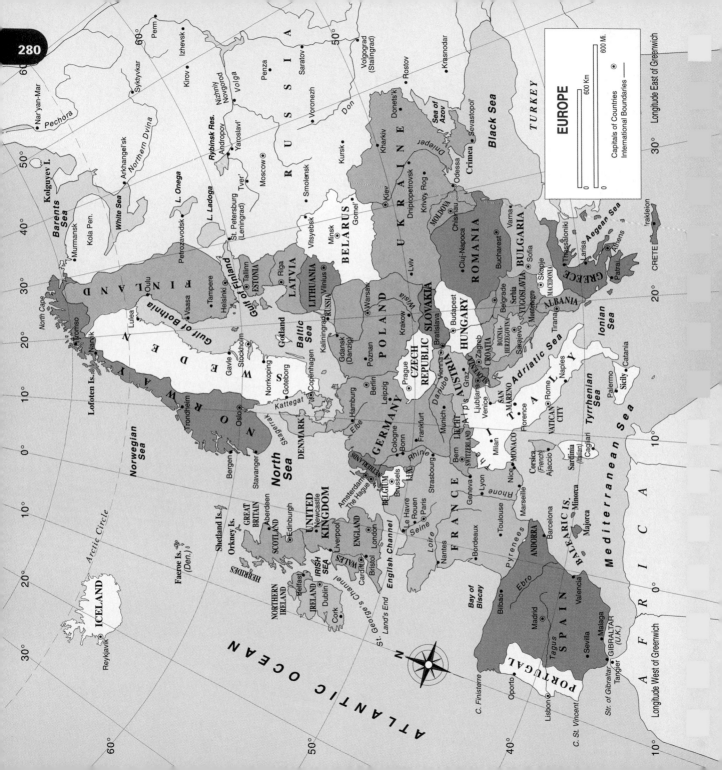

EUROPE

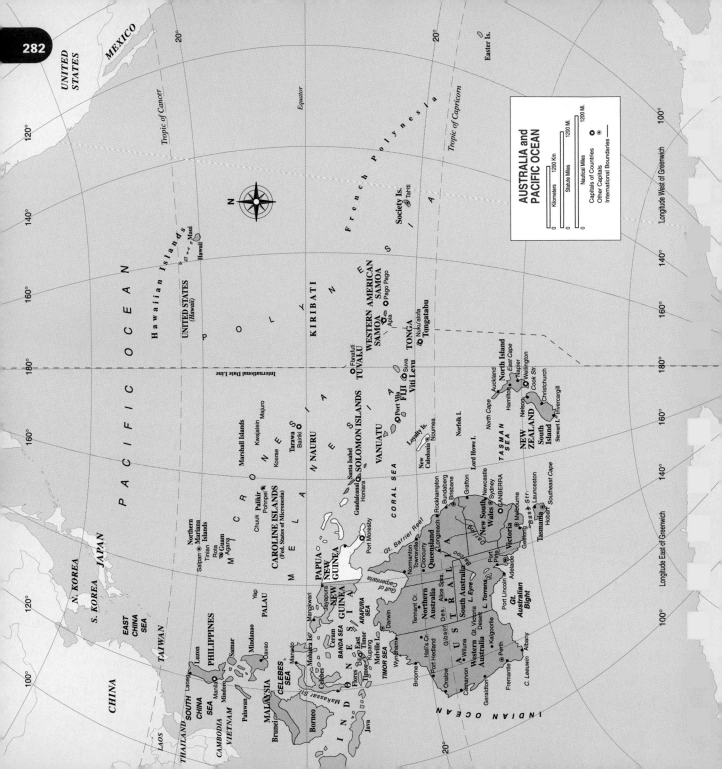

UNITED STATES
MEXICO
20°
Easter Is.

CHINA

N. KOREA
S. KOREA
JAPAN

EAST
CHINA
SEA

TAIWAN

THAILAND
SOUTH
CHINA
SEA

CAMBODIA
VIETNAM

LAOS

PHILIPPINES
Laoag
Luzon
Manila
Mindoro
Samar

Palawan
Mindanao
Davao

Yap
PALAU

BRUNEI
Borneo
MALAYSIA
CELEBES
SEA

Celebes
Manado

Ceram
East Timor
Kupang
Timor

Java

Mangkwari
Jayapura

MELANESIA

MICRONESIA

Hawaiian Islands

Maui
Hawaii

UNITED STATES
(Hawaii)

POLYNESIA

French Polynesia

Society Is.
Tahiti

WESTERN
SAMOA
AMERICAN
SAMOA
Apia
Pago Pago

TONGA
Nuku'alofa
Tongatabu

North Island
East Cape
Napier
Wellington
Cook Str.

NEW
ZEALAND
South Island
Christchurch
Invercargill
Stewart I.

Tropic of Cancer

Equator

Tropic of Capricorn

PACIFIC OCEAN

N

KIRIBATI

TUVALU
Funafuti

FIJI
Suva
Viti Levu

VANUATU
Port Vila

New
Caledonia
Loyalty Is.
Nouméa

Norfolk I.

Lord Howe I.

North Cape
Auckland
Hamilton
Nelson

TASMAN
SEA

CORAL SEA

Marshall Islands
Kwajalein
Majuro
Kosrae
Tarawa
Bairiki

NAURU

Santa Isabel
SOLOMON ISLANDS
Guadalcanal
Honiara

Chuuk
Palikir
Pohnpei

CAROLINE ISLANDS
(Fed. States of Micronesia)

Northern
Mariana
Islands
Saipan
Tinian Islands
Rota
Guam
Agana

PAPUA
NEW
GUINEA
Port Moresby

ARAFURA
SEA

BANDA SEA

Moluccas Is.

Flores

TIMOR SEA

INDONESIA

Gt. Barrier Reef
Townsville
Cloncurry
Longreach

Queensland

Rockhampton
Bundaberg
Brisbane
Grafton
Newcastle
New South
Wales
Sydney
CANBERRA

Victoria
Melbourne
Geelong

Tasmania
Launceston
Hobart
Southeast Cape

Bass Str.

Normanton

Gulf of
Carpentaria

Northern
Territory
Tennant Cr.
Alice Springs

Darwin

Melville I.

Wyndham

Broome

Hall's Cr.

Gibson Des.

Western
Australia

Gt. Victoria
Desert

AUSTRALIA

South Australia

L. Eyre
L. Torrens
Port Augusta
Port Pirie
Port Lincoln
Adelaide

Gt.
Australian
Bight

Wiluna

Kalgoorlie

Perth
Fremantle

Onslow

Carnarvon

Geraldton

C. Leeuwin
Albany

Port Hedland

INDIAN OCEAN

20°

INDONESIA

AUSTRALIA and
PACIFIC OCEAN

Kilometers   1200 Km
0

Statute Miles   1200 Mi.
0

Nautical Miles   1200 Mi.
0

⊛ Capitals of Countries
◉ Other Capitals
International Boundaries

International Date Line

Longitude West of Greenwich

Longitude East of Greenwich

120°   100°   20°   20°   140°   160°   180°   160°   140°   120°   100°

2003

```
      JANUARY              FEBRUARY               MARCH                 APRIL
S  M  T  W  T  F  S   S  M  T  W  T  F  S   S  M  T  W  T  F  S   S  M  T  W  T  F  S
         1  2  3  4                     1                     1          1  2  3  4  5
5  6  7  8  9 10 11    2  3  4  5  6  7  8    2  3  4  5  6  7  8    6  7  8  9 10 11 12
12 13 14 15 16 17 18   9 10 11 12 13 14 15    9 10 11 12 13 14 15   13 14 15 16 17 18 19
19 20 21 22 23 24 25  16 17 18 19 20 21 22   16 17 18 19 20 21 22   20 21 22 23 24 25 26
26 27 28 29 30 31     23 24 25 26 27 28      23 24 25 26 27 28 29   27 28 29 30
                                             30 31

        MAY                  JUNE                  JULY                 AUGUST
S  M  T  W  T  F  S   S  M  T  W  T  F  S   S  M  T  W  T  F  S   S  M  T  W  T  F  S
            1  2  3    1  2  3  4  5  6  7          1  2  3  4  5                  1  2
4  5  6  7  8  9 10    8  9 10 11 12 13 14    6  7  8  9 10 11 12    3  4  5  6  7  8  9
11 12 13 14 15 16 17  15 16 17 18 19 20 21   13 14 15 16 17 18 19   10 11 12 13 14 15 16
18 19 20 21 22 23 24  22 23 24 25 26 27 28   20 21 22 23 24 25 26   17 18 19 20 21 22 23
25 26 27 28 29 30 31  29 30                  27 28 29 30 31         24 25 26 27 28 29 30
                                                                    31

     SEPTEMBER              OCTOBER              NOVEMBER              DECEMBER
S  M  T  W  T  F  S   S  M  T  W  T  F  S   S  M  T  W  T  F  S   S  M  T  W  T  F  S
   1  2  3  4  5  6            1  2  3  4                     1       1  2  3  4  5  6
7  8  9 10 11 12 13    5  6  7  8  9 10 11    2  3  4  5  6  7  8    7  8  9 10 11 12 13
14 15 16 17 18 19 20  12 13 14 15 16 17 18    9 10 11 12 13 14 15   14 15 16 17 18 19 20
21 22 23 24 25 26 27  19 20 21 22 23 24 25   16 17 18 19 20 21 22   21 22 23 24 25 26 27
28 29 30              26 27 28 29 30 31       23 24 25 26 27 28 29   28 29 30 31
                                             30
```

2004

```
      JANUARY              FEBRUARY               MARCH                 APRIL
S  M  T  W  T  F  S   S  M  T  W  T  F  S   S  M  T  W  T  F  S   S  M  T  W  T  F  S
            1  2  3    1  2  3  4  5  6  7       1  2  3  4  5  6                1  2  3
4  5  6  7  8  9 10    8  9 10 11 12 13 14    7  8  9 10 11 12 13    4  5  6  7  8  9 10
11 12 13 14 15 16 17  15 16 17 18 19 20 21   14 15 16 17 18 19 20   11 12 13 14 15 16 17
18 19 20 21 22 23 24  22 23 24 25 26 27 28   21 22 23 24 25 26 27   18 19 20 21 22 23 24
25 26 27 28 29 30 31  29                     28 29 30 31            25 26 27 28 29 30

        MAY                  JUNE                  JULY                 AUGUST
S  M  T  W  T  F  S   S  M  T  W  T  F  S   S  M  T  W  T  F  S   S  M  T  W  T  F  S
                  1          1  2  3  4  5                1  2  3    1  2  3  4  5  6  7
2  3  4  5  6  7  8    6  7  8  9 10 11 12    4  5  6  7  8  9 10    8  9 10 11 12 13 14
9 10 11 12 13 14 15   13 14 15 16 17 18 19   11 12 13 14 15 16 17   15 16 17 18 19 20 21
16 17 18 19 20 21 22  20 21 22 23 24 25 26   18 19 20 21 22 23 24   22 23 24 25 26 27 28
23 24 25 26 27 28 29  27 28 29 30            25 26 27 28 29 30 31   29 30 31
30 31

     SEPTEMBER              OCTOBER              NOVEMBER              DECEMBER
S  M  T  W  T  F  S   S  M  T  W  T  F  S   S  M  T  W  T  F  S   S  M  T  W  T  F  S
         1  2  3  4                  1  2       1  2  3  4  5  6             1  2  3  4
5  6  7  8  9 10 11    3  4  5  6  7  8  9    7  8  9 10 11 12 13    5  6  7  8  9 10 11
12 13 14 15 16 17 18  10 11 12 13 14 15 16   14 15 16 17 18 19 20   12 13 14 15 16 17 18
19 20 21 22 23 24 25  17 18 19 20 21 22 23   21 22 23 24 25 26 27   19 20 21 22 23 24 25
26 27 28 29 30        24 25 26 27 28 29 30   28 29 30               26 27 28 29 30 31
                      31
```

2005

```
      JANUARY              FEBRUARY               MARCH                 APRIL
S  M  T  W  T  F  S   S  M  T  W  T  F  S   S  M  T  W  T  F  S   S  M  T  W  T  F  S
                  1          1  2  3  4  5          1  2  3  4  5                1  2
2  3  4  5  6  7  8    6  7  8  9 10 11 12    6  7  8  9 10 11 12    3  4  5  6  7  8  9
9 10 11 12 13 14 15   13 14 15 16 17 18 19   13 14 15 16 17 18 19   10 11 12 13 14 15 16
16 17 18 19 20 21 22  20 21 22 23 24 25 26   20 21 22 23 24 25 26   17 18 19 20 21 22 23
23 24 25 26 27 28 29  27 28                  27 28 29 30 31         24 25 26 27 28 29 30
30 31

        MAY                  JUNE                  JULY                 AUGUST
S  M  T  W  T  F  S   S  M  T  W  T  F  S   S  M  T  W  T  F  S   S  M  T  W  T  F  S
1  2  3  4  5  6  7            1  2  3  4                  1  2       1  2  3  4  5  6
8  9 10 11 12 13 14    5  6  7  8  9 10 11    3  4  5  6  7  8  9    7  8  9 10 11 12 13
15 16 17 18 19 20 21  12 13 14 15 16 17 18   10 11 12 13 14 15 16   14 15 16 17 18 19 20
22 23 24 25 26 27 28  19 20 21 22 23 24 25   17 18 19 20 21 22 23   21 22 23 24 25 26 27
29 30 31              26 27 28 29 30         24 25 26 27 28 29 30   28 29 30 31
                                             31

     SEPTEMBER              OCTOBER              NOVEMBER              DECEMBER
S  M  T  W  T  F  S   S  M  T  W  T  F  S   S  M  T  W  T  F  S   S  M  T  W  T  F  S
            1  2  3                     1       1  2  3  4  5                1  2  3
4  5  6  7  8  9 10    2  3  4  5  6  7  8    6  7  8  9 10 11 12    4  5  6  7  8  9 10
11 12 13 14 15 16 17   9 10 11 12 13 14 15   13 14 15 16 17 18 19   11 12 13 14 15 16 17
18 19 20 21 22 23 24  16 17 18 19 20 21 22   20 21 22 23 24 25 26   18 19 20 21 22 23 24
25 26 27 28 29 30     23 24 25 26 27 28 29   27 28 29 30            25 26 27 28 29 30 31
                      30 31
```

2006

```
      JANUARY              FEBRUARY               MARCH                 APRIL
S  M  T  W  T  F  S   S  M  T  W  T  F  S   S  M  T  W  T  F  S   S  M  T  W  T  F  S
1  2  3  4  5  6  7             1  2  3  4             1  2  3  4                  1
8  9 10 11 12 13 14    5  6  7  8  9 10 11    5  6  7  8  9 10 11    2  3  4  5  6  7  8
15 16 17 18 19 20 21  12 13 14 15 16 17 18   12 13 14 15 16 17 18    9 10 11 12 13 14 15
22 23 24 25 26 27 28  19 20 21 22 23 24 25   19 20 21 22 23 24 25   16 17 18 19 20 21 22
29 30 31              26 27 28               26 27 28 29 30 31      23 24 25 26 27 28 29
                                                                    30

        MAY                  JUNE                  JULY                 AUGUST
S  M  T  W  T  F  S   S  M  T  W  T  F  S   S  M  T  W  T  F  S   S  M  T  W  T  F  S
   1  2  3  4  5  6             1  2  3                     1          1  2  3  4  5
7  8  9 10 11 12 13    4  5  6  7  8  9 10    2  3  4  5  6  7  8    6  7  8  9 10 11 12
14 15 16 17 18 19 20  11 12 13 14 15 16 17    9 10 11 12 13 14 15   13 14 15 16 17 18 19
21 22 23 24 25 26 27  18 19 20 21 22 23 24   16 17 18 19 20 21 22   20 21 22 23 24 25 26
28 29 30 31           25 26 27 28 29 30      23 24 25 26 27 28 29   27 28 29 30 31
                                             30 31

     SEPTEMBER              OCTOBER              NOVEMBER              DECEMBER
S  M  T  W  T  F  S   S  M  T  W  T  F  S   S  M  T  W  T  F  S   S  M  T  W  T  F  S
                1  2   1  2  3  4  5  6  7             1  2  3  4                1  2
3  4  5  6  7  8  9    8  9 10 11 12 13 14    5  6  7  8  9 10 11    3  4  5  6  7  8  9
10 11 12 13 14 15 16  15 16 17 18 19 20 21   12 13 14 15 16 17 18   10 11 12 13 14 15 16
17 18 19 20 21 22 23  22 23 24 25 26 27 28   19 20 21 22 23 24 25   17 18 19 20 21 22 23
24 25 26 27 28 29 30  29 30 31               26 27 28 29 30         24 25 26 27 28 29 30
                                                                    31
```

2007

```
      JANUARY              FEBRUARY               MARCH                 APRIL
S  M  T  W  T  F  S   S  M  T  W  T  F  S   S  M  T  W  T  F  S   S  M  T  W  T  F  S
   1  2  3  4  5  6                1  2  3                1  2  3    1  2  3  4  5  6  7
7  8  9 10 11 12 13    4  5  6  7  8  9 10    4  5  6  7  8  9 10    8  9 10 11 12 13 14
14 15 16 17 18 19 20  11 12 13 14 15 16 17   11 12 13 14 15 16 17   15 16 17 18 19 20 21
21 22 23 24 25 26 27  18 19 20 21 22 23 24   18 19 20 21 22 23 24   22 23 24 25 26 27 28
28 29 30 31           25 26 27 28            25 26 27 28 29 30 31   29 30

        MAY                  JUNE                  JULY                 AUGUST
S  M  T  W  T  F  S   S  M  T  W  T  F  S   S  M  T  W  T  F  S   S  M  T  W  T  F  S
      1  2  3  4  5                  1  2   1  2  3  4  5  6  7             1  2  3  4
6  7  8  9 10 11 12    3  4  5  6  7  8  9    8  9 10 11 12 13 14    5  6  7  8  9 10 11
13 14 15 16 17 18 19  10 11 12 13 14 15 16   15 16 17 18 19 20 21   12 13 14 15 16 17 18
20 21 22 23 24 25 26  17 18 19 20 21 22 23   22 23 24 25 26 27 28   19 20 21 22 23 24 25
27 28 29 30 31        24 25 26 27 28 29 30   29 30 31               26 27 28 29 30 31

     SEPTEMBER              OCTOBER              NOVEMBER              DECEMBER
S  M  T  W  T  F  S   S  M  T  W  T  F  S   S  M  T  W  T  F  S   S  M  T  W  T  F  S
                  1      1  2  3  4  5  6                1  2  3                      1
2  3  4  5  6  7  8    7  8  9 10 11 12 13    4  5  6  7  8  9 10    2  3  4  5  6  7  8
9 10 11 12 13 14 15   14 15 16 17 18 19 20   11 12 13 14 15 16 17    9 10 11 12 13 14 15
16 17 18 19 20 21 22  21 22 23 24 25 26 27   18 19 20 21 22 23 24   16 17 18 19 20 21 22
23 24 25 26 27 28 29  28 29 30 31            25 26 27 28 29 30      23 24 25 26 27 28 29
30                                                                  30 31
```

2008

```
      JANUARY              FEBRUARY               MARCH                 APRIL
S  M  T  W  T  F  S   S  M  T  W  T  F  S   S  M  T  W  T  F  S   S  M  T  W  T  F  S
      1  2  3  4  5                  1  2                     1          1  2  3  4  5
6  7  8  9 10 11 12    3  4  5  6  7  8  9    2  3  4  5  6  7  8    6  7  8  9 10 11 12
13 14 15 16 17 18 19  10 11 12 13 14 15 16    9 10 11 12 13 14 15   13 14 15 16 17 18 19
20 21 22 23 24 25 26  17 18 19 20 21 22 23   16 17 18 19 20 21 22   20 21 22 23 24 25 26
27 28 29 30 31        24 25 26 27 28 29      23 24 25 26 27 28 29   27 28 29 30
                                             30 31

        MAY                  JUNE                  JULY                 AUGUST
S  M  T  W  T  F  S   S  M  T  W  T  F  S   S  M  T  W  T  F  S   S  M  T  W  T  F  S
            1  2  3   1  2  3  4  5  6  7          1  2  3  4  5                  1  2
4  5  6  7  8  9 10    8  9 10 11 12 13 14    6  7  8  9 10 11 12    3  4  5  6  7  8  9
11 12 13 14 15 16 17  15 16 17 18 19 20 21   13 14 15 16 17 18 19   10 11 12 13 14 15 16
18 19 20 21 22 23 24  22 23 24 25 26 27 28   20 21 22 23 24 25 26   17 18 19 20 21 22 23
25 26 27 28 29 30 31  29 30                  27 28 29 30 31         24 25 26 27 28 29 30
                                                                    31

     SEPTEMBER              OCTOBER              NOVEMBER              DECEMBER
S  M  T  W  T  F  S   S  M  T  W  T  F  S   S  M  T  W  T  F  S   S  M  T  W  T  F  S
   1  2  3  4  5  6            1  2  3  4                     1       1  2  3  4  5  6
7  8  9 10 11 12 13    5  6  7  8  9 10 11    2  3  4  5  6  7  8    7  8  9 10 11 12 13
14 15 16 17 18 19 20  12 13 14 15 16 17 18    9 10 11 12 13 14 15   14 15 16 17 18 19 20
21 22 23 24 25 26 27  19 20 21 22 23 24 25   16 17 18 19 20 21 22   21 22 23 24 25 26 27
28 29 30              26 27 28 29 30 31       23 24 25 26 27 28 29   28 29 30 31
                                             30
```